A CASEBOOK ON
THE ROMAN LAW OF DELICT

AMERICAN PHILOLOGICAL ASSOCIATION

CLASSICAL RESOURCES SERIES

John T. Ramsey, Series Editor

NUMBER 2
A CASEBOOK ON
THE ROMAN LAW OF DELICT

by
Bruce W. Frier

A CASEBOOK ON
THE ROMAN LAW OF DELICT

by
Bruce W. Frier
Professor of Classics and Roman Law
The University of Michigan

Scholars Press
Atlanta, Georgia

A CASEBOOK ON
THE ROMAN LAW OF DELICT

by
Bruce W. Frier

©1989
The American Philological Association

Library of Congress Cataloging in Publication Data

Frier, Bruce W., 1943-
    A casebook on the Roman law of delict.

    (Classical resources / American Philological
Association ; no. 2)
    Bibliography: p.
    Includes index.
    1. Torts (Roman law)--Cases. I. Title. II. Series:
Classical resources series ; no. 2.
KJA2612.F75 1989 346.45'63203   89-6076
                    344.5632063
ISBN: 1-55540-266-6
ISBN: 1-55540-267-4 (pbk.)

Printed in the United States of America
on acid-free paper

Iuris praecepta sunt haec: honeste vivere, alterum non laedere, suum cuique tribuere.

"The basic principles of law are these: to live uprightly, not to harm others, and to confer what is due to each person."

— Ulpian, D. 1.1.10.1

Classroom Notes

The author has prepared a set of teaching notes to accompany this book. Teachers may obtain a copy, free of charge, by sending a request on departmental stationery to the author, Law School, The University of Michigan, Ann Arbor, Michigan 48109.

Contents

Preface for Users

This casebook is designed to introduce the Roman law concerning delicts, private wrongs which broadly resemble torts in Anglo-American law. The Roman law of delict is unusually interesting, since many basic Roman principles of delict are still prominent in modern legal systems, while other Roman principles offer sharp and important contrasts with modern ideas. The influence of Roman law has been especially strong in the Civil Law systems of Continental Europe and its former dependencies, since these systems derive many basic principles from Roman law; but Roman influence on Anglo-American law has also been appreciable in some areas, although not usually in tort.

A casebook relies on direct use of primary sources in order to convey a clear understanding of what legal sources are like and how lawyers work. For Roman law, the primary sources are above all the writings of the early imperial Roman jurists. Almost all their writings date to the classical period of Roman law, approximately 30 B.C. to A.D. 235. Justinian's *Digest*, promulgated at Constantinople in A.D. 533, collects more than nine thousand lightly edited excerpts (totalling over eight hundred thousand words) that derive mainly from classical juristic writings; these excerpts vary in length from a few words to several pages. Modern knowledge of classical Roman law rests chiefly on the *Digest* and a few other sources — most prominent among them the *Institutes* of Gaius, an elementary textbook written about A.D. 160, which is the sole work of the classical jurists that has survived to us virtually intact.

The 171 Cases in this book all derive from the writings of pre-classical and classical jurists. The Roman jurists were not judges in our sense, nor were they like modern lawyers. They were, instead, a tiny elite of legal professionals who were charged with conserving and developing the private law that Romans used in lawsuits between themselves. Although the Cases often describe fact situations drawn from real life, they are, without exception, not judicial opinions on real legal cases; rather, the jurists write about hypothetical fact situations, as part of their effort to discuss and develop law. The jurists' writings were originally intended, in the main, for reading by their fellow jurists, not by lay persons. However, the law that the jurists created through their writings was applied directly to actual cases that arose in Roman courts, in order to settle questions of law.

During the classical period of Roman law, private lawsuits in the city of Rome were normally brought in the court of the Urban Praetor, a magistrate of the Roman State. So that potential plaintiffs could know which lawsuits he was willing to grant, the Praetor, at the start of his year in office, issued an Edict listing all the causes of action that he recognized as available. The Praetor used his Edict both to implement existing law and to create new actions.

Actual trials took place in two stages. A plaintiff first came before the Praetor and asked him to grant a lawsuit. If the plaintiff stated an acceptable cause of action, the Praetor granted a trial and assigned the case for decision by a "judge" (*iudex*), who was normally a lay person lacking any deep familiarity with law. The Praetor and the two parties to the lawsuit also prepared a special formula; this formula (which gives its name to Roman "formulary procedure") appointed the *iudex*, instructed him on the nature of the dispute, and ordered him to decide it. During the second stage of the trial, the *iudex* listened to argument from advocates for both parties and then decided the outcome of the case in accordance with the formula.

When important questions of law arose either before the Praetor or during the actual trial before the *iudex*, they were usually settled through reference to the opinions of jurists. Thus the Roman jurists, although they were not formally a part of the judicial system, played a pivotal role in determining law within Roman courts.

The "Case Law" Approach. In this casebook, students are exposed to the working methods of the Roman jurists, to their internal controversies, and to the principles and values that underlay their law. One important area, the law of delict, has been chosen to illustrate these points. The basic framework of the Roman law of delict initially derives from two sources: statutes (laws passed by the Roman people) and the Edict of the Urban Praetor. Some Cases (especially those in Chapter I) involve juristic interpretation of these fundamental sources. But in most Cases the jurists range well beyond this basic framework, into broader legal issues associated with personal legal responsibility for the harm or hurt that other people suffer; and most of Roman delictual law is in fact the jurists' own creation, not the result of direct statutory or edictal interpretation.

At the University of Michigan, I use this casebook as the basic text for a semester-long undergraduate course in Roman law. The course is organized mainly around classroom discussion of the individual Cases — usually about three to four Cases each hour. By delving into the Cases, students develop their own ability to examine legal rules and to assess them critically. Over a semester, the improvement in their legal skills is usually remarkable. Further, all law is to a large extent a seamless cloth, and this is no less true of Roman law; so students soon pick up a good deal of Roman law in other areas as well.

In order to encourage a deeper understanding of the Cases, I require students to purchase a general handbook on Roman law (e.g., Barry Nicholas, *An Introduction to Roman Law*, 1962). I also recommend that they purchase Edward Levi's *An Introduction to Legal Reasoning* (1949) and John Fleming's *An Introduction to the Law of Torts* (2d ed. 1985) — both excellent short treatments of their subjects. Students who not only participate in classroom discussion, but also read these three books, come away from the course with a good grasp of the nature of legal thinking in general, as well as an appreciation of the general content of both Roman and modern Anglo-American delictual law.

This casebook is modelled after the format of Herbert Hausmaninger's highly successful German casebooks on Roman contract and property law. To my mind, this format offers the best available method to communicate to modern students the content and character of classical Roman law. Direct exposure to original sources is far more exciting than lectures or a superficial reading of modern synthetic accounts; students also learn much more about law from the original sources than they could possibly learn from a mere summary.

How to Use This Casebook. The form of the Cases is invariable: first, the Latin text with the appropriate citation; second, an English translation of the text; third, for some Cases, a brief restatement of the main hypothetical problem in the Case; fourth, discussion questions that should orient students regarding the main legal problems raised by each Case.

The Cases are grouped by subject matter and presented in a definite order, usually so that legal questions can be explored on a progressively deeper basis. It is important to think about the interrelationship between the Cases and the various approaches that the jurists take within them.

The discussion questions have several forms. Some encourage accurate understanding of the Case itself, others involve application of the Case to different situations, and still others raise open-ended problems that invite a response based on broader considerations, including social morality and public policy. For this reason, not all of the questions have clear and specific answers; some, in fact, are intended mainly to stimulate thought and classroom discussion, and these questions may have no "correct" answer at all. Roman law, like all law, tends to raise difficulties on several levels simultaneously; students should learn to think about the connection between broad and narrow issues.

In the discussion of Cases, frequent reference is made to other legal texts, including many not quoted in this casebook. Although it is not necessary to look up these references in order to understand the questions, students who wish to learn more about Roman law are urged to consult these texts and the works discussed in the "Suggested Further Reading for Students" at the end of the book. To assist readers in becoming familiar with some of the more common technical terms of Roman law, a "Glossary" has been provided containing definitions of key Latin words and some unfamiliar English words.

Finally, students should remember that the Roman jurists wrote over more than three centuries, and that their writings accordingly display a development in legal ideas. The chronological list of jurists presented on the page following this preface should make it easier to observe this development. An "Appendix" to the casebook contains short biographies of the major Roman jurists. Fortunately, the number of major jurists is small, and students who look up the biographies will soon become familiar with their names.

In reading this casebook, students should think about not only the particular problems raised by the Cases, but also the larger issues they concern. On what principles does a civil society come to regard some acts (but not others) as delicts, and how does it use law to protect its citizens and itself against what it considers disruptive conduct? The jurists' thought on these matters is in some respects similar to our own, and in other respects sharply different. What explains the differences? Do they result chiefly from the relative social and economic "underdevelopment" of the Roman world, or from deeper disagreements about the way in which societies should be organized and governed? To what extent is the development of Roman law affected by accidents of its history or the conservatism of the jurists, and to what extent by the conscious or unconscious efforts of the jurists to achieve a socially beneficial body of rules? How close is the "fit" between Roman law and the social needs of Roman society? These are difficult questions, concerning which modern scholars still often disagree.

A Note on Translation. Throughout this casebook, "D." stands for the *Digesta* of Justinian, "C." for the *Codex* of Justinian, and "*Inst.*" for the *Institutiones* of Gaius or Justinian, as indicated. A few Cases come from two early post-classical collections of juristic sources: the *Collatio* (a "Comparison" of Roman with Mosaic law) and the *Sententiae* ("Sentences") of Paul. One Case is taken from the *Attic Nights* of Aulus Gellius, an antiquarian author of the mid-second century A.D. who sometimes cites juristic writings.

The translations in this casebook are intended to render the Latin sources into clear and comprehensible English, even at the cost of some wordiness. Where the Latin text is disputed, or its meaning ambiguous, I have opted for what I feel is the best solution. All translations are my own, although I have often been influenced by the renderings in *The Digest of Justinian* (a four-volume English translation edited by Alan Watson, 1985), *The Institutes of Gaius* (an English translation by Francis de Zulueta, 1946), F.H. Lawson's *Negligence in the Civil Law* (1950), and other earlier translations. I am very grateful to Profs. James O'Hara of Wesleyan University, John Ramsey of the University of Illinois, and the readers for the American Philological Association, who provided helpful criticism of my translations and of the casebook in general. I also want to thank Profs. Hardy Hansen of Brooklyn College and Marsh McCall of Stanford University for reading a late version of page proofs and for offering suggestions.

For a translator, the Lex Aquilia (the subject of Chapters I to III) causes particular difficulty. The First Section of this statute makes a defendant liable for wrongfully "slaying" (*occidere*) another person's slave or herd animal. In ordinary Latin, *occidere* means no more than "to kill"; but I have used the more archaic verb "to slay" because, in interpreting the Lex Aquilia, the jurists themselves give *occidere* a narrow and somewhat peculiar meaning, and because it is always important to realize when *occidere* occurs in the original Latin text. Similarly for the crucial verb *rumpere* in the Third Section; I have translated it, rather artificially, "to rend."

For reasons that should become clear, I have usually left untranslated the important technical terms *culpa* and *dolus*, along with a few others; any English translation of these terms would fatally prejudice understanding of them. It is preferable that students learn the meaning of these words from the contexts in which they appear. Likewise, in translating I have avoided the word "negligence" and its cognates, since they could result in misleading comparisons with the modern tort of neligence.

Ann Arbor   B.W.F.
July, 1988

Jurists Cited in this Casebook
(in Rough Chronological Order)

Pre-Classical (100–30 B.C.)

Q. MUCIUS Scaevola
C. Aquilius GALLUS
SERVIUS Sulpicius Rufus
P. ALFENUS Varus
A. OFILIUS
C. TREBATIUS Testa

Roman Emperors:

Early Classical (30 B.C.–A.D. 90)

M. Antistius LABEO	Augustus (31 B.C.–A.D. 14)
Fabius MELA	
Massurius SABINUS	Tiberius (14–37)
C. CASSIUS Longinus	Claudius (41–54)
PROCULUS	Nero (54–68)
PEGASUS	Vespasian (69–79)
PLAUTIUS	Domitian (81–96)

High Classical (A.D. 90–190)

L. JAVOLENUS Priscus	Trajan (98–117)
L. NERATIUS Priscus	Hadrian (117–138)
URSEIUS FEROX	
P. Juventius CELSUS	
OCTAVENUS	
VIVIANUS	
SEXTUS PEDIUS	
P. Salvius JULIANUS	Antoninus Pius (138–161)
Ulpius MARCELLUS	Marcus Aurelius (161–180)
GAIUS	
Sextus POMPONIUS	
Q. Cervidius SCAEVOLA	Commodus (180–192)

Late Classical (A.D. 190–235)

Aemilius PAPINIANUS	Septimius Severus (193–211)
CALLISTRATUS	
Julius PAULUS	Caracalla (211–217)
Domitius ULPIANUS	Alexander Severus (222–235)

(The usual Latin name of each jurist is capitalized. The Appendix contains further biographical information on these jurists.)

Introduction to the Roman Law of Delict

When one person inflicts harm or hurt on another, this act often results in a legal obligation: the offender must pay the offended party a sum of money that "makes up" for the misdeed. In Anglo-American law, this sort of obligation is called a tort; in Roman law and in the modern Civil Law systems that derive from Roman law, it is called a delict (*delictum*). Using technical language, we may define a delict in Roman law as a misdeed that is prosecuted through a private lawsuit brought by the offended individual and punished by a money penalty that the defendant must pay to the plaintiff. It is Roman law that determines, in the first instance, whether certain broad types of acts are treated as delicts; without such a legal determination, a harm or hurt does not result in delictual liability in Roman law.

A delict is not in itself a crime; it is not publicly prosecuted or sanctioned. Instead, a delict gives rise to a civil liability. The offended party alone decides whether or not to sue the offender, and then as plaintiff he or she receives whatever a court may order the defendant to pay. The role of the State, in other words, is limited to hearing arguments from the plaintiff and the defendant, and then to awarding money to the plaintiff if this is judged to be appropriate. Of course, the same act may at times lead to both a civil and a criminal liability; but in Roman law (as in modern law) these two liabilities are in principle kept distinct from one another.

Nonetheless, there was always in Roman law a markedly punitive aspect to delictual liability. Delictual liability is thought to have originated, in archaic Roman law, as a substitute for immediate personal vengeance; but vengeance can often involve not just satisfaction of the victim's sense of grievance, but also punishment of the offender, in order to admonish the offender and deter others from committing similar misdeeds. This concept survived until the end of classical Roman law, and it has, as we shall see, a powerful influence on how the Roman jurists think and write about delict.

The survival of punishment as an ordinary element of delictual law implies, from a modern perspective, that the Romans never completely separated the concepts of delictual and criminal liability. In a Roman delictual trial, the plaintiff is not so much seeking compensation for loss the delict has caused (in most delicts compensation is not even a central issue), as, in a sense, "avenging" a wrong done to him or herself; and at the same time the plaintiff is also often "avenging" a protected social interest that the defendant has violated. By contrast, in modern Anglo-American law, as in modern legal systems generally, punishment has become marginal in tort law, although courts still award punitive damages when a defendant's conduct is judged to have been particularly offensive to the community.

The three major delictual actions in Roman law all originate in statutes, a fact that suggests public recognition of the important social interests these actions protect. Broadly speaking, the protected social interests are three: persons should have confidence that their property will not be harmed by others; persons should be secure in their possession of property, and others must therefore be deterred from fraudulently taking it away from them; and persons should be protected from deliberate anti-social attacks on their dignity.

In classical Roman law, violation of the first of these social interests was actionable under the Lex Aquilia, a statute thought to date from the early third century B.C. The statute governed loss wrongfully inflicted (*damnum iniuria datum*), especially by damaging another person's property. This casebook discusses Aquilian liability in some detail (Chapters I–III) mainly because of its inherent interest for modern students; but this source of liability was much less important in the Roman world than in our own. Chapter IV deals with a related subject, the liability of owners when their animals inflict loss on others.

The other two major delicts are discussed more briefly in Chapter V. Both theft (*furtum*) and outrage (*iniuria*) were made actionable by the Twelve Tables (an archaic law code promulgated in 449 B.C.), and later, in a somewhat different form, by the Praetor's Edict. In the action on theft, the plaintiff could obtain a multiple of the value of property stolen by the defendant, this in addition to recovery of the stolen object or its value. It may seem strange to modern eyes that theft is punishable through a private action; but outrage (*iniuria*), intentional personal offense to someone else, has a more contemporary appearance. Persons commit *iniuria* by assaulting others physically, defaming them, violating exercise of their rights as citizens, and so on.

In addition to the three major delicts, the Praetor's Edict created many other delicts during the late Republic. Chapter VI treats two important praetorian delicts: deceit (*dolus*) and duress (*metus*) that result in loss to the plaintiff. These two praetorian delicts supplement the three major actions by catching some marginal cases. A few Cases on the action for corrupting a slave illustrate the numerous other minor Praetorian delicts.

Chapter VII deals with "quasi-delict," an amorphous catch-all category that was evidently proposed by Gaius, but did not become generally accepted until the post-classical period. Although there is little unity to this category, it does contain some liabilities that represent an evolution beyond the usual principles of Roman delict.

Chapter I: The Wording of the Lex Aquilia

The Lex Aquilia, proposed by an otherwise unknown plebeian tribune named Aquilius, was intended to replace most earlier statutory law on damage to another's property (Ulpian, D. 9.2.1). Its date is uncertain, but probably early third century B.C.

The new statute established liability under two heads: in the First Section, for the unlawful "slaying" (*occidere*) of slaves or four-footed herd animals; and in the Third Section, for the unlawful "burning, breaking, or rending" (*urere, frangere, rumpere*) of property in general, except for acts included under the First Section. (The statute's Second Section, on an apparently unrelated topic, soon became obsolete.) The Lex Aquilia thus attempted to create a general basis whereby a person could bring suit if his or her property was wrongfully damaged by a third party. The Urban Praetor implemented the statute by providing a private action in his Edict.

The Lex Aquilia was not skillfully drafted, and it soon required interpretation; this early and rather awkward interpretation exercised a strong influence on later juristic writing about the statute. In particular, the words "slaying" and "rending" were given rather unexpected meanings. "Slaying" was narrowly interpreted, and acts not strictly encompassed by the narrow meaning of the verb were excluded from coverage; by contrast, "rending" was very broadly interpreted. But both Sections required a high degree of physical directness; if this was not present, no action was available under the Lex Aquilia.

In order to prevent injustice, the Urban Praetor intervened by granting what are variously called, without distinction, either "analogous actions" (*actiones utiles*) or "actions on the facts" (*actiones in factum*) that were modelled after the statutory action. The Praetor gave such actions in situations where, for instance, a defendant had not directly "slain" a slave, but had indirectly caused his death to occur. The classical jurists struggled, without great success, to explain the legal basis of the distinction between statutory and analogous actions; the difficulties they encountered are somewhat similar to those involved in the older Common Law distinction between Trespass and Trespass on the Case, which was also based on the difference between direct and indirect causation of harm.

The later history of the Lex Aquilia is also heavily influenced by its ambiguous purpose: was it chiefly intended only to compensate the owner for property losses, or did it also aim to punish the offender for a wrongful act? The jurists concede that the Lex Aquilia has at least a partially punitive purpose, and this purpose is illustrated by one of its provisions, whereby a defendant who initially denies liability, and so forces the issue to trial, is condemned to pay to the plaintiff double the loss. Other punitive aspects of Aquilian liability will emerge in subsequent chapters of the casebook.

Part A: The Provisions of the Statute

Case 1: The First Section

D. 9.2.2 pr.–1 (Gaius, libro septimo ad Edictum Provinciale)

Lege Aquilia capite primo cavetur: 'ut qui servum servamve alienum alienamve quadrupedemve pecudem iniuria occiderit, quanti id in eo anno plurimi fuit, tantum aes dare domino damnas esto': (1) et infra deinde cavetur ut adversus infitiantem in duplum actio esset.

(Gaius in the seventh book on the Provincial Edict)

The First Section of the Lex Aquilia provides that: "if anyone wrongfully (*iniuria*) slays a male or female slave belonging to another person, or a four-footed herd animal, let him be condemned to pay to the owner as much money as the maximum the property was worth in the year (previous to the slaying)." (1) And it then provides that the action be for double against one who denies liability.

The Hypothetical Problem:

Titia has killed my slave. Under what circumstances will I be able to sue Titia, and what can I get from her?

Discussion:

1. What is the apparent purpose of this Section? Is the legislator aiming primarily to compensate the owner, or to punish the slayer? As we shall see, the jurists seem to waver in deciding this issue.

2. How clear are its terms? For instance, what meaning would you assign to the word "slays" (*occiderit*)? Does it cover only deliberate slaying, or also reckless or careless or accidental slaying? Originally, the Lex Aquilia may have applied only to deliberate slaying; but in classical law it includes all "wrongful" slaying, including many instances of careless (but not accidental) slaying. On other aspects of the definition of "slaying," see below, Part B, Section 1.

3. What reason might the legislator have had for singling out the slaying of slaves and four-footed herd animals as requiring special attention? Is it that this property is likely to have special importance to farmers?

4. What is a four-footed herd animal? Gaius, D. 9.2.2.2, includes the following: sheep, goats, cattle, horses, mules, and asses; also (but with some hesitation) pigs, elephants, and camels. Excluded are dogs and wild animals such as bears, lions, and panthers. What principles of selection seem to underlie this list?

5. The word "wrongfully" (*iniuria*) seems originally to have meant "without legal right." Under what circumstances do you suppose that a person might have a legal right to damage another's property? (Consider, for instance, killing in self-defense.) What is the difference between doing something

"without legal right" and doing something "wrongfully"? It is usually supposed that the late Republican jurists were responsible for the shift in the meaning of *iniuria*; see below, Chapter II, Parts A and B.

6. When a plaintiff came before the Praetor and claimed that someone else had wrongfully slain his slave, and the defendant denied liability, the Praetor granted a formulary action, the wording of which has been conjecturally reconstructed as follows:

> "If it appears that the defendant wrongfully slew this slave, whatever sum of money the defendant ought as a result to pay to the plaintiff, let the *iudex* condemn the defendant to the plaintiff for double this sum; if it does not appear, let him absolve."

The word "ought" tacitly refers to the Lex Aquilia, which had established the basis of the defendant's liability. What does the formula require the plaintiff to prove in order to win a judgment from the *iudex*? Similar formulas were used for other varieties of statutory and analogous Aquilian actions.

7. The Lex Aquilia also contained provisions concerning the result if the defendant admits liability (see below, Part C) and the limits on a person's liability for acts done by his slaves or by children who are in his power (Gaius, *Inst.* 4.76; Ulpian, D. 9.4.2 pr.–1; see below, Chapter III, Part B).

8. Before you begin to examine the Cases in which the jurists interpret the Lex Aquilia, you should give some thought to the general problem of interpreting a statute. In the case of a statute such as the Lex Aquilia, what principles ought to guide an interpreter (whether a jurist or, in modern law, a judge)? How does a statute differ from law established through the judicial system itself? What is the relationship between the words of the statute and its more general purpose? What degree of freedom does an interpreter have in giving meaning to the words of a statute? These are old and extremely difficult questions, and they are still live issues today. As you read the Cases below, try to determine how the jurists handled the problem, and also whether you approve of the way they handled it.

Case 2: The Third Section

D. 9.2.27.5 (Ulpianus, libro octavo decimo ad Edictum)

Tertio autem capite ait eadem lex Aquilia: 'Ceterarum rerum, praeter hominem et pecudem occisos, si quis alteri damnum faxit, quod usserit fregerit ruperit iniuria, quanti ea res erit in diebus triginta proximis, tantum aes domino dare damnas esto.'

(Ulpian in the eighteenth book on the Edict)

In the Third Section the Lex Aquilia states: "Of other property, apart from a slain slave and herd animal, if anyone causes loss to another by wrongfully (*iniuria*) burning, breaking, or rending, let him be condemned to pay the owner as much money as the matter (*res*) will be worth within the next thirty days (after the act in question)."

The Hypothetical Problem:

Sempronius knocks over and breaks my lamp. Can I demand compensation from him, and if so, how much?

Discussion:

1. The interpretation of this Section is notoriously difficult, and the correct translation is not certain. What problems do you see upon your first inspection of it?

2. What kinds of acts are included in the category "burning, breaking, or rending" (*usserit fregerit ruperit*)? What acts are excluded? Does this Section seem to apply if, for instance, someone pours out a vat of wine or spots clothing?

3. Is it likely that the legislator had in mind not only damage to movable objects (like slaves, herd animals, and vases), but also damage to land and buildings on land? See Case 14.

4. How clear is the law's description of the amount that the offender must pay to the object's owner? ("As much as the matter will be worth," *quanti ea res erit*, is a technical phrase, the meaning of which is discussed below in Chapter II, Part C.) The jurists normally allow the plaintiff to recover at least the reduction in value of the object as a result of the defendant's act. What additional losses should be recoverable? Must the plaintiff's property at least suffer some loss in value?

5. Did the Third Section allow for double damages if the defendant denied liability? (Probably yes; see Case 18.)

Part B: Interpretation of the Statute:
Actions *In Factum*

Section 1: Interpretation of the First Section

Case 3: The Meaning of "To Slay"

D. 9.2.7.1–2 (Ulpianus, libro octavo decimo ad Edictum)

Occisum autem accipere debemus, sive gladio sive etiam fuste vel alio telo vel manibus (si forte strangulavit eum) vel calce petiit vel capite vel qualiter qualiter. (2) Sed si quis plus iusto oneratus deiecerit onus et servum occiderit, Aquilia locum habet: fuit enim in ipsius arbitrio ita se non onerare. nam et si lapsus aliquis servum alienum onere presserit, Pegasus ait lege Aquilia eum teneri ita demum si vel plus iusto se oneraverit vel neglegentius per lubricum transierit.

(Ulpian in the eighteenth book on the Edict)

We should regard a person as "slain" (*occisum*) if someone struck (him) with a sword or also a club or other weapon, or with his hands — e.g., if he strangled him —, or with his boot or head, or in any like way. (2) But if someone who is excessively loaded throws down his burden and slays a slave, the Aquilian action is pertinent; for it was in his discretion not to burden himself so. For even if someone slips and crushes a slave with his burden, Pegasus says that he is liable under the Lex Aquilia if he either excessively loaded himself or walked carelessly on slippery ground.

The Hypothetical Problem:

Titius shrugs off a heavy backpack that he has been carrying. The backpack falls and crushes a slave belonging to Seia. Seia brings an Aquilian action against Titius, who defends himself by arguing that he has not "slain" the slave and hence is not liable under the Lex Aquilia. Will Seia win?

Discussion:

1. In this Case, Ulpian develops a definition of "slaying" by giving a number of examples. What are the common characteristics of the various actions described by Ulpian? On the basis of these characteristics, try to state what "slaying" means. To what extent does it appear to involve physical contact between the defendant and the victim?

2. A defendant is liable under the Lex Aquilia if he kills a slave by hitting him with a weapon. Will he also be liable if he throws the weapon and it strikes a passing slave when it descends? Alfenus (in Case 51) and Ulpian (in Case 60) indicate that he will be liable under the statute; why? Is this an extension of the core meaning of "slay"?

3. The implication of section (2) is that a person may not be liable under the Lex Aquilia if he is carrying a light burden and accidentally falls on non-slippery ground, thereby killing another's slave. Can this implication be justified from a straightforward reading of the statute? (Already at this stage, you might want to start thinking about the problem of fault. When one person "acts" by physically moving, and this "act" sets off a chain of causation that results in loss to somebody else, should the person acting always be liable for loss that results from the act? If not always, then when?)

4. In order for a statutory action to arise under the Lex Aquilia, must the defendant have intended to cause the loss? What does this Case indicate? As you will see in later Cases, the jurists almost never use intentionality as a basis for giving statutory Aquilian actions.

5. What happens when an action under the First Section is not available because the defendant did not "slay" within the definition this Case presents? Pomponius (D. 19.5.11) explains:

> But if a statute is just and necessary, the Praetor will supplement the actions instituted by statutes in areas where the statute is lacking; he does so in the case of the Lex Aquilia by according actions *in factum* adapted to the Lex Aquilia, something that is required for the statute to be beneficial.

Thus the Praetor undertook to extend the Lex Aquilia by recognizing other fact-situations as covered by its general intent, although not by its words. Much of the rest of this Part concerns the jurists' efforts to distinguish between statutory and *in factum* actions under the Lex Aquilia. As you read these Cases, try to determine why it was "just and necessary" to extend the Lex Aquilia in each instance. The sources on the Lex Aquilia provide a good illustration of Roman law-building in practice: the creative interaction between statutes, the Praetor, and the jurists.

Case 4: Pushing Someone Else

D. 9.2.7.3 (Ulpianus, libro octavo decimo ad Edictum)

Proinde si quis alterius inpulsu damnum dederit, Proculus scribit neque eum qui impulit teneri, quia non occidit, neque eum qui impulsus est, quia damnum iniuria non dedit: secundum quod in factum actio erit danda in eum qui impulit.

(Ulpian in the eighteenth book on the Edict)

Therefore if a person is pushed by another and so inflicts loss, Proculus writes that the one who pushed is not liable because he did not slay (*non occidit*), nor is the one who was pushed because he did not inflict loss wrongfully (*iniuria*). Accordingly an *in factum* action should be given against the one who pushed.

The Hypothetical Problem:

Cassia is elbowing her way through a crowd. She pushes Titia, who collapses onto a slave owned by Seia. The slave is killed. Whom can Seia sue, and how?

Discussion:

1. The person who pushes is not liable under the Lex Aquilia "because he did not slay"; that is, Cassia can argue that her act does not technically come within the terms of the Lex Aquilia. How does her action differ from that of a person who throws a burden onto someone else (see Case 3)?

2. The person who was pushed did inflict loss, but did not do so "wrongfully" (*iniuria*). In what sense is this true? What is the meaning of the word *iniuria* here? Is it only that Titia did not act voluntarily?

3. What is the practical consequence of bringing an action *in factum* rather than one on the statute itself? Surviving sources do not clearly indicate any difference in legal outcome; however, it is possible that a defendant in an *in factum* action did not have to pay double damages if he or she failed to admit liability. See the discussion on Case 15.

Case 5: Administering Drugs

D. 9.2.9 pr.–1 (Ulpianus, libro octavo decimo ad Edictum)

Item si obstetrix medicamentum dederit et inde mulier perierit, Labeo distinguit, ut si quidem suis manibus supposuit, videatur occidisse: sin vero dedit, ut sibi mulier offerret, in factum actionem dandam, quae sententia vera est: magis enim causam mortis praestitit quam occidit. (1) Si quis per vim vel suasum medicamentum alicui infundit vel ore vel clystere vel si eum unxit malo veneno, lege Aquilia eum teneri, quemadmodum obstetrix supponens tenetur.

(Ulpian in the eighteenth book on the Edict)

Again, if a midwife gives a drug to a woman who then dies of it, Labeo distinguishes: if she administered it with her own hands, she is held to have slain (*occidisse*); but if she gave it for the woman to take herself, an action *in factum* should be given. This view is correct, since she furnished the cause of death rather than slew. (1) If a person, using force or persuasion, injects a drug into another either orally or by syringe, or rubbed him with a foul poison, (a jurist held that) he is liable under the Lex Aquilia, just like the midwife who administers (a drug herself).

The Hypothetical Problem:

Sempronia is a midwife attending Pamphila, a pregnant slave woman who belongs to Cassia. Sempronia gives Pamphila a bottle of medicine, which she takes home and drinks some hours later. The "medicine" turns out to be a deadly poison, from which Pamphila dies immediately. What action can Cassia bring against Sempronia?

Discussion:

1. How is the distinction drawn in this Case similar to that between a person who drops a burden on another (Case 3) and a person who pushes someone else into another (Case 4)?

2. In justifying Labeo's decision, Ulpian notes the difference between "slaying" (*occidere*) and "furnishing the cause of death" (*causam mortis praestare*). Does this seem to you a valid distinction? What is the apparent basis of the distinction? (The distinction, which seems to have been favored especially by the jurist Celsus in the early second century A.D., is further discussed in the next Case.)

3. Should it be presumed that the midwife knew or ought to have known that the drug was toxic? What if she was unsure of the effect of the drug, but thought that it might have beneficial consequences? In short, what is required in order that the midwife's action be "wrongful"?

4. What situations are covered by the phrase "using force or persuasion"? Do you see any difference between forcibly administering a poisonous drug to a slave woman, and forcibly making the slave woman take the drug herself?

Is there any difference between someone persuading a slave woman to let a drug be administered to her, and persuading her to take the drug herself? In which of these four situations would Ulpian give a statutory action, and why?

Case 6: Furnishing the Cause of Death

D. 9.2.7.6–7: (Ulpianus, libro octavo decimo ad Edictum)

Celsus autem multum interesse dicit, occiderit an mortis causam praestit-
erit, ut qui mortis causam praestitit, non Aquilia, sed in factum actione teneatur. unde adfert eum qui venenum pro medicamento dedit et ait causam mortis
praestitisse, quemadmodum eum qui furenti gladium porrexit: nam nec hunc
lege Aquilia teneri, sed in factum. (7) Sed si quis de ponte aliquem praecipita-
vit, Celsus ait, sive ipso ictu perierit aut continuo submersus est aut lassatus vi
fluminis victus perierit, lege Aquilia teneri, quemadmodum si quis puerum
saxo inlisisset.

(Ulpian in the eighteenth book on the Edict)

Celsus says that there is a great difference between slaying and
furnishing the cause of death, in that a person who furnishes the
cause of death is liable not in an Aquilian action but by one *in
factum*. Thus he mentions a person who gave poison as a drug;
Celsus says that he furnished the cause of death, just like a person
who held out a sword to a lunatic; for this person is not liable under
the Lex Aquilia, but *in factum*. (7) But if a person hurled someone
from a bridge, Celsus says that whether he died by the blow itself
or was immediately drowned or was exhausted and died when
overcome by the river's current, there is liability under the Lex
Aquilia, just as if someone dashed a boy against a rock.

The Hypothetical Problem:

Titius knocks a slave woman off the Mulvian bridge. The slave falls into the
Tiber River, which carries her downstream. The slave woman, who is not a
skilled swimmer, struggles to reach shore, but she is weighed down by her
clothing. After ten minutes she is finally sucked under and drowns. Can her
owner bring a statutory Aquilian action against Titius?

Discussion:

1. What is the "great difference" that Celsus sees between "slaying" and "furnishing the cause of death"? Note that Celsus apparently holds that it is not slaying
   when one person gives a toxic drug to another, whereas Ulpian (in the previous Case) holds that it is slaying at least when one administers the drug
   oneself. Do Celsus and Ulpian disagree, or should Celsus rather be understood as including only cases where the victim takes the poison himself?

2. I give a sword to a lunatic, who then uses it to kill himself or somebody else.
   In what sense is it true that I have "furnished the cause of death"? To what
   extent does this seem more problematic? Why shouldn't we hold that the lunatic is the killer?

3. Why is it that a person is liable in a statutory action if he throws another from a bridge even when that person subsequently drowns because she cannot swim against the current? How clear is the chain of physical causation that ties the defendant's act to the victim's death? Can similar problems be raised about the boy who is dashed against a rock? Note that the person who pushed the boy may not have realized that he would fall against a rock.

4. You drive my cattle into a mountain pass and they then plunge off a cliff. Is the action statutory or *in factum*? (See Neratius, D. 9.2.53.)

5. My slave is riding a horse; you startle the horse, which throws the slave into a river; the slave drowns. Is the action statutory or *in factum*? Ulpian, D. 9.2.9.3, gives an *in factum* action; why?

6. A dog's owner incites it to bite a passing slave, who then dies of the wound. Under what circumstances should the dog's owner be held liable under a statutory Aquilian action? As Ulpian (D. 9.2.11.5) reports, Proculus held the owner always liable on a statutory action, while Julian thought him liable on the statutory action only if he was holding the dog, but *in factum* if he was not. Why is this hypothetical case more difficult than the previous one?

7. Ulpian (D. 9.2.49 pr.) writes: "If someone makes smoke and drives away or even kills another's bees, he is held to have furnished the cause of death rather than to have slain, and so he is liable in an action *in factum*." Is this ruling consistent with the present Case? An analogous action on the dead bees would lie under the Third Section of the Lex Aquilia, but the reasoning is applicable to the First Section as well. If Titius set a fire and as a result a slave died of smoke inhalation, would Titius be liable statutorily or *in factum*? What is the theory?

8. A highway robber strips a slave of his clothing; the slave then freezes to death. The highwayman has clearly stolen the clothing; has he also "furnished the cause" of the slave's death? See Ulpian, D. 19.5.14.1.

Case 7: Physical Directness

Gaius, *Institutiones* 3.219

Ceterum placuit ita demum ex ista lege actionem esse, si quis corpore suo damnum dederit; ideoque alio modo damno dato utiles actiones dantur, veluti si quis alienum hominem aut pecudem incluserit et fame necaverit, aut iumentum tam vehementer egerit ut rumperetur; item si quis alieno servo persuaserit ut in arborem ascenderet vel in puteum descenderet, et is ascendendo aut descendendo ceciderit et aut mortuus fuerit aut aliqua parte corporis laesus sit; item si quis alienum servum de ponte aut ripa in flumen proiecerit et is suffocatus fuerit; quamquam hic corpore suo damnum dedisse eo quod proiecerit non difficiliter intellegi potest.

(Gaius in the third book of his *Institutes*)

It is accepted that there is an action on this statute so long as a person gives loss with his own body (*corpore suo*). Therefore when loss is given otherwise, analogous actions are granted, e.g. if someone shuts up and starves to death a slave or herd animal, or drives a beast of burden so harshly that it is rent (*rumperetur*). And similarly, if someone persuades another's slave to climb a tree or go down a well, and in climbing or descending he is killed or is injured in some part of his body. And similarly, if someone hurls another's slave off a bridge or bank into a river and the slave is drowned; however, in this case it is not hard to interpret him as giving loss with his own body (*corpore suo*), in that he hurled him in.

The Hypothetical Problem:

Cassia borrows a mule from Sempronia and loads it with a heavy pack. She then drives the mule to market. Although the mule seems to be tiring, Cassia keeps pressing the mule to go faster. Finally the mule collapses in exhaustion and dies. Can Sempronia sue Cassia under the Lex Aquilia?

Discussion:

1. By contrast with Celsus (in the previous Case), Gaius explains the difference between statutory and *in factum* actions by emphasizing the degree of the defendant's physical contact with the victim. Does this seem more satisfactory? Why should physical contact make an important legal difference? (Julian also emphasizes direct physical contact; see Case 56.)

2. Can you justify drawing a distinction between administering poison to a slave (result: statutory action) and confining a slave until he starves to death (result: *in factum* action)? Haven't both offenders acted physically against the victim? Haven't both placed the victim in a life-threatening situation? Or are the jurists trying to get at some subtler distinction, such as that the first person directly altered the victim's body by administering poison, while the second merely put the victim into a position where nature could take its course? If this is so, why is one statutorily liable for hurling a slave into a

river when the slave later drowns because of the current? Gaius (unlike Celsus in Case 6) hesitates about this case; why?

3. The Lex Aquilia is a very early statute, and it may be that the restrictive meaning given to *occidere* ("to slay") simply resulted from archaic practice in interpreting. In any case, the jurists sometimes interpret the verb more broadly when handling criminal statutes of a later date. For instance, with regard to the use of *occidere* in the marriage legislation of Augustus, Ulpian (D. 48.8.15) remarks that "There is no difference between one who slays (*occiderit*) or who furnishes the cause of death." Further, Julian (D. 9.2.51 pr., = Case 56) asserts that: "Commonly a person is said to have 'slain' (*occidisse*) when he furnishes the cause of death in any manner"; in fact, the Latin verb *occidere* really just means "to kill." Why did the jurists accept a narrower interpretation of the verb in the Lex Aquilia?

4. If someone says to you that "Sally killed George," without adding further details, what image springs to your mind? Which of the following situations best corresponds to that image: 1) Sally beat George to death with a fireplace poker; or 2) Sally locked George in a room where he starved to death? In both cases, Sally "caused" George's death; but in ordinary speech the verb "kill" is most commonly used for situations in which there is a close and clear relation between an act and the results of the act, such that the act and its consequences are not readily distinguishable as separate events. Why is this so? Do you think that the distinction between statutory and *in factum* Aquilian actions might rest simply on the linguistic difference between the "core" meaning of "kill" and its more extended usages, rather than, say, upon some difference in the perceived "directness" of causation? See further G. Lakoff and M. Johnson, *Metaphors We Live By* (1980) 69–72, on the linguistic concept of "prototypical causation" in action verbs such as "kill."

5. As this fragment of Gaius shows, the problem of physical directness resurfaces in the juristic interpretation of the Third Section of the Lex Aquilia, which is discussed in the following Cases. How is a person who drives a mule too harshly, thereby injuring it physically, similar to a person who confines and starves to death a slave? Persuading a slave to do something dangerous (such as climbing a tree) is obviously different in that that the defendant's act is purely verbal; ought such purely verbal acts always to result in an *in factum* rather than a statutory action? Consider, for example, the proverbial case of the person who shouts "Fire!" in a crowded theater, thereby causing a panic.

Section 2: Interpretation of the Third Section

Case 8: The Meaning of "To Rend"

Gaius, *Institutiones* 3.217

...Si quid enim ustum aut ruptum aut fractum fuerit, actio hoc capite constituitur, quamquam potuerit sola rupti appellatio in omnes istas causas sufficere.
ruptum enim intellegitur quod quoquo modo corruptum est. unde non solum
usta aut rupta aut fracta, sed etiam scissa et collisa et effusa et quoquo modo vi-
tiata aut perempta atque deteriora facta hoc verbo continentur.

(Gaius in the third book of his *Institutes*)

...For if anything is burned or rent or broken, an action is established by this Section; but the term "rent" (*ruptum*) could suffice for
all these cases. For a thing is construed as "rent" (*ruptum*) when it
is "spoiled" (*corruptum*) in any way. Hence this word includes not
only things burned or rent or broken, but also things torn and
dashed and poured out and in any way harmed or destroyed and
(so) diminished in value.

The Hypothetical Problem:

Titius pours out a vat of wine belonging to Seius. Can Seius sue Titius under
the Third Section of the Lex Aquilia?

Discussion:

1. Ulpian (in the following Case) says that the late Republican jurists, in the
   second and first centuries B.C., already interpreted "rend" to mean "spoil";
   what might have been their reason for preferring this extended meaning?

2. According to Celsus (in Ulpian, D. 9.2.27.16), the legislator's intent was to
   list certain specific acts (burning and breaking), and then to give a more
   general term (spoiling) that embraced them. Does this seem a plausible interpretation of the words of the Third Section? Is it more plausible to suppose that the jurists gave the Third Section a meaning that the legislator
   probably had not intended?

3. Even under the extensive interpretation that the jurists give to the Third Section, do they still require that an offender commit some positive act (as op-
   posed to an act of omission) before statutory liability arises? Do they require
   that property be physically damaged by this act? As later Cases will suggest,
   the answers to both questions are usually affirmative. Only in special circumstances do the jurists consider acts of omission to be a source of
   Aquilian liability at all, and then the action is *in factum*. When property is
   not physically lowered in value but the owner sustains indirect financial
   loss, the jurists usually award an action *in factum*. Can their position on both
   questions be justified on the basis of the wording of the statute?

Case 9: Sowing Wild Oats; Pouring Out Wine

D. 9.2.27.13–15 (Ulpianus, libro octavo decimo ad Edictum)

Inquit lex 'ruperit.' rupisse verbum fere omnes veteres sic intellexerunt 'corruperit.' (14) Et ideo Celsus quaerit, si lolium aut avenam in segetem alienam inieceris, quo eam tu inquinares, non solum quod vi aut clam dominum posse agere vel, si locatus fundus sit, colonum, sed et in factum agendum, et si colonus eam exercuit, cavere eum debere amplius non agi, scilicet ne dominus amplius inquietet: nam alia quaedam species damni est ipsum quid corrumpere et mutare, ut lex Aquilia locum habeat, alia nulla ipsius mutatione applicare aliud, cuius molesta separatio sit. (15) Cum eo plane qui vinum spurcavit vel effudit vel acetum fecit vel alio modo vitiavit, agi posse Aquilia Celsus ait, quia etiam effusum et acetum factum corrupti appellatione continentur.

(Ulpian in the eighteenth book on the Edict)

The Lex (Aquilia) says "rends" (*ruperit*). Almost all the Republican jurists understood the word "rent" as "spoils" (*corruperit*). (14) Therefore Celsus also considers, if you sow darnel or wild oats in another's crop, thereby ruining it, the owner — or, if the farm has been leased out, the tenant farmer — can bring not only the interdict *quod vi aut clam*, but also an (Aquilian) action *in factum*; and if the tenant brought it, he should formally promise that there will be no further legal proceedings (against you by the farm's owner), obviously so that the owner not trouble (you) further. For (he adds) it is one type of loss to spoil and change an object, thus providing a basis for the Lex Aquilia; it is another when, without altering the object, one adds something that makes separation difficult. (15) Celsus says that the Aquilian action can obviously be brought against a person who polluted wine or poured it out or made it sour or otherwise harmed it; for even pouring it out and making it sour are included in the term "spoil."

The Hypothetical Problem:

Sempronius, who harbors a grudge against his neighbor Cassia, creeps onto Cassia's farm one night and sows wild oats in her newly planted grain field. The wild oats grow up together with the grain. As a result, Cassia's crop is ruined. What action should Cassia bring against Sempronius?

Discussion:

1. When the offender sows wild oats in a field of standing grain, the field's owner (or the tenant) has an option. She can bring a special type of legal action, called an interdict, which is available to recover damages resulting from "forcible or stealthy" interference with rights in immovable property such as land (the interdict *quod vi aut clam*). Alternatively, she can sue under an *in factum* Aquilian action. The Aquilian action is probably more advantageous, since it often results in double damages. Why must the tenant who brings an action on property damage make a judicial promise that the

owner will not also sue the offender?

2. How convincing is Celsus' reason for not allowing a statutory action when wild oats are sown among grain? Is there any clear basis for distinguishing this case from the pouring out of wine? Is the substance of the wine altered when it is poured out? How does Celsus' ruling derive from the wording of the Lex Aquilia?

3. In earlier Cases, the distinction between statutory and *in factum* actions was determined mainly by the physical directness of the defendant's act in harming the plaintiff's property. How is the criterion in this Case different? Try to state the criterion in this Case as clearly as you can. Is separability really the key issue, or is it rather that the defendant has not physically altered the grain? Is this criterion additional to that of direct physicality, or is it only supplemental?

4. In the following situations, should the Praetor grant a statutory or an analogous action?
   — the defendant has torn or spotted the plaintiff's clothes (Ulpian, D. 9.2.27.18).
   — the defendant has poured the plaintiff's grain into a river (D. 9.2.27.19).
   — the defendant has mixed sand into the plaintiff's grain (D. 9.2.27.20).

The third case is the most difficult. Ulpian says: "Again, if someone mixes sand or something else with grain, so that separation is difficult, action can be brought as for spoiling (of the grain)." The action is apparently statutory. How can this ruling be distinguished from the ruling in the main Case?

Case 10: Wine Runs Out of Damaged Cistern

D. 9.2.27.35 (Ulpianus, libro octavo decimo ad Edictum)
Item si tectori locaveris laccum vino plenum curandum et ille eum pertudit, ut vinum sit effusum, Labeo scribit in factum agendum.

(Ulpian in the eighteenth book on the Edict)

Likewise, if you contracted with a plasterer to mend a cistern full of wine, and he made a hole in it so that the wine ran out, Labeo writes that the action should be *in factum*.

Discussion:

1. This Case is considerably more difficult than it may appear to be at first sight. What reasons might Labeo have had for holding that a statutory action is not available, granted that the plasterer punctured the cistern? Is it that the wine is considerably more valuable than the cistern, or rather that the wine was not directly harmed by the plasterer's act?

2. I cut the mooring rope of your ship; the ship then drifts onto rocks and is lost. With regard to the ship, am I liable to you in a statutory or an *in factum* action? See Ulpian, D. 9.2.29.5, who gives an action *in factum*. Do you see why? Is the case similar to the one discussed above? How is cutting the mooring rope of a ship different from boring a hole in it and thereby causing it to sink (Ulpian, D. 9.2.27.24: statutory action)?

3. For other examples of *in factum* actions where loss is not directly inflicted, see Case 7 (driving a beast of burden too harshly; persuading a slave to climb a tree), Case 22 (waving a red flag and causing cattle to stampede), Case 42 (harming a party-wall with an oven), Case 50 (starting a fire on one's own property, if it spreads to a neighbor's), and Case 83 (holding a slave whom another person kills).

4. *In factum* actions are also granted when the defendant's failure to act is primarily responsible for the loss: Case 71 (a magistrate starves wrongly confiscated cattle) and Case 89 (a furnace tender falls asleep without banking a fire). (See also Case 35.) How is failing to act similar to causing damage indirectly?

Case 11: Striking Coins Out of a Hand

D. 9.2.27.21 (Ulpianus, libro octavo decimo ad Edictum)

Si quis de manu mihi nummos excusserit, Sabinus existimat damni iniuriae esse actionem, si ita perierint, ne ad aliquem pervenirent, puta si in flumen vel in mare vel in cloacam ceciderunt: quod si ad aliquem pervenerunt, ope consilio furtum factum agendum, quod et antiquis placuit. idem etiam in factum dari posse actionem ait.

(Ulpian in the eighteenth book on the Edict)

If someone strikes coins out of my hand, Sabinus thinks that there is an action on wrongful loss if they are lost in such a way that no one receives them, e.g., if they fall into a river, the sea, or a sewer; but if someone received them, then an action must be brought for aiding and abetting a theft, a view that the Republican jurists shared. He says that (in the first case) an *in factum* action can also be granted.

The Hypothetical Problem:

Titius knocks coins out of my hand, and they fall to the bottom of the Tiber River. Efforts to retrieve them are unsuccessful. What action can I bring?

Discussion:

1. Why does Sabinus hold that I can bring a statutory action for wrongful loss? Is an *in factum* action more appropriate? Compare Case 29, where an *in factum* action is also given. What is the principle?

2. I deliberately throw your cup over the side of a ship into the sea. The jurists regard this not as theft (since I do not intend to profit), but as wrongful infliction of loss actionable *in factum*: Ulpian, D. 19.5.14.2. Do you see why?

3. Is the action *in factum* if I release a boar from your net, or free your chained slave, and the boar or slave runs away? See Proculus, D. 41.1.55; Ulpian, D. 4.3.7.7.

4. Titius knocks coins out of my hand; Maevius picks them up and runs away. On the action for aiding and abetting a theft, see Case 110. If an action on theft is not available against Titius, can I bring an action on wrongful damage against him if I cannot recover the coins from Maevius?

Case 12: Drinking Wine; Eating Grain

D. 9.2.30.2 (Paulus, libro vicensimo secundo ad Edictum)

Si quis alienum vinum vel frumentum consumpserit, non videtur damnum iniuria dare ideoque utilis danda est actio.

(Paul in the twenty-second book on the Edict)

If someone consumes another's wine or grain, he is not understood to give a wrongful loss, and so the analogous action (*actio utilis*) should be given.

The Hypothetical Problem:

Titius sets a bottle of wine on his windowsill. I uncork the bottle and drink the wine. What action can Titius bring against me?

Discussion:

1. Doesn't the offender alter the substance of the wine or grain? What reason might Paul have for declining to give a statutory action on the Lex Aquilia? Is it relevant that the wine or grain was, so to speak, put to its proper use by being consumed, and was not really damaged?

2. In this Case, as in many others, the fact situation is obviously incomplete as stated; Paul presumes, for instance, that the defendant has not been invited to have dinner at the plaintiff's house. What other presumptions might Paul be making about, for instance, the defendant's awareness that he was eating another person's food?

3. Acorns drop from your tree onto my land; although they still belong to you, I let my cows feed on them. Is the action against me statutory or *in factum*? See Ulpian, D. 19.5.14.3.

Case 13: Packing Stones Improperly in a Cart

D. 9.2.27.33 (Ulpianus, libro octavo decimo ad Edictum)

Si ex plostro lapis ceciderit et quid ruperit vel fregerit, Aquiliae actione plostrarium teneri placet, si male composuit lapides et ideo lapsi sunt.

(Ulpian in the eighteenth book on the Edict)

If stone falls from a cart and rends or breaks something, the prevailing view is that the carter is liable under the Aquilian action if he improperly packed the stones and they fell for this reason.

The Hypothetical Problem:

Seius loads his cart with building stone. The stone is improperly packed, and it falls out of the cart, thereby injuring a slave owned by Cassia. What action can Cassia bring?

Discussion:

1. Why does Ulpian grant a statutory action rather than one *in factum*? Is the physical action of the carter in loading the stones improperly the effective equivalent of his throwing down the stones? (See Case 4.)

2. Is the carter liable because, as a carter, he ought to have known how to load stones properly? In that event, could he also be liable for misperforming a contract of carriage (*locatio conductio*)? See Gaius (D. 19.2.25.7), who describes a contractual liability when the mover of a column damages it:

   If it broke while being raised or carried or repositioned, he is held responsible for the risk if this happens due to his own fault (*culpa*) or that of those whose labor he employs; but there is no fault (*culpa*) if all precautions were taken which a very careful person would have observed.

   How does this contractual liability differ from a liability in delict?

Case 14: Damage to Buildings

D. 9.2.27.31–32 (Ulpianus, libro octavo decimo ad Edictum)

Si quis aedificii mei fores confregerit vel refregerit aut si ipsum aedificium diruit, lege Aquilia tenetur. (32) Si quis aquae ductum meum diruerit, licet cementa mea sunt quae diruta sunt, tamen quia terra mea non sit, qua aquam duco, melius est dicere actionem utilem dandam.

(Ulpian in the eighteenth book on the Edict)

If someone destroyed or broke open the door of my building, or if he demolished the building itself, he is liable under the Lex Aquilia. (32) If someone demolishes my aqueduct, although the demolished materials are mine, nonetheless because I do not own the land over which I am bringing water, the better solution is to say that an analogous action (*actio utilis*) should be given.

Discussion:

1. Although the jurists usually discuss wrongful damage to movable property, this text indicates that the Aquilian action also applied to immovables such as land and the buildings atop land. Does this represent an extension of the original statute? (Compare also Cases 9, 39.)

2. In section (32), the plaintiff has a servitude, a property right that permits him to bring water over a neighbor's property; he has constructed an aqueduct in order to use his servitude. Since in Roman law structures built atop land belong to the owner of the land as long as they remain in place, the neighbor is the technical owner of the aqueduct until it is demolished; but after demolition ownership of its materials reverts to the plaintiff. Why is this relevant to Ulpian's decision that an analogous action is preferable to a statutory action?

3. Could the neighbor bring a statutory suit against the offender? What if anything has the neighbor lost?

4. Ulpian says that this is "the better solution" (*melius*), which indicates that he is aware of an alternative view. What might that view be?

5. For other instances where *in factum* actions are granted to non-owners, see Cases 79–81; also, rather more bizarrely, Case 48. Does the Lex Aquilia require that the plaintiff have owned the damaged property?

Part C: The Defendant's Admission of Liability

Case 15: The Quasi-Punitive Nature of Aquilian Actions

Gaius, *Institutiones* 4.6, 9

Agimus autem interdum ut rem tantum consequamur, interdum ut poenam tantum, alias ut rem et poenam.... (9) Rem vero et poenam persequimur velut ex his causis ex quibus adversus infitiantem in duplum agimus; quod accidit per actionem ... damni iniuriae legis Aquiliae....

(Gaius in the fourth book of his *Institutes*)

We sue sometimes just to obtain our property (*res*), sometimes to obtain a penalty, sometimes to obtain both our property (*res*) and a penalty.... (9) We obtain our property and a penalty in those cases where we sue for double against a person who denies liability; this happens in the action ... for wrongful loss under the Lex Aquilia....

Discussion:

1. In the context of wrongful damage to property, suing for "our property" means receiving material compensation for the damage; obtaining a "penalty" means punishing the defendant for wrongful conduct. Explain the point that Gaius is making here. What is the penalty for? Will it encourage a defendant to admit liability?

2. When someone wrongfully damages property, what should the victim be able to recover? What reasons might a lawmaker have for limiting recovery to the actual damages received? What reasons might influence extending recovery to include a penalty?

3. The action for wrongful loss is often at least partially punitive in Roman law; what effect is that fact likely to have on the breadth of acts for which a defendant may be held liable? What concept of "culpability" is likely to result?

4. The action for double is clearly available under the Lex Aquilia; but is it also available in an action *in factum*? Curiously, no classical source gives a clear answer either way to this question, although the number of sources is very small. If it were not available, would this fact help to explain the jurists' emphasis on the distinction between statutory and *in factum* actions? How?

Case 16: Judicial Effect of Admitting Liability

D. 9.2.25.2 (Ulpianus, libro octavo decimo ad Edictum)

Notandum, quod in hac actione, quae adversus confitentem datur, iudex non rei iudicandae, sed aestimandae datur: nam nullae partes sunt iudicandi in confitentes.

D. 9.2.26 (Paulus, libro vicensimo secundo ad Edictum)

Puta enim, quod qui convenitur fateatur se occidisse et paratus sit aestimationem solvere, et adversarius magni litem aestimat.

(Ulpian in the eighteenth book on the Edict)

It should be noted that when an action is given against someone who admits liability, the *iudex* is appointed not to decide the issue (of liability), but to evaluate the loss; for there is no room for deciding (the issue of liability) against persons who admit liability.

(Paul in the twenty-second book on the Edict)

For suppose that the defendant admits having slain and is ready to pay the evaluation, and his adversary evaluates the claim at an amount that is (excessively) high.

The Hypothetical Problem:

Sempronia admits slaying my slave, but she argues that I am setting the value of the slave much too high. What form of Aquilian action should I have?

Discussion:

1. In the view of Ulpian and Paul, what is the role of the *iudex* when the defendant admits liability? On what issue can the trial go forward anyway?

2. Suppose that the defendant admits liability with regard to some of the losses suffered by the plaintiff, but not as to others. What is the outcome?

Case 17: Falsely Admitting Liability for Slaying

D. 9.2.23.11, 25 pr. (Ulpianus, libro octavo decimo ad Edictum)

Si quis hominem vivum falso confiteatur occidisse et postea paratus sit ostendere hominem vivum esse, Iulianus scribit cessare Aquiliam, quamvis confessus sit se occidisse: hoc enim solum remittere actori confessoriam actionem, ne necesse habeat docere eum occidisse: ceterum occisum esse hominem a quocumque oportet. (25 pr.) Proinde si occisus quidem non sit, mortuus autem sit, magis est ut non teneatur in mortuo, licet fassus sit.

(Ulpian in the eighteenth book on the Edict)

If someone falsely admits having slain a slave who is (actually) alive, and later he is ready to show that the slave is alive, Julian writes that the Aquilian action fails even though he admitted having slain (the slave); for the action on a confession only relieves the plaintiff from having to prove that the defendant slew, but it is still required that the slave have been slain by someone. (25 pr.) Therefore if he is dead but was not in fact slain, the better view is that despite his confession the defendant is not liable for the dead slave.

The Hypothetical Problem:

Cassia's slave is dead. At the time of his death, I was out drinking with the slave, and although my memory of the incident is cloudy, I think that I slew him; so I admit liability when Cassia sues me. After the trial begins, credible witnesses come forward to testify that the slave fell down and accidentally killed himself. Am I liable to Cassia?

Discussion:

1. If the slave is still alive, but the defendant has admitted slaying him, what must the defendant prove to the *iudex* in order to escape liability? Explain the basis of Julian's distinction.

2. If the slave is dead but was not slain, what must the defendant prove to the *iudex* if he wishes to escape liability? How does Ulpian's ruling follow from Julian's distinction? What alternatives might there be to this "better view"?

3. What if the defendant admits liability, but the slave was in fact slain by someone else? Paul, D. 42.2.4, holds that if the slave was slain, the defendant who has confessed is liable even if he can show that somebody else slew the slave. Is Paul's view consistent with this Case? What is the underlying rationale?

4. In light of this Case, formulate exactly what it is that the defendant does when he admits liability under the Lex Aquilia.

Case 18: Falsely Admitting Liability for Wounding

D. 9.2.24 (Paulus, libro vicensimo secundo ad Edictum)

Hoc apertius est circa vulneratum hominem: nam si confessus sit vulnerasse nec sit vulneratus, aestimationem cuius vulneris faciemus? vel ad quod tempus recurramus?

(Paul in the twenty-second book on the Edict)

This point is more obvious still in the case of a wounded slave. For if he (the defendant) has admitted having wounded, but the slave was not wounded, what wound will we evaluate? Or to what time period should we go back?

Discussion:

1. If the defendant has admitted wounding a slave, what must he prove to the *iudex* in order to escape liability? Why does Paul consider this a "more obvious" case than the false admission of slaying?

2. In light of the preceding Cases, assess the purposes and the likely effectiveness of the statutory rule allowing double damages if a defendant denies liability, but simple (compensatory) damages if he admits liability.

3. What happens if a plaintiff sues on a wounded slave, and the slave later dies of the wound? See Case 52, where Julian and Ulpian allow a second lawsuit on the slaying. If the defendant admits liability and pays the loss in the first trial, can he or she then deny liability in the second trial? Suppose, for example, that the injured slave died because the master failed to provide adequate medical care; see Case 53.

Chapter II:
The Components of Aquilian Liability

The Cases in the previous chapter concentrated on two questions that the Urban Praetor had to settle in the first stage of the trial, when he assisted the parties in constructing a formula: whether a statutory or an *in factum* action should be granted, and whether the action should be for simple or double damages. In this chapter, the central focus is on a group of issues that were normally dealt with not by the Praetor, but instead by a *iudex* during the second stage of the trial. These issues constitute the essence of Aquilian liability.

In the standard Anglo-American analysis of the tort of negligence, five crucial elements are required for liability:

1) a preexisting legal duty to take care, in acting, that the plaintiff not suffer injury or harm of a specific type (the duty of care);

2) a breach of that duty by the defendant (the negligence);

3) an actual injury or harm suffered by the plaintiff (the loss);

4) a reasonably close causal connection between the defendant's breach and the plaintiff's loss (causation); and

5) the absence of special circumstances that the defendant can raise to escape from liability (absence of excuses).

Aquilian liability differs in significant respects from the tort of negligence. For one thing, Aquilian liability originally involved only loss related to property (including slaves), but did not cover wrongful death or injury of free persons (though the jurists modified this somewhat; see Part C, Section 4). More important, the jurists construct Aquilian liability on a somewhat different basis from the modern tort of negligence; since the Lex Aquilia had defined certain acts as delicts, the jurists tend to focus on the defendant's act and on its wrongfulness, rather than on the pre-existing duty of care that the defendant owes the plaintiff. The Anglo-American categories are thus of limited usefulness in discussing Aquilian liability, and in fact they could conceivably lead to misunderstanding.

Nonetheless, the modern categories are at least helpful for organizing discussion of Aquilian liability. The jurists have important things to say about all five categories, even if what they say is sometimes very different from what modern lawyers believe. What emerges above all from juristic discussion is the central principle of Aquilian liability, namely that no one can be held legally liable for loss not demonstrably caused by his or her own fault (however "loss," "caused," and "fault" may be defined). The principle of "no liability without fault," which ranks among the greatest intellectual achievements of Roman jurists, has only come to be seriously questioned in this century.

Part A: The Duty of Care

As the jurists commonly put it, Aquilian liability arises out of "loss wrongfully inflicted" (*damnum iniuria datum*). *Iniuria*, a word used in the Lex Aquilia (see Cases 1–2), originally meant "without legal right"; a defendant was liable if he or she had inflicted loss on the plaintiff and had no offsetting legal defense for having done so. This meaning of *iniuria* was still important in juristic discussions of the defenses to Aquilian liability (below, Part E).

However, under juristic influence the word *iniuria* took on the additional meaning "wrongfulness." The defendant was liable for inflicting loss "without right," but only if he or she had also acted in a way that was somehow positively improper and worthy of legal reproach. Unless the defendant had acted "wrongfully" in this sense, he or she was not liable for the loss inflicted. Since in practice it was the plaintiff who had to prove the wrongfulness of the defendant's conduct, this juristic interpretation of *iniuria* narrowed the range of actions that gave rise to Aquilian liability.

Although the jurists do not often express the problem in this manner, the concept of "wrongfulness" clearly implies the existence of legal rules that roughly define what constitutes the conduct that is expected in various situations. The Lex Aquilia itself only sketchily described the content of such rules; and in fact, the Roman rules are mostly of juristic creation. Today, the "duty of care" that such rules define is regarded primarily as a device whereby judicial control is exercised over the questions of public policy that are often raised by suits on negligence; and this is also a plausible way of thinking about what the Roman jurists say on the subject.

Clearly, we are not the keepers of our brothers and sisters; in living our daily lives we have no general obligation to see to it that other people not suffer material loss. On the other hand, the prerequisites of social life require that we act with care in situations where our acts might cause others to sustain material loss. In Roman law, the legal line between these two principles comes to be expressed especially with the word *culpa*, literally "fault" or "responsibility." A person who crosses this line is "at fault" and hence "responsible." A person who steps over the line with the deliberate intent to inflict harm on another is responsible for *dolus*, literally "intentional fault." But these standards of care apply only if the defendant has a preexisting legal duty of care not to cause particular types of loss to the plaintiff.

In the Cases that follow, the jurists deal, in a casuistic fashion, with the extent of the duty of care that Romans are obliged to exercise toward others. Plainly, this duty is considerably more extensive in some circumstances than in others; the Cases invite generalization about what criteria determine the limits of the duty of care. Further, at times a defendant is liable for actions that are characterized by *culpa* (including *dolus*); at other times a defendant is liable only for actions characterized by *dolus*. The jurists say a good deal about what constitutes *culpa* or *dolus* in specific circumstances, a subject dealt with in more detail in Part B.

Case 19: Defining the Duty of Care: A Tree-Trimmer

D. 9.2.31 (Paulus, libro decimo ad Sabinum)

Si putator ex arbore ramum cum deiceret vel machinarius hominem prae-tereuntem occidit, ita tenetur, si is in publicum decidat nec ille proclamavit, ut casus eius evitari possit. sed Mucius etiam dixit, si in privato idem accidisset, posse de culpa agi: culpam autem esse, cum quod a diligente provideri potuerit, non esset provisum aut tum denuntiatum esset, cum periculum evi-tari non possit. secundum quam rationem non multum refert, per publicum an per privatum iter fieret, cum plerumque per privata loca vulgo iter fiat. quod si nullum iter erit, dolum dumtaxat praestare debet, ne immittat in eum, quem viderit transeuntem: nam culpa ab eo exigenda non est, cum divinare non potuerit, an per eum locum aliquis transiturus sit.

(Paul in the tenth book on Sabinus)

If a tree-trimmer threw down a branch from a tree and killed a passing slave — so too for a man on scaffolding —, he is clearly liable if it falls on public land and he did not call out so that the acci-dent to him could be avoided. But Mucius also said that if this oc-curred on private land, there could be an action for *culpa*; for it is *culpa* not to have foreseen what a careful person could have fore-seen, or to have called out only when the danger could not be avoided. According to this reasoning, there is not much difference between a path over public or private land, since paths quite com-monly run through private land. But if there was no path, he ought to be liable only for (an act of) *dolus*, that he not aim at someone whom he sees passing; (a standard of) *culpa* should not be required of him, since he could not foretell whether someone would pass through this place.

Discussion:

1. Leaving aside for the moment the reasoning of the Case, work out exactly what Paul requires of the tree-trimmer, depending on the circumstances. How do these rules arise?

2. Paul requires the tree-trimmer, in certain circumstances, to call out that a branch is about to fall. Could the tree-trimmer instead erect a sign warning passers-by that the tree is being trimmed? Note that calling out will not help a passer-by who is deaf; but a sign will not help a passer-by who is blind or illiterate. What social considerations should determine what is required in particular situations?

3. Paul first sets his rule for a tree-trimmer on public land, and then extends it to private land over which people commonly pass. How persuasive is the reason that he and Q. Mucius give for regarding these two situations as es-sentially identical? What counterarguments could be made?

4. The translation conceals a grammatical problem with the Latin text; this

problem has led many scholars to believe that Q. Mucius' definition of *culpa* ("not to have foreseen what a careful person could have foreseen") was not written by him, but was inserted into the text by the *Digest*'s compilers. If this definition were removed, would it make a difference to your interpretation of the Case?

5. Supposing that Q. Mucius' definition of *culpa* is substantially genuine, what kind of duty does it impose on the tree-trimmer, and on Romans generally in other situations? Does this duty seem appropriate? Why should people in general be held to the standards of a "careful" person? Would it not be enough to say, as Common Law does, that people should be held to the standards of a "reasonable" person? Or are these two standards in fact the same?

6. How extensive is the tree-trimmer's duty of care? Does it embrace all "foreseeable" losses resulting from a specific act? Suppose that he dropped a branch without calling out, and the passing slave saw the branch falling, jumped back, slipped, and struck his head on a rock. Is the tree-trimmer liable? Is he liable if the slave is not physically injured, but either suffers a nervous breakdown or is unable to complete a task set by his master?

7. Why is a tree-trimmer on private property, over which there are usually no passers, liable only for *dolus*? Paul casts his reason in terms of foreseeability; how does this link to Q. Mucius' definition of *culpa*? Why doesn't Paul instead say that the passers-by are trespassing on private property, and the tree-trimmer therefore owes them no duty of care beyond not injuring them deliberately?

8. Because the Lex Aquilia defines certain acts as delicts in themselves, Roman law does not need a "duty of care" to explain why such acts result in liability. But as the jurists expanded the scope of Aquilian liability, they had to consider its possible limits, since they were unwilling to hold that all loss caused by the arguably wrongful behavior made that person liable. At this point, the "duty of care" becomes helpful in understanding the limits of Aquilian liability. For example, why did Roman law, like later legal systems, find it easier to impose a duty of care for physical injury than for emotional injury or purely economic loss?

Case 20: Digging Pits

D. 9.2.28 (Paulus, libro decimo ad Sabinum)

Qui foveas ursorum cervorumque capiendorum causa faciunt, si in it- ineribus fecerunt eoque aliquid decidit factumque deterius est, lege Aquilia obligati sunt: at si in aliis locis, ubi fieri solent, fecerunt, nihil tenentur. (1) Haec tamen actio ex causa danda est, id est si neque denuntiatum est neque scierit aut providere potuerit: et multa huiusmodi deprehenduntur, quibus summovetur petitor, si evitare periculum poterit.

(Paul in the tenth book on Sabinus)

Those who make pits in order to catch bears and stags are liable under the Lex Aquilia if they made them on paths and something fell in and was (thereby) lowered in value. But if they made them in other places where they are usually made, they are not liable. (1) Nonetheless, this action should only be given for cause, i.e., if there was no warning and he (the victim) neither knew nor was able to foresee (the danger); and many such cases are found in which the plaintiff is defeated if he could avoid the danger.

Discussion:

1. What duties does this text impose on a person who digs pits? Does Paul assume that the pits are concealed? Does it really matter why the pits were dug? Why does the plaintiff have a statutory and not an *in factum* Aquilian action?

2. How, if at all, does the rule in this Case differ from that in Case 19? What general duty of care do the jurists develop?

3. Section (1) introduces the problem of the contributory negligence of the victim, which is examined below in Part E, Section 2. What is the legal effect of contributory negligence? Does this Case suggest that persons have a duty to look out for themselves and their own property? What is the relation between this duty and that of persons who dig pits?

4. In this Case the defendant physically dug the pits. What if the defendant only knew where others had dug pits, but told the plaintiff's slave to walk in this area; the slave then fell into a pit and was injured. Is the defendant liable? His act was purely verbal; but Case 7 (persuading slave to climb tree) implies a duty of care for at least some verbal acts that may result in physical injury to others.

Case 21: Driving Off Animals

D. 9.2.39 (Pomponius, libro septimo decimo ad Quintum Mucium)

Quintus Mucius scribit: equa cum in alieno pasceretur, in cogendo quod praegnas erat eiecit: quaerebatur, dominus eius possetne cum eo qui coegisset lege Aquilia agere, quia equam in iciendo ruperat. si percussisset aut consulto vehementius egisset, visum est agere posse. (1) POMPONIUS. Quamvis alienum pecus in agro suo quis deprehendit, sic illud expellere debet, quomodo si suum deprehendisset, quoniam si quid ex ea re damnum cepit, habet proprias actiones. itaque qui pecus alienum in agro suo deprehenderit, non iure id includit, nec agere illud aliter debet quam ut supra diximus quasi suum: sed vel abigere debet sine damno vel admonere dominum, ut suum recipiat.

(Pomponius in the seventeenth book on Q. Mucius)

Q. Mucius writes: A pregnant mare, which was grazing on another's land, miscarried in being driven off. It was asked whether her owner can sue the person who drove her off under the Lex Aquilia, because he rent the mare in striking her. If he had struck her or deliberately drove her off too harshly, it was held that an action was possible. (1) Pomponius adds: Although a person finds another's domestic animal on his land, he ought thus to drive it out as if he had found his own animal, since if he suffered some loss from this fact, he has appropriate actions. So a person who finds another's animal on his own land has no right to pen it up, nor should he act otherwise than as I said above, as if it were his own; he should either lead it away without inflicting loss, or warn the owner to pick up his property.

The Hypothetical Problem:

I find Titius' mare grazing in my wheat field. What should I do?

Discussion:

1. What duty of care do I ordinarily have with respect to my neighbor's animals? Does this duty change because the animals are on my land? Where does this duty come from?

2. The rule with regard to miscarriage is very early; according to Ulpian (D. 9.2.27.22), the jurist Brutus (second century B.C.) held that there was a statutory action on the Lex Aquilia if a slave woman or a mare miscarried as a result of a blow, the theory being that the victim was "rent." Does this ruling seem to extend the statute's application? Does it matter whether the offender knew that the mare was pregnant?

3. To what standard of care (*culpa* or *dolus*) do Q. Mucius and Pomponius hold the landowner? Q. Mucius seems to refer only to acts involving either physical contact (striking the mare) or *dolus* (deliberately driving it too harshly), while Pomponius describes a broader standard. Which jurist's view is more in accord with Case 19?

4. Gaius, *Inst.* 3.219 (= Case 7) holds that if a mule is driven too harshly and is thereby "rent," an *in factum* action lies. However, Q. Mucius seems to envisage a statutory action. Which seems more appropriate? Are the two situations different? Q. Mucius Scaevola is a very early jurist; in granting a statutory Aquilian action, does he seem to be influenced by the fact that the neighbor "deliberately" drove the mare too harshly, i.e., that his act was arguably *dolus*? If so, how does Q. Mucius' perspective differ from that of later jurists? (It is not certain that *in factum* actions were yet available when Q. Mucius wrote; the earliest source on them dates from about fifty years after his death in 82 B.C.)

5. Pomponius states that the landowner "ought thus to drive it out as if he had found his own animal." Do these words imply that he is held to a standard determined by his own normal conduct? For instance, if he is normally brutal with his own animals, can he also be brutal with his neighbor's? Or does Pomponius simply presume that people will normally be quite careful with their own property?

6. Pomponius speaks of "appropriate actions" available to the landowner. He has in mind the Aquilian action (Diocletian, C. 3.35.6) and the action for recovering damage done by animals pasturing on one's land. Does the availability of these actions really explain why the landowner cannot harm the animal in driving it out? Why can't the landowner claim "self-defense" in protecting his own crops? If the landowner has sustained loss from the animal, should he at least be able to hold the animal until its owner pays for the loss?

7. Would the neighbor's duty of care change if, for instance, the horse had strayed repeatedly onto his land, or if he notified the owner to come get the horse and the owner failed to do so?

Case 22: Causing a Stampede

D. 47.2.50.4 (Ulpianus, libro trigensimo septimo ad Edictum)

Cum eo, qui pannum rubrum ostendit fugavitque pecus, ut in fures incideret, si quidem dolo malo fecit, furti actio est: sed et si non furti faciendi causa hoc fecit, non debet impunitus esse lusus tam perniciosus: idcirco Labeo scribit in factum dandam actionem.

D. 47.2.51 (Gaius, libro tertio decimo ad Edictum Provinciale)

Nam et si praecipitata sint pecora, utilis actio damni iniuriae quasi ex lege Aquilia dabitur.

(Ulpian in the thirty-seventh book on the Edict)

There is an action of theft against a person who held up a red flag and put to flight a herd in order that it fall into the hands of thieves, so long as he acted intentionally (*dolo malo*). But even if he did not act in order to steal, so dangerous a game should not go unpunished; therefore Labeo writes that an *in factum* action should be given.

(Gaius in the thirteenth book on the Provincial Edict)

For also if the animals fell headlong, an analogous action (*actio utilis*) for wrongful loss, as if under the Lex Aquilia, will be given.

Discussion:

1. This Case sets out the difference between liability for aiding and abetting a theft (see Case 110) and liability for wrongful damage. Explain this difference as clearly as you can.

2. Is the defendant liable if he was unaware that cattle may stampede when a red flag is waved? Would he be liable if he knew that the cattle would stampede, but thought that he owned them? If the answer to both these questions is yes (as it seems to be), then to what extent does the defendant's duty of care include a duty to know certain common facts about the world, as well as who owns what property?

3. Is the defendant liable if the cattle stampede, but no harm comes to them? Suppose, for instance, that the owner of the cattle had spent considerable time and money in rounding them up again; should the defendant pay for these expenses?

4. Why is the action *in factum* rather than statutory?

Case 23: A Brutal Schoolmaster

D. 9.2.5.3 (Ulpianus, libro octavo decimo ad Edictum)

Si magister in disciplina vulneraverit servum vel occiderit, an Aquilia teneatur, quasi damnum iniuria dederit? et Iulianus scribit Aquilia teneri eum, qui eluscaverat discipulum in disciplina: multo magis igitur in occiso idem erit dicendum. proponitur autem apud eum species talis: sutor, inquit, puero discenti ingenuo filio familias, parum bene facienti quod demonstraverit, forma calcei cervicem percussit, ut oculus puero perfunderetur. dicit igitur Iulianus iniuriarum quidem actionem non competere, quia non faciendae iniuriae causa percusserit, sed monendi et docendi causa: an ex locato, dubitat, quia levis dumtaxat castigatio concessa est docenti: sed lege Aquilia posse agi non dubito:

D. 9.2.6 (Paulus, libro vicensimo secundo ad Edictum)

praeceptoris enim nimia saevitia culpae adsignatur.

(Ulpian in the eighteenth book on the Edict)

If, while teaching, a schoolteacher wounds or slays a slave, is he liable under the Lex Aquilia for giving wrongful loss? Julian writes that a person who had blinded a pupil while teaching him is liable under the Lex Aquilia; thus the same thing is much more true if he slew him. Julian also proposes this variant: A shoemaker, he says, had a student who was a freeborn son in his father's power. The boy was badly performing what he (the shoemaker) had demonstrated, and he struck his neck with a shoe last, thereby putting the boy's eye out. Julian accordingly says that there is no action on outrage (*iniuria*) since he struck not to insult him but to correct and instruct him; he is unsure about the action on hire of services (*ex locato*), since a teacher is allowed to punish (students), though only lightly. But I do not doubt that an action can be brought under the Lex Aquilia,

(Paul in the twenty-second book on the Edict)

since a teacher's excessive brutality is counted as *culpa*.

The Hypothetical Problem:

Cassius, a master shoemaker, becomes exasperated at the poor performance of his young apprentice. He strikes the apprentice with a shoe last and severely injures the boy. Is Cassius liable?

Discussion:

1. Ulpian (following Julian) sets two cases. The first concerns the wounding or killing of a slave student. Here Ulpian sees no difficulty in allowing an Aquilian action. Explain why this is so. Should we presume that the schoolmaster deliberately intended to harm the slave? Or is he liable even for the

unexpected consequences of a light blow which he had intended to be harmless?

2. The second case is the famous one of the shoemaker's apprentice. The putting out of the apprentice's eye sounds rather like a freak accident; how clear is the sequence of events? Is it significant that the shoemaker struck his apprentice with a shoe last rather than, say, with his hand? Did the shoemaker intend to injure the apprentice?

3. As Julian holds, the shoemaker is not liable for the delict of outrage (*iniuria*) because his blow was not intentionally insulting; the action on outrage requires *dolus*, the intent to insult (see Case 137). Julian's opinion is also reported by Ulpian in D. 19.2.13.4, where it is clear that Julian did favor giving an action on the contract of hire (*ex locato*) to the boy's father. How has the shoemaker violated his contract to teach the boy?

4. With regard to Aquilian liability, the case of the shoemaker's apprentice is famous in part because it is the earliest clear case in which the jurists extend a teacher's Aquilian liability (and hence his duty of care) from slaves to free persons; see below, Part C, Section 4. Julian tentatively affirmed Aquilian liability (the compilers evidently struck out his opinion); two generations later, Ulpian is no longer in doubt. What is the shoemaker liable for? (Julian's answer is given below in Case 47.)

5. What does this Case show about the extent to which corporal punishment was permissible in Roman education? Where does the limit come from? Was a teacher allowed to do things that an ordinary Roman could not do? Why or why not?

6. In this Case, as in the next one, the defendant can be sued either on contract or on delict. For the legal problems raised by such concurrence of actions, see Cases 94–95.

Case 24: A Doctor's Duties

D. 9.2.7.8 (Ulpianus, libro octavo decimo ad Edictum)

Proculus ait, si medicus servum imperite secuerit, vel ex locato vel ex lege Aquilia competere actionem.

D. 9.2.8 pr. (Gaius, libro septimo ad Edictum Provinciale)

Idem iuris est si medicamento perperam usus fuerit. sed et qui bene secuerit et dereliquit curationem, securus non erit, sed culpae reus intellegitur.

(Ulpian in the eighteenth book on the Edict)
Proculus says that if a doctor unskillfully operates on a slave, an action lies either on the contract for services (*ex locato*) or under the Lex Aquilia.

(Gaius in the seventh book on the Provincial Edict)
The rule is the same if he uses a drug improperly. But also if he operated correctly and then abandoned treatment, he does not get off but is considered guilty of *culpa*.

Discussion:

1. What does this Case establish about the general duties of a doctor in treating a sick slave? Where do these duties come from? Are they the normal standards of the medical profession, or legal standards that are being imposed on doctors?

2. A doctor is liable if he operates, but then fails to follow up on the operation. Why is this a reasonable exception to the usual rule that one is not liable for failing to do something? Should the action be statutory or *in factum*? Ulpian (*Collatio* 12.7.7) says that doctors are liable *in factum* for careless treatment of any type; why? Is the doctor being held to a higher duty of care because he is a doctor, or because he is offering medical treatment? Suppose, for instance, that the defendant had no medical training but offered emergency treatment to a slave.

3. Would the doctor's Aquilian liability be different if he did not charge a fee for his services?

4. Why were the Romans usually reluctant to impose a duty of care for omissions, failures to act that may foreseeably result in loss for other persons?

Part B: The Standards of Care: *Culpa* and *Dolus*

In interpreting the Lex Aquilia's requirement that loss be inflicted "wrongfully" (*iniuria*), the jurists began requiring that a defendant's conduct be characterized by *culpa* (literally "fault" or "responsibility") or, in some cases, by *dolus* (literally "malice"). In ordinary use, these Latin words had a moral connotation, and so they invite the view that the defendant's conduct was being morally evaluated, by what is called a subjective standard: the defendant is personally at fault for what he or she did, and this fault is determined by reference to the defendant's unique personality, intelligence, physical capacity, and so on. Since *dolus* implies the existence of an intent to do harm, it accords fairly well with a subjective standard of care.

However, juristic texts usually look at *culpa* (short of *dolus*) not from a subjective but from an objective perspective; the jurists regard not what an individual defendant was capable of, but rather whether he or she behaved in a way that accords with the performance expected of Romans generally. Thus, a defendant is not held to a lower standard because he or she is stupider or less skillful than most Romans; nor is an unusually gifted defendant held to a higher standard. Because carelessness, for instance, is a fairly common characteristic of human behavior, the amount of moral blame that attaches to it may be very small indeed; often no more is involved than simple lapse of attention, the failure swiftly and accurately to calculate the implications of one's acts for others. But such failure can still frequently be a source of legal liability if others thereby suffer loss. As Ulpian puts it (D. 9.2.44 pr.), "Under the Lex Aquilia, even the slightest *culpa* counts."

In fact, carelessness (*neglegentia*) is far and away the most common form of *culpa*. But in certain circumstances, especially when a defendant is acting as a professional, the jurists also grant liability if a defendant does not know what professionals should know, or is insufficiently experienced, or is too weak for the physical demands of the task. Here the carelessness lies not in the act itself, but rather in the defendant's undertaking the act when he or she is evidently unready to perform it successfully.

On the other hand, the subjective standard returns in juristic discussion of the liability of those who simply cannot understand the consequences of their actions, such as young children or the insane. In their case no moral blame is imputable even under the most extreme conditions; and the absence of moral blame apparently leads the jurists to deny their legal liability as well.

The objective understanding of *culpa* makes Aquilian liability look somewhat like liability under the Anglo-American tort of negligence. However, it should not be forgotten that the Aquilian action, unlike its modern counterpart, was partially punitive in its design (see above, Case 15). One could therefore argue that the jurists should have preferred a subjective understanding of *culpa*, in which genuine blame attaches to the defendant's conduct.

Section 1: Iniuria

Case 25: Lack of Right

D. 9.2.3 (Ulpianus, libro octavo decimo ad Edictum)

Si servus servave iniuria occisus occisave fuerit, lex Aquilia locum habet. iniuria occisum esse merito adicitur: non enim sufficit occisum, sed oportet iniuria id factum.

D. 9.2.4 pr. (Gaius libro septimo ad Edictum Provinciale)

Itaque si servum tuum latronem insidiantem mihi occidero, securus ero: nam adversus periculum naturalis ratio permittit se defendere.

(Ulpian in the eighteenth book on the Edict)
If a slave of either sex is unlawfully (*iniuria*) slain, the Lex Aquilia applies. The requirement that he be slain unlawfully (*iniuria*) is rightly added; for slaying is not alone enough, it must also be done unlawfully (*iniuria*).

(Gaius in the seventh book on the Provincial Edict)
And so if I slay your slave who was lying in wait to rob me, I will get off. For natural reason allows a person to defend himself against danger.

Discussion:

1. In this Case, Gaius and Ulpian are interpreting the word *iniuria* in the First Section of the statute. This original sense of the word is the foundation of the theory of excuses discussed in more detail below in Part E.

2. Reconstruct the reasoning of the Case. How does Gaius derive the victim's right to slay a robber? What does Gaius mean by "natural reason" (*naturalis ratio*)? Can you think of other ways to explain this legal right?

3. What is the "danger" against which "natural reason" allows you to defend yourself: being robbed, or being physically harmed? For example, can you kill the slave even if the slave has no weapon or does not resist being apprehended? (For the answer, see Cases 62–63, 69 below.)

Section 2: Culpa

Case 26: Unlawfulness, *Dolus*, and *Culpa*

Gaius, *Institutiones* 3.211

Iniuria autem occidere intellegitur cuius dolo aut culpa id acciderit; nec ulla alia lege damnum quod sine iniuria datur reprehenditur; itaque impunitus est qui sine culpa et dolo malo casu quodam damnum committit.

(Gaius in the third book of his *Institutes*)

A person is deemed to slay wrongfully (*iniuria*) when this occurs by his *dolus* or *culpa*; nor does any other statute punish loss which is inflicted without *iniuria*. And so a person who inflicts loss by some accident, without *culpa* and *dolus malus*, goes unpunished.

Discussion:

1. In this Case, Gaius attempts to explain why it is that the statutory requirement of *iniuria* means that the defendant must be at fault in causing the loss. Reconstruct his reasoning. How convincing do you find it?

2. Give an example of how one can cause loss by accident, without committing *dolus* or *culpa*. Is it necessary to think in terms of a duty of care?

3. Gaius seems to regard Aquilian liability as punitive in nature. Is this consistent with an objective understanding of *culpa*? Why or why not?

Case 27: Unlawfulness and *Culpa*

D. 9.2.5.1 (Ulpianus, libro octavo decimo ad Edictum)

Iniuriam autem hic accipere nos oportet non quemadmodum circa iniuriarum actionem contumeliam quandam, sed quod non iure factum est, hoc est
contra ius, id est si culpa quis occiderit: et ideo interdum utraque actio concur-
rit et legis Aquiliae et iniuriarum, sed duae erunt aestimationes, alia damni, alia
contumeliae. igitur iniuriam hic damnum accipiemus culpa datum etiam ab eo,
qui nocere noluit.

(Ulpian in the eighteenth book on the Edict)

We should understand *iniuria* here not as some insult, like in the
action on outrage (*iniuria*), but rather as something not done by
right (*ius*), in other words contrary to right (*contra ius*), i.e., if someone slays by *culpa*. And so sometimes both the action under the Lex
Aquilia and the action on outrage lie simultaneously, but there are
two evaluations, one of the loss and the other for the insult. We will
therefore construe *iniuria* here as loss inflicted by *culpa*, even by
one who did not wish to do harm.

Discussion:

1. Ulpian tries a different way to derive the requirement of *culpa* from the
wording of the statute. Reconstruct his reasoning. Do you find it more convincing than Gaius' in the previous Case? Could it be argued that, on
Ulpian's argument, *culpa* ought to be conceived as subjective fault rather
than as objective breach of a duty of care?

2. The action on outrage (*actio iniuriarum*) covers deliberate offenses to the
personality of the victim; see Case 23, and below, Chapter IV, Part B. Examples are defamation of character, interference with normal rights, assault
and battery, and so on. The victim is allowed to recover on the basis of his
distress caused by the defendant's antisocial conduct. Construct an example
in which a plaintiff could bring suit both under the Lex Aquilia and on outrage.

3. It is important to note that, as Ulpian observes, the meaning of *iniuria* is
much different within the context of the Lex Aquilia than in the delict of outrage. Outrage (*iniuria*) is an "injury" to the feelings of the victim.

Case 28: Setting a Brushfire

D. 9.2.30.3 (Paulus, libro vicensimo secundo ad Edictum)

In hac quoque actione, quae ex hoc capitulo oritur, dolus et culpa punitur: ideoque si quis in stipulam suam vel spinam comburendae eius causa ignem immiserit et ulterius evagatus et progressus ignis alienam segetem vel vineam laeserit, requiramus, num imperitia eius aut neglegentia id accidit. nam si die ventoso id fecit, culpae reus est (nam et qui occasionem praestat, damnum fecisse videtur): in eodem crimine est et qui non observavit, ne ignis longius procederet. at si omnia quae oportuit observavit vel subita vis venti longius ignem produxit, caret culpa.

(Paul in the twenty-second book on the Edict)

Also in the action arising from the Third Section, *dolus* and *culpa* are punished. Wherefore if a person sets fire to his stubble or thorns in order to burn them up, and the fire escapes more widely and by spreading damages another's grain or vines, we should ask whether this occurred by his lack of skill or carelesness. For if he did it on a windy day, he is guilty of *culpa*, since even a person who provides the opportunity seems to have brought about the loss. Open to the same charge is someone who did not guard against the fire's spreading out. But if he saw to everything that he should have, or a sudden burst of wind spread the fire out, he is free of *culpa*.

The Hypothetical Problem:

I set a brushfire to burn up the stubble in my field. While the fire is burning, I go inside my house to get a drink of water. During my absence the fire spreads onto my neighbor Cassia's property and it then burns up her grain field. Am I liable to her?

Discussion:

1. What duties does Paul impose on a landowner who decides to burn stubble? Where do these duties come from?

2. This Case clearly illustrates the ambiguous character of *culpa* and Aquilian liability. On the one hand, the defendant is "punished" if he is "guilty of *culpa*" — strongly moralistic language that may imply a subjective concept of *culpa*. On the other hand, Paul specifies general rules and allows the defendant to escape only if "he saw to everything that he should have" — a generalized and rule-oriented approach that suggests an objective concept of *culpa*. Which conception of *culpa* seems to prevail in the text? Does the inherently dangerous nature of a brushfire lead Paul to regard carelessness in its regard as more reprehensible than ordinary carelessness?

3. Paul says that a person who sets a brushfire on a windy day is guilty of *culpa*, "since even a person who provides the opportunity seems to have brought about the loss." It is possible to interpret these words as implying a rather

broad duty not to create, through carelessness, a situation that increases the risk of loss to others — even, perhaps, through the act of a third party. (One example would be a driver who leaves the keys in her car in a crime-ridden part of a city; her car is then stolen by some joy-riding teenagers who ram it into another car. Should the owner of the first car be liable to the owner of the second?) On the basis of other Cases, do you think it likely that the jurists imposed such a wide duty of care? Should they have?

4. Note the wording of the final sentence: the defendant is free of *culpa* if "he saw to everything that he should have, or a sudden burst of wind spread the fire out." The text reads "or," not "and." Suppose that Titius sets a fire which he then watches carelessly; but the fire spreads to his neighbor's field not because of Titius' carelessness but rather because of a sudden burst of wind that is so strong the fire would have spread even had Titius not been careless. Is Titius liable? Why or why not? (On the general problem of an intervening event, see also below, Part D, Section 2.)

5. On brushfires, see also Case 50, where the problem of the appropriate action (statutory or *in factum*) is discussed.

Case 29: Dropping a Ring

D. 19.5.23 (Alfenus, libro tertio Digestorum a Paulo Epitomatorum)

Duo secundum Tiberim cum ambularent, alter eorum ei, qui secum ambulabat, rogatus anulum ostendit, ut respiceret: illi excidit anulus et in Tiberim devolutus est. respondit posse agi cum eo in factum actione.

(Alfenus in the third book of his *Digests*, as Epitomized by Paul)

While two men were walking by the Tiber, one of them, at his companion's request, held out a ring for him to see; the ring slipped away from the other man and rolled into the Tiber. He (Servius) responded that the man can be sued by an action *in factum*.

The Hypothetical Problem:

Seius and Cassius are walking by the Tiber River. Cassius asks Seius to show him his ring. Seius takes off the ring and gives it to Cassius, who drops it into the Tiber; efforts to recover the ring are unsuccessful. Can Seius sue Cassius for the ring's value?

Discussion:

1. Why does Servius, Alfenus' teacher, grant an action *in factum*, rather than a statutory Aquilian action? Compare Case 11.

2. It can be presumed that the defendant dropped the ring by accident. Wherein does his *culpa* lie? Is it related to the fact that he requested to see the ring? Would the outcome be different if the ring's owner had spontaneously given it to the other man, who was unprepared and dropped it into the Tiber?

3. Is this Case most easily reconcilable with an objective or a subjective concept of *culpa*?

Case 30: Killing a Slave Who You Think Is Free

D. 9.2.45.2 (Paulus, libro decimo ad Sabinum)

Si meum servum, cum liberum putares, occideris, lege Aquilia teneberis.

(Paul in the tenth book on Sabinus)

If you slay my slave who you think is free, you will be liable under the Lex Aquilia.

Discussion:

1. Should it be presumed that you killed the slave deliberately? Could it be that you killed him through carelessness?

2. Why is it no defense to an Aquilian action to assert that you believed another's property was not involved? On the general problem raised by this text, see below, Cases 48, 73.

3. This Case may suggest to you some further problems in defining the concept *culpa*. Is Paul holding that it is *culpa* to be mistaken about the juridical status of one's victim? Or is he rather holding that the *culpa* involved in slaying a person whom you believe to be free is sufficient to justify an Aquilian action when your victim turns out to be in fact a slave? Or is Paul's point just that it is irrelevant for Aquilian liability whether or not one is aware that another person's property is involved? If this last view is correct, how can it be justified?

4. Julian (cited by Ulpian, D. 9.2.13.1) discusses the following case, which raises the opposite problem: Titius, who is in fact a Roman citizen, is serving you as a slave in good faith (both he and you think that he is a slave); he damages your property. If Titius' true status is subsequently discovered, will he be liable to you? Julian holds that he is. Can you explain this ruling through analogy with the present Case?

Section 3: Lack of Skill or Weakness

Case 31: A Muleteer

D. 9.2.8.1 (Gaius, libro septimo ad Edictum Provinciale)

Mulionem quoque, si per imperitiam impetum mularum retinere non potuerit, si eae alienum hominem obtriverint, volgo dicitur culpae nomine teneri. idem dicitur et si propter infirmitatem sustinere mularum impetum non potuerit: nec videtur iniquum, si infirmitas culpae adnumeretur, cum affectare quisque non debeat, in quo vel intellegit vel intellegere debet infirmitatem suam alii periculosam futuram. idem iuris est in persona eius, qui impetum equi, quo vehebatur, propter imperitiam vel infirmitatem retinere non poterit.

(Gaius in the seventh book on the Provincial Edict)

Likewise a muleteer is commonly held to be liable for *culpa* if through lack of skill (*imperitia*) he cannot check the movement of his mules and they trample another's slave. The same is held also if through physical weakness (*infirmitas*) he cannot check the movement of his mules. Nor does it seem unfair to count weakness as *culpa*, since a person ought not to undertake something when he knows or ought to know that his weakness will be dangerous to another. The same rule holds for a person who through lack of skill or weakness cannot check the movement of a horse he is riding.

Discussion:

1. Gaius says that it is not unfair to count weakness as *culpa*. He also holds that "lack of skill is counted as *culpa*" (D. 50.17.132, probably originally from this passage). Does Gaius mean that one is at fault simply for being weak or unskilled? What else is required?

2. Does Gaius presume that any person who tries to control a mule team, or to ride a horse, will realize from the start that experience and strength are required? Or does he rather require such knowledge as a matter of law, whether or not a particular person is aware of it in fact?

3. Gaius justifies his ruling by referring to the defendant's duty of care: "he knows or ought to know that his weakness will be dangerous to another." Is the defendant still liable if he could not have known this?

Case 32: Filigreeing a Cup

D. 9.2.27.29 (Ulpianus, libro octavo decimo ad Edictum)

Si calicem diatretum faciendum dedisti, si quidem imperitia fregerit, damni iniuria tenebitur: si vero non imperitia fregit, sed rimas habebat vitiosas, potest esse excusatus: et ideo plerumque artifices convenire solent, cum eiusmodi materiae dantur, non periculo suo se facere, quae res ex locato tollit actionem et Aquiliae.

(Ulpian in the eighteenth book on the Edict)

If you gave a cup to be filigreed, he (the artisan) will be liable for wrongful damage if he breaks it through lack of skill (*imperitia*). But if he broke it not through lack of skill but because it had defective cracks, he can be excused. Accordingly artisans customarily provide, when they receive materials of this sort, that they do not act at their own risk; this eliminates the action on hire of services (*ex locato*) and the Aquilian action.

Discussion:

1. In the absence of a contract clause specifying that he bears no risk, under what circumstances may an unskilled artisan be liable if the cup breaks while he is filigreeing it? What is the basis of his liability? How easy will it normally be to prove how the cup came to be broken?

2. Would a very skilled artisan be liable if he broke a cup while filigreeing it? Could such an artisan still be careless in handling the cup?

3. What is the effect of the contract clause that artisans customarily use? Does it eliminate Aquilian liability for lack of skill? Should artisans be able to escape Aquilian liability in this way?

4. In this Case, the artisan was working under contract; that is, he received a fee for his efforts. How would it affect his Aquilian liability if he undertook to filigree the cup without being paid?

Case 33: Setting or Engraving a Gem

D. 19.2.13.5 (Ulpianus, libro trigensimo secundo ad Edictum)

Si gemma includenda aut insculpenda data sit eaque fracta sit, si quidem vitio materiae factum sit, non erit ex locato actio, si imperitia facientis, erit. huic sententiae addendum est, nisi periculum quoque in se artifex receperat: tunc enim etsi vitio materiae id evenit, erit ex locato actio.

(Ulpian in the thirty-second book on the Edict)

If a gem was given for setting or engraving and it was broken, there will be no action on hire of services (*ex locato*) if this happened because of a defect in the material; but if through the workman's lack of skill (*imperitia*), there will be. To this rule should be added: unless the artisan also took the risk on himself; for then there will be an action on hire of services even if it happened because of a defect in the material.

Discussion:

1. This Case discusses only liability on the contract. In light of the preceding Case, discuss the implications for Aquilian liability.

2. How does the contract clause that Ulpian mentions differ from the contract clause in the preceding Case? What effect will such clauses probably have on the fee the artisan receives?

3. If the artisan takes on himself the risk of faulty materials, will he also be liable under the Lex Aquilia if the gem breaks because of a flaw? Why or why not?

4. Curiously, although the jurists consider inexperience and physical weakness as forms of *culpa*, surviving sources do not discuss the consequences of intoxication. If a drunk person causes loss, should he or she be held to the standard of conduct for sober persons? How is this problem similar to that of inexperience or weakness, and how is it different?

Section 4: Dolus

Case 34: Cutting Off an Eave; Ripping Out an Aqueduct

D. 9.2.29.1 (Ulpianus, libro octavo decimo ad Edictum)

Si protectum meum, quod supra domum tuam nullo iure habebam, recci-
disses, posse me tecum damni iniuria agere Proculus scribit: debuisti enim
mecum ius mihi non esse protectum habere agere: nec esse aequum damnum
me pati recisis a te meis tignis. aliud est dicendum ex rescripto imperatoris
Severi, qui ei, per cuius domum traiectus erat aquae ductus citra servitutem,
rescripsit iure suo posse eum intercidere, et merito: interest enim, quod hic in
suo protexit, ille in alieno fecit.

(Ulpian in the eighteenth book on the Edict)

If without legal right I had an eave projecting over your house
and you had cut it off, Proculus writes that I can sue you for wrongful loss; for you ought to have brought suit against me that I had no
right to have such an eave, nor is it fair that I suffer loss when my
roofbeams are cut off by you. A different ruling must be given in
accord with a rescript of the Emperor Septimius Severus, who, in
reply to a person through whose house an aqueduct had been
brought across without a servitude, wrote that he can rightfully cut
it off. This is correct, for there is a difference: the former person
constructed the eave on his own land, the latter on another's.

Discussion:

1. In Roman law, the owner of land has property rights that extend upward and
   downward from the borders; he or she also owns whatever is constructed
   on the land. When a third party, who has no legal right to do so, constructs
   an eave that projects over a neighbor's land, or an aqueduct that runs
   through or atop it, this is a violation of the neighbor's property rights. According to this Case, what can the neighbor do to stop such violations?

2. What explains the difference in treatment between the eave and the aqueduct? Why shouldn't the aggrieved owner be required to contact the builder
   of the aqueduct and try to reach a mutually satisfactory agreement concerning it? Note that the builder of the aqueduct may not have realized that another person's property rights were being violated, and that the ownership
   of the materials from which the aqueduct is constructed reverts to the
   builder after the aqueduct is destroyed (see Case 14).

3. The eave and the aqueduct are both structures, and in this they differ from,
   e.g., a slave that walks across another person's property (Case 19) or a horse
   that strays onto a neighbor's land (Case 21). Is there nonetheless an underlying pattern to the rules? Suppose, for instance, that the landowner, in the
   normal use of his property, carelessly damaged the projecting eave; would
   he be liable under the Lex Aquilia? Would the answer depend on the exact
   circumstances (e.g., whether the landowner knew that the eave projected

over his property)? To what extent does Roman law permit carelessness toward the property of others when a landowner is on his or her own land?

4. Besides the type of situation described in this Case, a defendant is also liable only for intentional *dolus*, and not for *culpa*, when he or she has a legitimate excuse for inflicting loss that would otherwise result in Aquilian liability, for instance to a partner in an athletic contest (Case 59), to someone acting carelessly (Case 60), to someone who has started a fight (Cases 62, 64), or to a thief caught in the act (Cases 63, 69). What is the principle underlying these Cases?

Section 5: Subjective Incapacity

Case 35: Lunatics and Minors

D. 9.2.5.2 (Ulpianus, libro octavo decimo ad Edictum)

Et ideo quaerimus, si furiosus damnum dederit, an legis Aquiliae actio sit? et Pegasus negavit: quae enim in eo culpa sit, cum suae mentis non sit? et hoc est verissimum. cessabit igitur Aquiliae actio, quemadmodum, si quadrupes damnum dederit, Aquilia cessat, aut si tegula ceciderit. sed et si infans damnum dederit, idem erit dicendum. quodsi inpubes id fecerit, Labeo ait, quia furti tenetur, teneri et Aquilia eum: et hoc puto verum, si sit iam iniuriae capax.

(Ulpian in the eighteenth book on the Edict)

Hence we ask whether there is an action under the Lex Aquilia if a lunatic (*furiosus*) inflicts loss? Pegasus denied this; for what *culpa* can a person have who is not in his right mind? This view is exactly correct. Therefore the Aquilian action will fail, just as it fails if a four-footed animal inflicts loss, or if a rooftile falls. But also if a young child inflicts loss, the same will be held. But if an older child does this, Labeo says that because he is liable for theft (*furtum*), he is also liable in the Aquilian action; I think this view correct if he is already capable of wrongful conduct (*iniuria*).

The Hypothetical Problem:

Sempronia kills your slave. It emerges that Sempronia is a lunatic under the control of a guardian. Is she liable for the loss you have suffered?

Discussion:

1. Explain why Pegasus and Ulpian hold that lunatics and young children are not liable under the Aquilian action. What conception of *culpa* do they rely on in reaching this outcome?

2. How convincing is their argument? Suppose, for instance, that a wealthy lunatic sets fire to a neighbor's house; why should the neighbor have to bear the loss?

3. Ulpian compares the loss caused by a lunatic to the loss caused by a four-footed animal. What point is he getting at? Note that the owner of a four-footed animal has no Aquilian liability for loss caused by the animal (unless, of course, he was somehow responsible for the animal's causing loss: e.g., Ulpian, D. 9.2.11.5, sicking one's dog on someone). However, under the action on *pauperies*, he is obliged either to make good the loss or to surrender the animal to the victim. Ulpian, D. 9.1.1.3 (= Case 96) explains: "*Pauperies* is loss given without the doer's wrongfulness (*iniuria*); for an animal cannot act wrongfully, since it lacks understanding." Does this help to clarify Ulpian's point with regard to the absence of a lunatic's Aquilian liability? On the action on *pauperies*, see further Chapter IV, Part A.

4. How is the act of a lunatic like a falling rooftile? This Case is one of many that imply no Aquilian liability for acts of omission, such as failure to keep up one's property. Ulpian (D. 9.2.29.2) discusses a ship that collides with a skiff. According to Proculus, the sailors are liable to the skiff's owner if they let the ship run loose or they steered badly; but there is no Aquilian liability if the ship was adrift because, e.g., a rope broke. Why?

5. Where would Labeo set the line between very young and older children? How does Ulpian differ from him? In other texts. the jurists seem to be unsure whether to use a fixed age (such as seven), or to judge on a case-by-case basis. Which view seems more practical? Which is more in accord with the logic of the exception?

6. In this Case, the Lex Aquilia is held inapplicable to large groups of persons; young children, or adult lunatics, are defined as lacking judgment and are therefore not liable under the Lex Aquilia. Is this approach fully reconcilable with the words of the statute? Does a block approach at least have the virtue of softening the contradictions between the competing objective and subjective concepts of *culpa*?

7. Are there other groups of persons for whom a subjective standard should be used? Consider, for example, those suffering from a physical handicap (e.g., the blind) or a mental handicap (e.g., the feeble-minded); should they be held to the same standard as non-handicapped persons? Why or why not?

8. Do you think that the jurists should have used subjective standards more widely in deciding Aquilian liability? What might have been the advantages of doing so? What disadvantages might have resulted?

Part C: Loss (*Damnum*)

Many acts of *culpa*, or even of *dolus*, do not result in Aquilian liability. Someone who commits a wrongful act is not liable unless two additional things are true: the plaintiff has suffered a measurable loss (*damnum*), and this loss was more or less clearly caused by the defendant's act. The first of these requirements is discussed in the present part, the second in the following part.

The Lex Aquilia evidently envisaged liability only for physical injury to the plaintiff's property. However, especially in relation to the Third Section, which allowed the plaintiff to recover "as much money as the matter (*res*) will be worth," the concept of loss was gradually extended. *Damnum* came to mean not just the loss directly associated with physical injury, but also the loss stemming more indirectly from the wrongful act, since this loss was part of "the matter." Accordingly, the plaintiff became entitled to claim his or her "interest" (*interesse*) in the defendant's act not having occurred. In time, this measure of damages came to be applied also in actions arising under the First Section of the Lex Aquilia.

However, the jurists continue to insist that objectively measurable loss must be sustained if the defendant is to be held liable; where such loss has not occurred, there is no Aquilian liability even if the defendant has fairly drastically altered the plaintiff's property in a way that the plaintiff had not contemplated or desired. Further, the jurists usually require that the defendant's act affect the plaintiff's tangible property, even if the property itself is not lowered in value.

The Cases illustrate the way in which the plaintiff's loss is calculated. The jurists gradually developed methods whereby the plaintiff could recover not only the true economic value of the damaged object, but also losses inflicted indirectly as a result of the defendant's act (so-called *damnum emergens*) and profits lost as a result of the act (so-called *lucrum cessans*). However, the extent of the losses covered is still limited by the rule that the defendant's act must have caused the loss.

Perhaps the most remarkable extension comes in the late classical period, when the jurists finally recognize that there may be limited recovery for loss at least when a free person in the power of his or her *paterfamilias* is killed or injured. At the end of the classical period this sort of Aquilian liability is still strictly limited; there is no recovery for the wrongful death or injury itself (since, as the jurists reason, free persons are not property), but only for the losses, such as medical expenses or lost income, that stem therefrom.

Section 1: Loss Measurable in Money

Case 36: Reckoning the Value of a Dead Slave

D. 9.2.21 pr.–1 (Ulpianus, libro octavo decimo ad Edictum)

Ait lex: 'quanti is homo in eo anno plurimi fuisset.' quae clausula aestimationem habet damni, quod datum est. (1) Annus autem retrorsus computatur, ex quo quis occisus est: quod si mortifere fuerit vulneratus et postea post longum intervallum mortuus sit, inde annum numerabimus secundum Iulianum, ex quo vulneratus est, licet Celsus contra scribit.

(Ulpian in the eighteenth book on the Edict)

The statute says: "as much money as the maximum the property was worth in that year." This clause tells how to evaluate the loss (*damnum*) that was inflicted. (1) The year is counted backwards from when someone was slain. But if he was mortally wounded and then died after a long interval, then according to Julian we will count backward from when the wounding occurred, although Celsus writes the opposite.

Discussion:

1. The clause is quoted from the First Section of the Lex Aquilia. Case 1 gives the complete Section, which you should re-read in order to understand the context.

2. Ulpian (D. 9.2.23.3) gives the following example, drawn from Julian: A slave, who is a valuable painter, loses a thumb, and thereby also his skill; less than a year later he is slain by a third party. What can the slave's owner recover from the third party? How can this measure of recovery be justified? See also Gaius, *Inst.* 3.214: a slave who has lost an eye or gone lame within the past year.

3. What effect on a slave's worth if: 1) within the past year he lost his reputation for honesty (Ulpian, D. 9.2.23.5); 2) he is killed before reaching his first birthday (ibid. 7)?

4. Summarize the conflict between Julian and Celsus with regard to slaves who die long after an injury. Which jurist sticks closer to the wording of the statute? Which jurist's view makes more practical sense? Does the controversy come down to determining the legal definition of "slaying"?

Case 37: A Natural Son; Market Value Vs. Sentimental Value

D. 9.2.33 pr. (Paulus, libro secundo ad Plautium)

Si servum meum occidisti, non affectiones aestimandas esse puto, veluti si filium tuum naturalem quis occiderit quem tu magno emptum velles, sed quanti omnibus valeret. Sextus quoque Pedius ait pretia rerum non ex affectione nec utilitate singulorum, sed communiter fungi: itaque eum, qui filium naturalem possidet, non eo locupletiorem esse, quod eum plurimo, si alius possideret, redempturus fuit, nec illum, qui filium alienum possideat, tantum habere, quanti eum patri vendere posset. in lege enim Aquilia damnum consequimur: et amisisse dicemur, quod aut consequi potuimus aut erogare cogimur.

(Paul in the second book on Plautius)

If you have slain my slave, I think that evaluation should not be of personal feelings — e.g., if someone slays your natural son whom you would buy for a high price — but rather of the worth to everybody. Sextus Pedius also says that the prices of property stem not from personal feelings or individual needs, but from general usage; thus, he who possesses a natural son is not wealthier because he would repurchase him for a very large amount if another possessed him, nor does someone who possesses another's son have as much as he could sell him for to the father. For under the Lex Aquilia we recover loss (*damnum*); and we shall be held to have lost what we either could gain or were forced to pay out.

The Hypothetical Problem:

Stichus is my natural son by a slave woman, and he has always been a particular favorite of mine. You slay him. What can I recover from you?

Discussion:

1. A natural son is most commonly the product of a sexual relationship between an owner and his slave woman. Such children were born slaves, but as this text suggests (and other sources confirm), there could be a real affective relationship between natural fathers and children. Why does the existence of this relationship have no effect on the owner's recovery when his natural son is killed? Do you think that courts should be suspicious of a claim by a plaintiff that his or her property has a value higher than its apparent market value?

2. What concept of "loss" (*damnum*) is being developed in this Case? Is there any inconsistency with the concept developed in the preceding Case?

3. Sextus Pedius says that the price or value of property is "estimated not from personal feelings or individual needs, but in a general way." What is the difference between "personal feelings" and "individual needs"? Does the latter phrase refer just to some particular use that the master was putting the slave to?

4. The last sentence of this Case refers to some other things that the owner may recover, in addition to the direct value of the slain slave; he may also recover what he could have gained (lost profit, *lucrum cessans*) or what he was forced to pay out (ensuing loss, *damnum emergens*). These losses may vary from case to case. Is there any contradiction between allowing recovery for them and refusing compensation for personal feelings? See also below, Sections 2–3.

5. The jurists often speak of "price" (*pretium*) as if it was the equivalent of value. What point do they seem to be getting at? What sorts of evidence would be useful for proving the value of a slave?

Case 38: Actual Loss and Ensuing Loss

D. 9.2.27.17 (Ulpianus, libro octavo decimo ad Edictum)

Rupisse eum utique accipiemus, qui vulneraverit, vel virgis vel loris vel pugnis cecidit, vel telo vel quo alio, ut scinderet alicui corpus, vel tumorem fecerit, sed ita demum, si damnum iniuria datum est: ceterum si nullo servum pretio viliorem deterioremve fecerit, Aquilia cessat iniuriarumque erit agendum dumtaxat: Aquilia enim eas ruptiones, quae damna dant, persequitur. ergo etsi pretio quidem non sit deterior servus factus, verum sumptus in salutem eius et sanitatem facti sunt, in haec mihi videri damnum datum: atque ideoque lege Aquilia agi posse.

(Ulpian in the eighteenth book on the Edict)

We will certainly understand a person to have "rent" (*rupisse*) if he wounded, or struck with rods or lashes or blows, or with a weapon or elsewise so as to cut a person's body, or made a bruise; but so only if loss was wrongfully inflicted. But if he does not make the slave less in price or usefulness, the Aquilian action fails and only the action on outrage (*iniuria*) can be brought; for by the Aquilian action one claims only those "rendings" that inflict loss. Therefore even if the slave was not lowered in price, but there were expenses for his health and safety, to this extent I think that loss was inflicted, and so action can be brought under the Lex Aquilia.

Discussion:

1. Outline the holding of this Case. Why does Ulpian hold that the owner can recover for medical expenses even if the slave is not lowered in value? The *Digest* compilers obviously altered Ulpian's opinion (the word "Therefore" makes no sense); in *Collatio* 2.4.1, which gives the original version of this Case, Ulpian refuses the statutory action if the slave is not lowered in value, but does not say whether he would give an *in factum* action. Does an *in factum* action seem appropriate? Or should the slave's owner have no action at all? On medical expenses, see Cases 47, 102.

2. If the slave was injured mentally but not physically, would Ulpian allow recovery? Suppose, for example, that the defendant jumped out and scared a slave, who then required costly treatment for a nervous disorder. No Roman source gives recovery for such losses; why?

Case 39: Picking Grapes

D. 9.2.27.25 (Ulpianus, libro octavo decimo ad Edictum)

Si olivam inmaturam decerpserit vel segetem desecuerit inmaturam vel vineas crudas, Aquilia tenebitur: quod si iam maturas, cessat Aquilia: nulla enim iniuria est, cum tibi etiam impensas donaverit, quae in collectionem huiusmodi fructuum impenduntur: sed si collecta haec interceperit, furti tenetur. Octavenus in uvis adicit, nisi, inquit, in terram uvas proiecit, ut effunderentur.

(Ulpian in the eighteenth book on the Edict)

If someone picks unripe olives or cuts unripe grain or grapes, he will have Aquilian liability; but if they are ripe, the Aquilian action fails, since there is no wrongfulness (*iniuria*) when he saves you the expenses that are made on gathering fruits of this kind. But if he carries off what he has gathered, he is liable for theft (*furtum*). As to the grapes, Octavenus adds: "unless he hurled the grapes to the ground, thereby destroying them."

Discussion:

1. What underlying principle makes one liable under the Lex Aquilia for cutting unripe grapes, but not for cutting ripe grapes? Does the additional point made by Octavenus substantially modify this principle?

2. Ulpian says that there is no "wrongfulness" (*iniuria*). Should he not have rather said that there is no "loss" (*damnum*)? What might explain Ulpian's way of putting the point? (This question is more important than it may seem. Is Ulpian suggesting that unless loss results, it is not possible to describe an act as "wrongful" within the context of the Lex Aquilia?)

3. Why might someone cut another's grapes, other than to steal them? Similarly, in the preceding Case, what reason might one have for deliberately striking another person's slave, other than to injure the slave?

4. Would the defendant have Aquilian liability if he had eaten the grapes? See Case 12.

Case 40: Castrating a Slave

D. 9.2.27.28 (Ulpianus, libro octavo decimo ad Edictum)

Et si puerum quis castraverit et pretiosiorem fecerit, Vivianus scribit cessare Aquiliam, sed iniuriarum erit agendum aut ex edicto Aedilium [aut] in quadruplum.

(Ulpian in the eighteenth book on the Edict)

Also, if someone, by castrating a slave boy, makes him more valuable, Vivianus writes that the Aquilian action fails. But action should be brought on outrage (*iniuria*) or for quadruple under the Edict of the Curule Aediles.

Discussion:

1. Explain the decision. Would it matter if the slave's master had purchased the slave in the hope that he would sire children?

2. By a special provision in the Praetor's Edict, defendants were held liable for outrage (*iniuria*) if they injured another person's slave; note, however, that this action requires the intent (*dolus*) to offend the owner. The provision of the Curule Aediles' Edict, to which Ulpian refers, is not otherwise known; but castration of slaves was also often a criminal offense.

Case 41: Piercing Pearls

D. 9.2.27.30 (Ulpianus, libro octavo decimo ad Edictum)

Si cum maritus uxori margaritas extricatas dedisset in usu eaque invito vel inscio viro perforasset, ut pertusis in linea uteretur, teneri eam lege Aquilia, sive divertit sive nupta est adhuc.

(Ulpian in the eighteenth book on the Edict)

If a husband had given unstrung pearls to his wife for her use, and without his knowledge or against his will she had pierced them so that, after boring them through, she could string them, (a jurist held) that she is liable under the Lex Aquilia, no matter whether she is divorced or still married.

Discussion:

1. In Roman marriages, the estates of husband and wife are in principle kept separate, and they are not allowed to co-mingle their estates by giving gifts of large value. Thus the pearls remain the husband's after he has given them to his wife. According to Paul (D. 9.2.56), "If a wife damages her husband's property, she is liable in accord with the Lex Aquilia." (The converse is presumably also true.) Discuss the advantages and disadvantages of this rule from the perspective of public policy with regard to marriage. Are the jurists holding that protecting the property of the individual spouses is more important than discouraging them from bringing suit against one another?

2. Why is the wife liable for piercing the pearls? Could she argue that they are otherwise unusable? Think about this issue in terms of her duty of care toward the pearls; how is Ulpian tacitly defining her duty?

3. Ulpian says that she is liable if she pierced them "without (her husband's) knowledge or against his will." If he knew that she was having them pierced, but said nothing, is his silence presumed to be consent? Would this normally be true for Aquilian liability?

4. Does Ulpian presume that piercing the pearls will lower their value? Would the wife be liable if they increased in value as a result of being pierced?

5. The Latin text is clearly in some disarray, and it is possible that the *Digest*'s compilers have suppressed an alternate juristic view. What might that view have been?

Case 42: An Oven Against a Party Wall

Collatio 12.7.8 (Ulpianus, libro octavo decimo ad Edictum)

Item libro vi ex Viviano relatum est: si furnum secundum parietem communem haberes, an damni iniuria teneris? Et ait (Proculus) agi non posse Aquilia
lege, quia nec cum eo qui focum haberet: et ideo aequius putat in factum actionem dandam. Sed non proponit exustum parietem. Sane enim quaeri potest,
si nondum mihi damnum dederis et ita ignem habeas ut metuam ne mihi des,
an aequum sit me interim actionem, id est in factum, impetrare? Fortassis enim
de hoc senserit Proculus. Nisi quis dixerit damni non facti sufficere cautionem.

(Ulpian in the eighteenth book on the Edict)

Again, it was reported in the sixth book from Vivianus: If you
have an oven against a party wall, are you liable for wrongful
damage? And Proculus says there is no liability under the Lex
Aquilia, since there also is none with one who has a fireplace; and
so he thinks an action should be given *in factum*. But he does not
hypothesize that the wall was burnt up. For indeed, if you have not
yet inflicted loss on me but have a fire in such a way that I fear you
will inflict loss on me, it can be asked whether it is fair that I mean-
while obtain an action, i.e. *in factum*. Perhaps Proculus was thinking about this situation. Unless someone might say that the undertaking against threatened damage suffices.

The Hypothetical Problem:

You and I share ownership of a party wall. You construct an oven against the
wall. I become alarmed that the oven may damage the wall. What can I do?

Discussion:

1. This is a complex and confusing text, which is reported in a somewhat different version in the *Digest* (9.2.27.10). A party wall is common property of
   two persons, who share the use of it. In the hypothetical, one owner has
   built an oven against it, and the other is concerned about actual or potential
   damage to the wall resulting from the oven's use. On Aquilian liability in
   cases of co-ownership, see Case 74.

2. As Ulpian observes, Proculus' hypothetical does not mention damage to the
   party wall. Is he, as Ulpian suggests, simply presuming that the wall has been
   damaged? If so, why does he hold that the action should be *in factum*, rather
   than statutory? (See, on this point, Case 50.)

3. Is Ulpian willing to allow an *in factum* action if the party wall has not in fact
   been damaged?

4. The undertaking against threatened damage (*cautio damni infecti*) is a
   formal promise that the promissor will pay for any damage that the rundown condition of his or her building may cause to the promissee in the
   future. A neighbor who fears such damage can demand that the owner give

this *cautio*. Once the *cautio* has been given, the neighbor can sue on it and does not need to bring an Aquilian action if damage then occurs; the Aquilian action can be hard to win because there is usually no liability for failing to maintain property (see Case 35). The *cautio* would be available in the case of an oven (Ulpian, D. 39.2.24.7). If the undertaking were not available, would that strengthen the case for allowing an *in factum* action before damage occurred? What loss could the plaintiff then claim?

Section 2: Determining What the Defendant Must Pay

Case 43: Associated Losses

D. 9.2.21.2 (Ulpianus, libro octavo decimo ad Edictum)

Sed utrum corpus eius solum aestimamus, quanti fuerit cum occideretur, an potius quanti interfuit nostra non esse occisum? et hoc iure utimur, ut eius quod interest fiat aestimatio.

D. 9.2.22 (Paulus, libro vicensimo secundo ad Edictum)

Proinde si servum occidisti, quem sub poena tradendum promisi, utilitas venit in hoc iudicium. (1) Item causae corpori cohaerentes aestimantur, si quis ex comoedis aut symphoniacis aut gemellis aut quadriga aut ex pari mularum unum vel unam occiderit: non solum enim perempti corporis aestimatio facienda est, sed et eius ratio haberi debet, quo cetera corpora depretiata sunt.

(Ulpian in the eighteenth book on the Edict)

But do we evaluate only the physical worth of him (a dead slave) when he was slain, or rather the extent of our interest in his not being slain? Our law is that evaluation is made of the interest.

(Paul in the twenty-second book on the Edict)

Therefore if you slew a slave whom I had promised to deliver under a stipulation, this trial includes his usefulness to me. (1) Likewise circumstances related to the body are evaluated if somebody slays a man or woman from a troupe of actors or musicians, or one from a set of twins or a chariot team or a pair of mules. For not only must evaluation be made of the destroyed body, but also account should be taken of how the other bodies are lowered in value.

The Hypothetical Problem:

I promised Titius that I would deliver the slave Pamphilus to him, and that I would pay him a penalty of 10,000 sesterces if I failed to deliver Pamphilus. You wrongfully slew Pamphilus before I could deliver him to Titius. What can I recover from you in an Aquilian action? Does the result depend on whether Pamphilus is worth 5,000 sesterces or 15,000 sesterces?

Discussion:

1. How clear is the method Paul uses for arriving at an evaluation? To what extent does the rule for evaluating a slain slave (highest value within the past year) conflict with the rule for assessing the plaintiff's interest? Do the two standards reflect different understandings of Aquilian liability?

2. Paul (D. 9.2.55) puts the following case: I promised Titius that I would deliver either Stichus or Pamphilus to him; the slave Stichus was worth 10,000,

the slave Pamphilus was worth 20,000. Before I was obliged to carry out my promise, Titius wrongfully slew Stichus. Am I still obliged to deliver Pamphilus to Titius? What, if anything, can I recover from Titius for the slain slave? Suppose that Pamphilus had died of natural causes less than a year before Titius slew Stichus; would the amount of liability be different?

3. Javolenus (D. 9.2.37.1) discusses another case: A four-footed animal has done extensive damage to another's property. Under the action on *pauperies* (see Chapter IV), the animal's owner can choose either to surrender the animal or pay for the damage. Suppose that the animal is worth 2,000 sesterces, and the damage it did is evaluated at 20,000 sesterces. If the animal is wrongfully slain by Sempronia before Titius can bring suit, what can the animal's owner recover?

4. A troupe of four slave actors are worth 50,000 sesterces if sold as a unit, and 10,000 apiece if sold separately. What can their owner recover if someone wrongfully slays one of the slaves? Would it matter if the three remaining slaves could be sold together for 35,000 sesterces?

5. In this Case (and also in those that follow), how do the jurists go about determining the true amount of the loss sustained by the plaintiff? In Case 37, Ulpian allows recovery for "what we either could gain (= lost profit, *lucrum cessans*) or were forced to pay out (= ensuing loss, *damnum emergens*)." Do these categories have any major influence on most juristic descriptions of how loss should be evaluated?

6. In Case 37, Ulpian quotes Sextus Pedius as holding that "the prices of property stem not from personal feelings or individual needs, but from general usage." Why does Case 43 allow the plaintiff to recover his individual interest in the damaged property? To what extent do Cases 37 and 43 involve two different concepts of "interest"?

Case 44: Killing a Slave Accountant

D. 9.2.23.4 (Ulpianus, libro octavo decimo ad Edictum)

Sed et si servus, qui magnas fraudes in meis rationibus commiserat, fuerit occisus, de quo quaestionem habere destinaveram, ut fraudium participes eruerentur, rectissime Labeo scribit tanti aestimandum, quanti mea intererat fraudes servi per eum commissas detegi, non quanti noxa eius servi valeat.

(Ulpian in the eighteenth book on the Edict)

But likewise if a slave was killed who had made great falsifications in my account books and whom I had intended to question (under torture) in order to discover his accomplices in deceit, Labeo writes quite correctly that the evaluation should be of my interest in detecting the slave's falsifications [committed through him], not of the value of the harm the slave did.

The Hypothetical Problem:

Stichus was keeping my account books. Recently I learned that he had been systematically forging entries in my accounts in order to cheat me; as a result I have lost a substantial amount of money. I also suspected that Stichus had accomplices, and decided to question him under torture. Before I could do so, Titia killed Stichus. What can I recover from her?

Discussion:

1. Explain the distinction made by Labeo. How is it possible to evaluate the owner's interest in detecting the slave's falsifications? Why is there no recovery of the amount lost by the slave's fraud? (The words in brackets probably were not written by Ulpian, but were added later to his text.)

2. Do Labeo and Ulpian think of the owner's interest in detecting the slave's falsifications as "lost profit" or "ensuing loss," or do they rather think of the owner's interest as part of the value of the slave himself?

Case 45: Losing an Inheritance When a Slave Is Killed

D. 9.2.23.2 (Ulpianus, libro octavo decimo ad Edictum)

Idem Iulianus scribit, si institutus fuero sub condicione 'si Stichum manumisero' et Stichus sit occisus post mortem testatoris, in aestimationem etiam hereditatis pretium me consecuturum: propter occisionem enim defecit condicio: quod si vivo testatore occisus sit, hereditatis aestimationem cessare, quia retrorsum quanti plurimi fuit inspicitur.

(Ulpian in the eighteenth book on the Edict)

The same Julian writes that, if I was instituted heir under the condition that I manumit Stichus, and Stichus was slain after the testator's death, in the evaluation (of Stichus) I will also obtain the value of the inheritance, since the condition failed because of the slaying. But if he had been killed while the testator lived, no evaluation is made of the inheritance, since maximum value is determined by reckoning backward.

The Hypothetical Problem:

Titius appoints me his heir on the condition that I manumit my slave Stichus. After Titius' death, but before I can free Stichus and so take the inheritance, Stichus is wrongfully killed by Seia. What can I recover from her?

Discussion:

1. Because I cannot complete the condition, I lose the inheritance. In what sense is the inheritance part of the value of the slain Stichus? In what sense is it not? If the inheritance is worth 100,000 and Stichus is worth 10,000, what can I recover from the defendant: 90,000; 100,000; or 110,000?

2. Is the lost inheritance describable as "lost profit"? Note that I never actually had the inheritance, and that if Stichus had, say, died of natural causes after Titius' death but before I could free him, I would not have inherited. How does the inheritance differ from, for instance, wages that a wounded slave doesn't earn?

3. Why can't I recover the inheritance if Stichus is slain before Titius' death? Do you find Julian's argument convincing? Why doesn't he treat the inheritance as "lost profit"?

Case 46: Erasing Proof of a Debt

D. 9.2.40 (Paulus, libro tertio ad Edictum)

In lege Aquilia, si deletum chirographum mihi esse dicam, in quo sub condicione mihi pecunia debita fuerit, et interim testibus quoque id probare possim, qui testes possunt non esse eo tempore, quo condicio extitit, et si summatim re exposita ad suspicionem iudicem adducam, debeam vincere: sed tunc condemnationis exactio competit, cum debiti condicio extiterit: quod si defecerit, condemnatio nullas vires habebit.

(Paul in the third book on the Edict)

Under the Lex Aquilia, if I allege that a handwritten receipt was erased that recorded money owed to me under a condition, and I can now prove this debt through witnesses who cannot be available when the condition is fulfilled, and if, in sum, by setting out the facts I persuade the *iudex* to believe me, I should win. But the execution of the judgment is available when the debt's condition is fulfilled; if the condition fails, the judgment has no force.

Discussion:

1. This Case is one of a number of sources dealing with the erasure of legal documents such as receipts; see also D. 9.2.41–42; 47.2.27.3, 32.1. The recurrent problem is that the erasure causes loss that may far outstrip the physical damage. The plaintiff has a dilemma: either other proofs of the legal point are available, in which case the erased document is superfluous; or they are not available, in which case the fact and value of the loss are hard to prove. How does Paul handle the dilemma? Should it count as loss simply that the debt is more difficult to prove without the document?

2. A debt owed under a condition is payable only if the condition is fulfilled. How does Paul deal with the fact that the plaintiff has incurred no loss at the time of the lawsuit on the Lex Aquilia? (The rough-and-ready solution suggested in this Case may not have been possible under Roman procedural law; the compilers of the *Digest* may have altered the text.)

3. A loan receipt is erased, and in consequence my suit to recover the loan fails; later I find witnesses who can prove the loan. I cannot sue the debtor again; but can I sue the person who erased the receipt? See Ulpian, D. 47.2.32.1.

Section 3: Injury to a Free Person

Case 47: An Injured Son

D. 9.2.7 pr. (Ulpianus, libro octavo decimo ad Edictum)

Qua actione patrem consecuturum ait, quod minus ex operis filii sui propter vitiatum oculum sit habiturus, et impendia, quae pro eius curatione fecerit.

(Ulpian in the eighteenth book on the Edict)
In this action he (Julian) says that the father will obtain what he lost from his son's services because of the eye being harmed, as well as his expenses in caring for him.

Discussion:

1. This Case is the conclusion of Julian's famous hypothetical about the shoemaker's apprentice (above, Case 23). Julian now turns to discuss what the boy's father can claim as a result of the injury. No recovery is given for the "decline in value" of the boy himself; as Gaius (Case 102) elsewhere explains, "a free person's body does not admit of evaluation." Does what the father can recover provide an adequate substitute?

2. To what degree is this extension of Aquilian liability explained by the nature of the Roman family? A son who is in the power of his father owns nothing, and all his earnings accrue to his father. To what extent is he in a position analogous to that of a slave? Would there be a similar Aquilian liability for injury to a free person not in power?

3. The father can recover medical expenses and the lost prospective wages of his son. How can they be estimated? Is recovery of these items also possible in the case of an injured slave? See Case 37.

4. This Case deals with liability under the Third Section of the Lex Aquilia for an injured son. Is liability under the First Section for a slain son also possible?

Case 48: An Injured Free Man

D. 9.2.13 pr. (Ulpianus, libro octavo decimo ad Edictum)

Liber homo suo nomine utilem Aquiliae habet actionem: directam enim non habet, quoniam dominus membrorum suorum nemo videtur. fugitivi autem nomine dominus habet.

(Ulpian in the eighteenth book on the Edict)

A free man has the analogous form of Aquilian action in his own name; for he does not have the statutory action, since no one is regarded as owning his own limbs. However the owner has (an action) in the name of a fugitive slave.

Discussion:

1. On its face, this Case seems to hold that any free person can bring an Aquilian action to recover for wrongful personal injury to him. This is the only classical text that expressly states such a view, although in a few other texts (Alfenus, D. 9.2.52.1 = Case 62; Ulpian, D. 9.2.7.7 = Case 6; Ulpian, D. 9.2.11.5) the legal status of the victim is unclear. If recovery is possible, what ought the measure of damage to be? See also Case 102.

2. How does Ulpian justify awarding an analogous action (*actio utilis*) rather than a statutory one? Is he convincing? (Compare Case 14, and Cases 79–81; but also Case 38.)

3. Many scholars believe that this text was altered by the *Digest*'s compilers, and that Ulpian originally discussed not "free men" generally, but rather a very specific situation: a free man who, at the time of the injury, is being held as a slave by someone who is unaware of the truth about his status. If this narrower interpretation of the Case is correct, is it perhaps easier to understand why Ulpian awards the free man an *in factum* Aquilian action if he is injured while ostensibly serving as a slave?

4. The final sentence deals with the converse of the situation described in the preceding question: a fugitive slave, ostensibly acting as a free person, is injured or killed. The fugitive's owner has a statutory action; why? Does this ruling help to clarify the earlier part of the Case?

Part D: Causation

The final requirement for Aquilian liability is that the defendant's wrongful act have caused the loss inflicted on the plaintiff. If the loss was directly caused, then the plaintiff can sue under the Lex Aquilia itself; if indirectly caused, then through an *in factum* action. (See Chapter 1, Part B.)

Apart from this distinction between direct and indirect causation, what the jurists say about causation is, from a modern viewpoint, not wholly adequate. In particular, although they do recognize that the chain of causation should not be extended to include remote or speculative losses (cf. Case 67), the jurists do not really come to grips with the problem of the sufficiency of the causal relationship — one of the major issues in modern negligence law because, in the complex and frequently dangerous world we inhabit, not only do losses often result from events that involve numerous interlinked causes, but losses may also be extremely high in relation to the gravity of the specific acts producing them. Thus the tangle of questions surrounding "proximate cause" (the Anglo-American theory that limits liability to the "foreseeable" or "direct" results of acts) is never really addressed by the jurists, although their hypothetical cases usually lie well within the perimeter of "proximate cause."

Nonetheless, in juristic discussions of causation many of the themes of earlier sections begin to be tied together. The jurists can avoid intricate analysis of causation in part because they restrict the duty of care that Romans owe toward the property of others, in part because they confine Aquilian liability chiefly to positive acts involving the defendant's more or less obvious misconduct, and in part because they define fairly narrowly the types of loss for which the plaintiff can recover. These prior moves make it much easier in practice to recognize the chain of causation.

But the jurists were unable to avoid controversies altogether. These become particularly intense over cases where the chain of causation does not run to its likeliest outcome, but is instead interrupted by a second event, and particularly by a second wrongful act of another person. The sharp controversy between Celsus and Julian (perhaps the two greatest jurists of the high classical period in the early second century A.D.) brings into sharp focus the historical ambiguity of Aquilian liability: is it primarily punitive or loss-compensating? Although late classical jurists probably resolved this controversy in favor of Celsus, the compilers of the *Digest* nonetheless included a long and difficult passage to attest the dissenting views of Julian.

Section 1: Chain of Causation

Case 49: A Sick Slave

D. 9.2.7.5 (Ulpianus, libro octavo decimo ad Edictum)

Sed si quis servum aegrotum leviter percusserit et is obierit, recte Labeo dicit lege Aquilia eum teneri, quia aliud alii mortiferum esse solet.

(Ulpian in the eighteenth book on the Edict)

But if a person lightly strikes a sick slave who then dies, Labeo rightly holds that he is liable under the Lex Aquilia, since different things are fatal for different people.

Discussion:

1. Is it to be presumed that the light blow was strong enough to have done at least some injury to a healthy slave? That the defendant knew or ought to have known that the slave was sick?

2. In the Common Law of negligence, it is often said that "the tortfeasor takes his victim as he finds him"; this means that if, for instance, you negligently strike the head of a person who (unknown to you) has an eggshell-thin skull, you are liable for the unexpected and disastrous consequences of your negligence. To what extent does this Case suggest that the Romans had a similar doctrine?

3. Re-express Labeo's ruling in terms of causation. What arguments can be used to support his ruling?

4. Suppose that the defendant in this case did not strike the slave, but stole his clothing, as a result of which the slave died of cold. Would there be Aquilian liability? On what theory of causation? See Ulpian, D. 19.5.14.1, who gives an *in factum* action.

Case 50: Setting a Fire

Collatio 12.7.1–5 (Ulpianus, libro octavo decimo ad Edictum)

Item si insulam meam adusseris vel incenderis, Aquiliae actionem habebo, idemque est et si arbustum meum vel villam meam. (2) Quod si dolo quis insulam exusserit, etiam capitis poena plectitur quasi incendiarius. (3) Item si quis insulam voluerit exurere et ignis etiam ad vicini insulam pervenerit, Aquilia tenebitur lege vicino etiam non minus inquilinis ob res eorum exustas, et ita Labeo libro xv Responsorum refert. (4) Sed si stipulam in agro tuo incenderis ignisque evagatus ad praedium vicini pervenerit et illud exusserit, Aquilia lex locum habeat an in factum sit fuit quaestio. (5) Sed plerisque Aquilia lex locum habere non videtur, et ita Celsus libro xxxvii Digestorum scribit. ait enim 'Si stipulam incendentis ignis effugit, Aquilia lege eum non teneri, sed in factum agendum, quia non principaliter hic exussit, sed dum aliud egit, sic ignis processit.'

(Ulpian in the eighteenth book on the Edict)

Likewise if you burn or set fire to my apartment house, I will have the Aquilian action, and the same is true if (you burn) my orchard or villa. (2) But if someone deliberately (*dolo*) burnt my apartment house, he is also punished by capital punishment as an arsonist. (3) Likewise if someone wishes to burn an apartment house and the fire also spreads to a neighbor's apartment house and burns it up, he will be liable to the neighbor under the Aquilian law, and also to the tenants for their burned property, and so Labeo writes in the fifteenth book of his *Responses*. (4) But if you burn stubble in your field and the fire spreads until it comes to a neighbor's property, there was a question whether the Lex Aquilia applies or (rather) an action *in factum*. (5) But many hold that the Lex Aquilia does not apply, and so Celsus writes in the thirty-seventh book of his *Digests*. For he says: "If someone burns stubble and the fire escapes, he is not liable under the Aquilian law, but the action must be *in factum*; for he did not burn it directly, but the fire spread while he did something else."

Discussion:

1. This passage, reproduced in much abbreviated form by D. 9.2.27.7–8, is a good example of how the jurists develop law through casuistry. Set out the logic of the Case.

2. The text deals with three problems. The first is easy: you set fire to my apartment house. If you do so carelessly, you are liable to me under the Lex Aquilia; if you do so deliberately, you face both an Aquilian suit from me and criminal liability as an arsonist.

3. The second problem raises more difficulties. Titius deliberately sets fire to an apartment house; the fire then spreads to an adjacent apartment house.

Ulpian, supported by the early classical jurist Labeo, holds that both the neighbor and his tenants can sue Titius with a statutory Aquilian action. Why can they bring a statutory rather than an *in factum* lawsuit? Is it because Titius is regarded as directly inflicting the loss to the neighbor, or rather because Titius' act of arson was intentional? Suppose, for instance, that Titius carelessly sets fire to A's house (e.g., by knocking over a lamp), and the fire spreads to B's house; would B's action against Titius be statutory or *in factum*?

4. The third problem raises still more difficulties. Titius is burning the stubble in his field; because of his failure to pay attention, the fire escapes and damages a neighbor's property. Case 28 has already established that Titius is liable for *culpa* in carelessly allowing the fire to escape; but is the action statutory or *in factum*? Celsus, whom Ulpian quotes, holds that there cannot be a statutory action "because he did not burn it directly." What does he mean? Is it possible to distinguish between Titius' wrongfully setting fire to another person's property, and Titius' setting fire to his own property (which he has a right to do) but then wrongfully allowing this fire to spread to another person's property? In the latter case, would it be correct to describe the damage done to the neighbor as "indirectly caused"?

5. But Ulpian may also be suggesting that the distinction between statutory and *in factum* actions is somehow related to the difference between *dolus* and *culpa*. Try to reconstruct a possible argument along these lines. Ulpian indicates that earlier jurists had found the issue difficult; what might opponents of his view have argued? Is this Case entirely consistent with the Cases in Chapter I, Part B?

6. What does this Case say about the interrelationship of duty of care, standards of care, causation, and loss? To what extent is one held liable for the entirely unintended or unforeseeable consequences of one's wrongful acts?

Case 51: Traffic Accident on the Capitoline Hill

D. 9.2.52.2 (Alfenus, libro secundo Digestorum)

In clivo Capitolino duo plostra onusta mulae ducebant: prioris plostri muliones conversum plostrum sublevabant, quo facile mulae ducerent: superius
plostrum cessim ire coepit et cum muliones, qui inter duo plostra fuerunt, e
medio exissent, posterius plostrum a priore percussum retro redierat et
puerum cuiusdam obtriverat: dominus pueri consulebat, cum quo se agere op-
erteret. respondi in causa ius esse positum: nam si muliones, qui superius
plostrum sustinuissent, sua sponte se subduxissent et ideo factum esset, ut
mulae plostrum retinere non possint atque onere ipso retraherentur, cum
domino mularum nullam esse actionem, cum hominibus, qui conversum plostrum sustinuissent, lege Aquilia agi posse: nam nihilo minus eum damnum
dare, qui quod sustineret mitteret sua voluntate, ut id aliquem feriret: veluti si
quis asellum cum agitasset non retinuisset, aeque si quis ex manu telum aut
aliud quid immisisset, damnum iniuria daret. sed si mulae, quia aliquid re-
formidassent, recessissent et muliones timore permoti ne opprimerentur
plostrum reliquissent, cum hominibus esse actionem nullam esse, cum
domino mularum esse. quod si neque mulae neque homines in causa essent,
sed mulae retinere onus nequissent aut cum coniterentur lapsae concidissent
et ideo plostrum cessim redisset atque hi quo conversum fuisset onus
sustinere nequissent, neque cum domino mularum neque cum hominibus
esse actionem. illud quidem certe, quoquo modo res se haberet, cum domino
posteriorum mularum agi non posse, quoniam non sua sponte, sed percussae
retro redissent.

(Alfenus in the second book of his *Digests*)

Mules were pulling two loaded carts up the ascent to the Capitoline hill. The front cart had tilted back, and the muleteers lifted it
up so that the mules could pull it easily; the front cart began to go
back, and when the muleteers who were between the two carts
moved out from between, the front cart struck the rear one, which
then moved backward and ran over somebody's slave boy. The
boy's owner asked whom he should sue.

I replied that the law depended on the circumstances. For if the
muleteers who had held up the front cart got out of the way of their
own accord, and for this reason it came about that the mules could
not hold the cart and were dragged back by the load, there is no
action against the owner of the mules, but the men who held up
the tilted cart can be sued under the Lex Aquilia; for a man does
damage no less when of his own accord he lets go of what he is
holding up, and it then strikes someone. For example, if a man did
not control an ass that he was driving, he gives wrongful loss, just
like someone who lets fly from his hand a weapon or something.

But if the mules backed up because they shied at something, and
the muleteers abandoned the cart from fear they would be

crushed, the men cannot be sued, but the owner of the mules can be.

But if neither the mules nor the men were responsible, but the mules were unable to hold the weight, or they slipped and fell when they tried to do so, so that the cart moved backwards and those where the load was tilted back were unable to hold it, there is no action either against the mules' owner or the men.

In any case this is clear: however the event occurred, there can be no action against the owner of the rear mules, since they moved back not of their own accord but because they were struck.

Discussion:

1. The Case (which is probably based on a real incident) is reported in the form of a juristic response to a legal question (*responsum*). Alfenus gives three possible scenarios. Which best matches the facts as stated?

2. Reconstruct the first scenario. The muleteers are presumably free employees of the owner of the mules. To what extent is their Aquilian liability explained by the analogy Alfenus draws with a man who fails to control an ass he is driving, or who lets fly a spear? Why does Alfenus grant a statutory action, rather than one *in factum*? (Compare Cases 3 and 4.) Note that in many instances the muleteers are likely to have no assets to pay the plaintiff, and therefore a lawsuit against them will be of little value.

3. Reconstruct the second scenario. The owner of the mules would most probably be liable under the action on *pauperies*, which covers damage done by four-footed animals; cf. Case 35, and below, Chapter IV. He might also have Aquilian liability if he were somehow responsible for the mules' conduct.

4. Reconstruct the third scenario, which is probably the most difficult; why? Does it seem reasonable that no one is at fault for having overloaded the cart? Does it matter whether the fear of the muleteers was reasonable? Was this just an unavoidable accident?

5. On the basis of the three reconstructed scenarios, describe the duty of care that Alfenus imposes on muleteers. Is this duty owed to anyone on whom loss may be inflicted if the duty is violated? Trace the chain of causation that leads from a wrongful act by the muleteers to the slave boy. How direct is the line?

6. Why is the owner of the rear mules not liable? Are the muleteers of the rear cart also not liable? What if they were following so closely that an accident was more likely to occur?

7. By varying the facts given above, it is possible to attenuate the chain of causation. Suppose that, because of the muleteers' carelessness, their cart rolled backward and:
   — struck a stone wall that collapsed onto and killed the slave boy, who by chance had been standing underneath the wall; or:

— bore down on the slave boy, who, in jumping backward to get out of the way, fell, struck his head against a rock, and died; or:

— set off a panic among bystanders, who, in attempting to flee the careening cart, upset a bronze statue that fell on the slave boy and crushed him; or:

— frightened the slave boy, who, although he was in no direct physical danger, had a congenital heart condition and died of a heart attack; or:

— blocked the ascent to the Capitoline hill, as a result of which the slave boy's master, who lived on the slopes of the Capitoline, could not obtain medicine and the slave boy died of pneumonia.

At what point does the chain of causation become so attenuated that the jurists will no longer hold the muleteers liable for the dead slave boy? Although it is not easy to answer this question, one can at least approximate an answer by looking at the Roman conception of Aquilian liability. In a particular case, it may be undeniable that the defendant's act "caused" the plaintiff's loss, and that the defendant's act was "wrongful" with respect to someone; but there may still be no recovery if the act is not "wrongful" with respect to the actual plaintiff. As Benjamin Cardozo observed in the landmark 1928 case of *Palsgraf v. Long Island Railroad Co.* (248 N.Y. 339), quoting an earlier decision: "In every instance, before negligence can be predicated of a given act, back of the act must be sought and found a duty to the individual complaining, the observance of which would have averted or avoided the injury." Do the jurists generally seem to follow this theory? Is the basic problem the remoteness of cause, or the duty of care?

Case 52: Two Actions Under the Lex Aquilia

D. 9.2.46 (Ulpianus, libro quinquagensimo ad Sabinum)

Si vulnerato servo lege Aquilia actum sit, postea mortuo ex eo vulnere agi lege Aquilia nihilo minus potest.

D. 9.2.47 (Iulianus, libro octagensimo sexto Digestorum)

Sed si priore iudicio aestimatione facta, postea mortuo servo, de occiso agere dominus instituerit, exceptione doli mali opposita compelletur, ut ex utroque iudicio nihil amplius consequatur, quam consequi deberet, si initio de occiso homine egisset.

(Ulpian in the fiftieth book on Sabinus)
If action is brought under the Lex Aquilia for a wounded slave, there can still be an action under the Lex Aquilia if the slave later dies from the wound.

(Julian in the eighty-sixth book of his *Digests*)
But if an evaluation was made in the first trial, and after the slave dies the owner starts to sue for the slaying, then through interposition of the defense of deceit (*exceptio doli mali*) he is forced to recover no more from both trials than he ought to recover if he had sued from the start on the slain slave.

Discussion:

1. The defense of deceit (*exceptio doli*) is a formal device, inserted into the formula for the trial, whereby the defendant asserts that the plaintiff's claim cannot be granted as it stands because the claim is somehow tainted by deceit or fraud; see Cases 150–151. What is the deceit in this Case?

2. According to Julian, when did the act of slaying take place? (See above, Case 36.) What is the appropriate measure of damages in the second trial, and how is it affected by the fact that the plaintiff won the first trial?

3. If in the first trial the defendant denied liability for the wounding and he lost, can he reassert his denial of liability when he is sued under the First Section of the Lex Aquilia?

Section 2: Intervening Acts

Case 53: Inadequate Care for an Injured Slave

D. 9.2.52 pr. (Alfenus, libro secundo Digestorum)

Si ex plagis servus mortuus esset neque id medici inscientia aut domini neglegentia accidisset, recte de iniuria occiso eo agitur.

(Alfenus in the second book of his *Digests*)

If a slave had died from wounds and this did not occur because of a doctor's lack of knowledge or his master's carelessness, action is properly brought for his wrongful slaying.

The Hypothetical Problem:

Seius wounded Pamphila, a slave who belonged to Cassia. Cassia thought that the wound was slight and decided not to have it treated by a doctor. In fact, the wound was much more serious than it appeared, and Pamphila soon died of the wound. What can Cassia recover from Seius?

Discussion:

1. According to this Case, what obligations does the owner of a slave have when a third party injures the slave? What is the source of these obligations?

2. On the Aquilian liability of doctors, see above, Case 24. If the injured slave dies because of the doctor's ignorance, will the owner be able to sue both the injurer and the doctor? What will be the measure of damages in these actions?

3. Paul (D. 9.2.30.4) puts the converse case of a wound that is clearly not mortal, of which the slave dies because of the master's carelessness. For what is the defendant liable?

Case 54: A Second Mortal Wound

D. 9.2.11.3 (Ulpianus, libro octavo decimo ad Edictum)

Celsus scribit, si alius mortifero vulnere percusserit, alius postea exanimaverit, priorem quidem non teneri quasi occiderit, sed quasi vulneraverit, quia ex alio vulnere periit, posteriorem teneri, quia occidit. quod et Marcello videtur et est probabilius.

(Ulpian in the eighteenth book on the Edict)

Celsus writes that if one person strikes with a mortal wound and a second person then kills, the first person is not liable as for having slain but as for having wounded, since the slave died of the second wound; the second person is liable because he slew. This view also seemed best to Marcellus, and it is the more reasonable one.

The Hypothetical Problem:

Sempronia mortally wounds a slave; but before the slave can die, he is killed by Titius. What can the slave's owner recover from Sempronia and from Titius?

Discussion:

1. What does Celsus mean by "a mortal wound" — one from which the slave would certainly have died, or one from which he would quite probably have died, or one from which he could die? How sure can one be that a wound is mortal before the slave actually dies?

2. According to Celsus, what can the owner recover from each of the defendants? Note that Celsus had strong views on what an owner can recover when a slave dies of a slow-acting wound; see above, Case 36.

3. How convincing do you find Celsus' reasoning in support of his decision? As the last sentence shows, Celsus' decision was controversial, although later jurists seem to have preferred it; the compilers of the *Digest* have apparently eliminated the alternative view. What might that view have been?

4. The problem that Celsus raises has important modern implications, since it is quite possible that an act of negligence may, for instance, cause medical bills that will predictably last for the remainder of the plaintiff's life. Is Celsus saying that a plaintiff cannot recover compensation until he or she has actually sustained such losses? What practical problems might result from this position?

Case 55: A Building Collapses on an Injured Slave

D. 9.2.15.1 (Ulpianus, libro octavo decimo ad Edictum)

Si servus vulneratus mortifere postea ruina vel naufragio vel alio ictu maturius perierit, de occiso agi non posse, sed quasi de vulnerato, sed si manumissus vel alienatus ex vulnere periit, quasi de occiso agi posse Iulianus ait. haec ita tam varie, quia verum est eum a te occisum tunc cum vulnerabas, quod mortuo eo demum apparuit: at in superiore non est passa ruina apparere an sit occisus....

(Ulpian in the eighteenth book on the Edict)

If a slave is mortally wounded and afterwards dies more quickly owing to the collapse of a building or a shipwreck or another blow, an action can be brought not for slaying, but as for wounding; but if the slave was manumitted or alienated, and then died of the wound, Julian says that an action can be brought as for slaying. The reason for this difference is that in truth the slave was slain by you when you wounded him, but this fact became clear when he later died; but in the former case the building's collapse did not allow it to become clear whether the slave was slain....

Discussion:

1. Ulpian discusses two cases. In the first, the mortally injured slave is killed sooner than might have been expected when a building collapses on him or he is lost in a shipwreck. In Roman law, these are standard examples of *vis maior*, an irresistible force against which human effort is regarded as vain. Why does the intervention of *vis maior* relieve the original defendant of liability for slaying? Do Ulpian's reasons differ substantially from those given by Celsus in the preceding Case?

2. In the text as it stands, Ulpian also says that the original defendant is relieved of liability if the slave dies prematurely from "another blow." This would appear to be a blow struck by a third party. In what sense is such a second act similar to an irresistible force? How do they differ?

3. In the second case that Ulpian discusses, a slave receives a slow-acting mortal blow; his master then frees or sells him, after which the slave dies. Why does Julian hold that the former master can bring an Aquilian action for slaying despite the fact that he no longer owns the slave? (See Case 36.) Why might anyone have believed that there is any contradiction between the holdings in the two cases Ulpian discusses?

4. At this point, try to summarize the position in Cases 54–55 with regard to the effects of an intervening event on the chain of causation. How reasonable is this position?

5. There is a significant and much debated problem with the Latin text of this fragment. Many scholars believe that Ulpian cited Julian for both of the positions quoted above, and the Latin would in fact make good sense on this

view. But other scholars believe that the position taken on the first case (namely, that an intervening cause relieves the defendant from liability for the slave's death) is impossible to reconcile with Julian's views in Case 56 (see below). These scholars suppose that the first part of the first sentence reports Ulpian's own views or those of Celsus. After you read Case 56, make up your own mind on this question.

Case 56: A Second Mortal Wound (Julian's View)

D. 9.2.51 (Iulianus, libro octagensimo sexto Digestorum)

Ita vulneratus est servus, ut eo ictu certum esset moriturum: medio deinde tempore heres institutus est et postea ab alio ictus decessit: quaero, an cum utroque de occiso lege Aquilia agi possit. respondit: occidisse dicitur vulgo quidem, qui mortis causam quolibet modo praebuit: sed lege Aquilia is demum teneri visus est, qui adhibita vi et quasi manu causam mortis praebuisset, tracta videlicet interpretatione vocis a caedendo et a caede. rursus Aquilia lege teneri existimati sunt non solum qui ita vulnerassent, ut confestim vita privarent, sed etiam hi, quorum ex vulnere certum esset aliquem vita excessurum. igitur si quis servo mortiferum vulnus inflixerit eundemque alius ex intervallo ita percusserit, ut maturius interficeretur, quam ex priore vulnere moriturus fuerat, statuendum est utrumque eorum lege Aquilia teneri. (1) Idque est consequens auctoritati veterum, qui, cum a pluribus idem servus ita vulneratus est, ut non appareret cuius ictu perisset, omnes lege Aquilia teneri iudicaverunt. (2) Aestimatio autem perempti non eadem in utriusque persona fiet: nam qui prior vulneravit, tantum praestabit, quanto in anno proximo homo plurimi fuerit repetitis ex die vulneris trecentis sexaginta quinque diebus, posterior in id tenebitur, quanti homo plurimi venire poterit in anno proximo quo vita excessit, in quo pretium quoque hereditatis erit. eiusdem ergo servi occisi nomine alius maiorem, alius minorem aestimationem praestabit, nec mirum, cum uterque eorum ex diversa causa et diversis temporibus occidisse hominem intellegatur. quod si quis absurde a nobis haec constitui putaverit, cogitet longe absurdius constitui neutrum lege Aquilia teneri aut alterum potius, cum neque impunita maleficia esse oporteat nec facile constitui possit, uter potius lege teneatur. multa autem iure civili contra rationem disputandi pro utilitate communi recepta esse innumerabilibus rebus probari potest: unum interim posuisse contentus ero. cum plures trabem alienam furandi causa sustulerint, quam singuli ferre non possent, furti actione omnes teneri existimantur, quamvis subtili ratione dici possit neminem eorum teneri, quia neminem verum sit eam sustulisse.

(Julian in the eighty-sixth book of his *Digests*)

A slave was so seriously wounded that it was certain he would die from this blow; then, in the meantime, he was instituted heir, and afterwards he was struck by another person and died. I ask whether an action under the Lex Aquilia can lie against both men for the slaying.

He (Julian) responded: Commonly a person is said to have "slain" (*occidisse*) when he furnishes the cause of death in any manner; but under the Lex Aquilia a person is held liable only if he furnished the cause of death by applying force and, so to speak, by hand. That is, the word is interpreted by reference to "hew" (*caedere*) and "slaughter" (*caedes*).

On the other hand, persons are held liable under the Lex Aquilia not only when they wound so seriously that they take life immediately, but also when, because of their wound, it is certain that someone will lose life.

Therefore if someone inflicts a mortal wound on a slave, and after an interval a second person so strikes him that he dies sooner than he would have died from the first wound, it must be determined that both of them are liable under the Lex Aquilia.

(1) And this follows logically from the authority of the Republican jurists, who ruled that, when the same slave was so wounded by several persons that it was unclear by whose blow he died, all were liable under the Lex Aquilia.

(2) But the evaluation of the dead slave will not be the same for both persons. For the one who first wounded him will owe as much as the man's maximum value in the past year, counting back 365 days from the date of the wound. But the second person will be liable for the maximum value of the man in the year preceding his death; and the value of the inheritance will be included.

Therefore, on account of the same slain slave, one man will owe a larger evaluation and the other a smaller; nor is this surprising, since each of them is understood to have slain the man under different circumstances and at different times.

But if someone thinks that my decision is preposterous, let him consider that it would be far more preposterous if neither was liable under the Lex Aquilia, or just one, since it ought not to be that misdeeds go unpunished and it cannot easily be determined which one is rather liable by statute.

For it can be proved by countless examples that many rules which have been received in the Civil Law (*ius civile*) are contrary to legal logic but benefit the common good. I will content myself for the moment with giving one: When several persons, who could not individually carry another person's wooden beam, lift it up (together) in order to steal it, all of them are considered to be liable in an action on theft (*furtum*), although by narrow logic it can be said that none of them is liable since it is true that none (individually) lifted it up.

Discussion:

1. This very long passage is unusual in that it represents a sustained argument on a single legal point. Try to follow Julian's reasoning as he drives to his conclusion. The Case has the form of a juristic response (statement of facts; question of law; answer); but it is very doubtful that a real case is involved. Although Julian does not name Celsus, he is clearly attacking the earlier jurist's views.

2. Suppose the following hypothetical: Stichus, a slave painter, lost his thumb in an accident on 1 July (cf. Case 36); as a consequence his value fell from 20,000 sesterces to 10,000. Five days later Maevius wrongfully gave Stichus a blow from which he was certain eventually to die. On the following 1 August, a wealthy Roman died, and her will made Stichus sole heir to an estate worth 100,000 sesterces; but before Stichus' master could order Stichus to accept the inheritance, Titius wrongfully killed Stichus. According to Julian, what is the minimum that Stichus' owner can recover from each defendant?

3. Julian says that "it was certain" that the slave would die from the first wound. Does this mean that it was absolutely certain, or that it was extremely probable, or that it was a good deal more likely than not? Should we rule out the possibility of a miracle cure? How would Julian deal with Celsus' point (in Case 54) that death is never certain until it occurs?

4. Julian begins his response by discussing the problem of "furnishing a cause of death." Does he agree more closely with Celsus (in Case 6) or with Gaius (in Case 7)? What is the relevance of this discussion to his response?

5. In justifying his argument that both defendants should be held liable for slaying, Julian states that "it should not be that misdeeds go unpunished." What view is he taking with regard to the nature of Aquilian liability? How might his view differ from Celsus'?

6. By way of analogy, Julian invokes the Republican rule that when it was impossible to tell which of several simultaneous assailants had slain a slave, each of them is cumulatively liable under the Lex Aquilia; that is, each of them is liable to pay the full amount owed under the Lex Aquilia. (This rule is further discussed below, in Case 83.) How does this analogy reinforce Julian's point? Is his point further strengthened by the parallel treatment of multiple thieves under the action on theft (*actio furti*)?

7. Suppose that Maevius gave Stichus a blow from which it was certain that Stichus would die, and that a few days later Maevius killed Stichus outright. Would Julian allow Stichus' owner to recover twice from Maevius for the slaying of Stichus?

8. In the last part of this Case, Julian appears to admit that his ruling may seem absurd and "contrary to legal logic"; but he argues that it is in accord with "common good" (*utilitas communis*). Why does he think this to be true? What aspect of public policy is he invoking?

9. Finally, examine Julian's reasoning as an example of statutory construction. Is it in accord with the words and the spirit of the First Section of the Lex Aquilia? What argument would you use against Julian's reasoning?

Case 57: A Defendant Strikes Twice

D. 9.2.32.1 (Gaius, libro septimo ad Edictum Provinciale)

Si idem eundem servum vulneraverit, postea deinde etiam occiderit, tenebitur et de vulnerato et de occiso: duo enim sunt delicta. aliter atque si quis uno impetu pluribus vulneribus aliquem occiderit: tunc enim una erit actio de occiso.

(Gaius in the seventh book on the Provincial Edict)

If the same man wounds and then later also slays the same slave, he will be liable for both the wounding and the slaying; for there are two delicts. It is different if he slays someone with several wounds in a single attack, for then there will be one action for the slaying.

Discussion:

1. In the first example, does Gaius presume that the wound was not mortal? What would Gaius allow the plaintiff to recover in the two actions? How does his ruling accord with the debate between Celsus and Julian in Cases 54–56?

2. How easy is it in practice to determine whether a slave was slain "in a single attack"? Can you think of instances where it could be difficult to determine this?

3. Ulpian (D. 9.2.27 pr.) puts the following case: A man carries off another's slave (this is theft, *furtum*) and then later slays the slave. Both Julian and Celsus agree (!) that the slave's master can sue the defendant twice: once for theft, a second time under the Lex Aquilia. Is it clear to you why these are two separate delicts? What if the defendant carried off the slave with the intention of killing him, and did so very soon thereafter?

Part E: Defenses

In particular situations a defendant can argue that an act does not give rise to Aquilian liability, although it ordinarily would do so. The Roman jurists have no formal theory of defenses to Aquilian liability, and indeed they often treat legitimate defenses more obliquely, by blandly holding that, under the circumstances, the defendant's act was not blameworthy (there is no *culpa*); the core of this point goes back to the wording of the Lex Aquilia, which required that loss be inflicted "without right" (*iniuria*). In any case, for our purposes it is more convenient to look at the defenses as a separate category.

One of the most common ways that Aquilian defendants could seek to excuse their conduct was by asserting that the plaintiff (or the plaintiff's slave) had essentially brought the loss on him or herself: either by voluntarily accepting the risk that the loss would occur, or by being also at fault in causing the loss, or by having somehow provoked the defendant's conduct. Here the jurists seem to rely on what has been called, perhaps somewhat misleadingly, "*culpa*-equivalence": the *culpa* of the defendant is balanced, or more exactly cancelled out, by the plaintiff's own *culpa*, and hence the plaintiff cannot recover for the loss. But some limits must obviously be placed on the operation of this sort of balancing, especially when one party's fault takes the more insidious form of deliberate *dolus*.

In other circumstances, however, a defendant can escape liability even for deliberate destruction of the plaintiff's property. One way of escape is to argue that a particular situation compelled the defendant to damage the plaintiff's property; but this defense of necessity requires narrow scrutiny, and the jurists vary somewhat in permitting it. A second way is to argue that law expressly gave one a positive legal right to act as one had; this defense is available in fairly restricted circumstances. Finally, for their official acts magistrates enjoyed a limited measure of immunity from Aquilian liability.

In some respects, the reconstructed Roman defenses resemble many of the defenses available in modern Anglo-American negligence law. The Roman defenses also largely elaborate the theory of wrongfulness, and so provide a convenient opportunity to review that theory.

Section 1: Assumption of Risk

Case 58: Slave Injured While Playing Ball

D. 9.2.52.4 (Alfenus, libro secundo Digestorum)

Cum pila complures luderent, quidam ex his servulum, cum pilam percipere conaretur, impulit, servus cecidit et crus fregit: quaerebatur, an dominus servuli lege Aquilia cum eo, cuius impulsu ceciderat, agere potest. respondi non posse, cum casu magis quam culpa videretur factum.

(Alfenus in the second book of his *Digests*)

While several persons were playing ball, one of them pushed a slave boy when he tried to catch the ball; the slave fell and broke his leg. Question was raised whether the slave boy's owner can bring suit under the Lex Aquilia against the person through whose push he fell. I responded that this is not possible, since the event is held to have occurred more by accident than by *culpa*.

Discussion:

1. Does it matter whether the potential defendant was obeying the rules of the game? Whether he used unnecessary roughness?

2. Why is it significant that this was a "slave boy"? Is the questioner suggesting that, although they are both playing together, the defendant may owe a duty of care to an obviously young slave?

3. Alfenus says that there is no Aquilian liability "since it seems to have occurred more by accident than by (the defendant's) *culpa*." How convincing is this explanation? In what sense is it right to regard the slave's fall as merely a non-wrongful "accident" (see Case 26)? Can you think of a better way to explain Alfenus' ruling? Would it be more accurate to hold that, by deciding to participate in the game, the slave boy had accepted the risk that he might be injured?

4. There are two ways to regard situations such as these. Either we can hold that the alleged offender's conduct was justified (it was legally unobjectionable); or we can say that the conduct is excused by special circumstances (it was objectionable, but the defendant has a valid excuse for escaping liability). Which way do the jurists think of the matter? Which do you prefer? Does it really matter?

Case 59: Athletic Competitions

D. 9.2.7.4 (Ulpianus, libro octavo decimo ad Edictum)

Si quis in colluctatione vel in pancratio, vel pugiles dum inter se exercentur alius alium occiderit, si quidem in publico certamine alius alium occiderit, cessat ̃Aquilia, quia gloriae causa et virtutis, non iniuriae gratia videtur damnum datum. hoc autem in servo non procedit, quoniam ingenui solent certare: in filio familias vulnerato procedit. plane si cedentem vulneraverit, erit Aquiliae locus, aut si non in certamine servum occidit, nisi si domino committente hoc factum sit: tunc enim Aquilia cessat.

(Ulpian in the eighteenth book on the Edict)

If one person slays another in a wrestling match or in the pancratium, or while boxers are contesting — if in general one person slays another in a public contest —, the Aquilian action fails, since loss is evidently inflicted in pursuit of fame and valor, not to be wrongful. But this rule does not apply in the case of a slave, since it is freeborn persons who normally compete; it does apply in the case of a wounded son in his father's power. Clearly the Aquilian action lies if he wounds a person who has yielded, or if he slew a slave not in the contest, except if this happened when the owner entered him; for then the Aquilian action fails.

Discussion:

1. The text appears to be somewhat confused, probably because of the *Digest*'s compilers. What is the rule for free persons? How convincing is Ulpian's explanation of the rule, that "loss is evidently inflicted in pursuit of fame and valor, not to be wrongful"? Can you provide a better explanation?

2. As to slaves, they did not normally compete in this type of contest. The last sentence would make more sense if the text read: "if he slew a slave in the contest," omitting "not." What would the rule then be? Is it presumed that the slayer knew his opponent was a slave?

3. "Assumption of risk" means that a person voluntarily accepts the possibility that someone else may injure him or her. How has a person "assumed the risk" by entering a game? See Paul, D. 47.10.1.5, writing of the delict of outrage (*iniuria*): "there is no *iniuria* when the victim consents."

Section 2: Contributory Negligence

Case 60: Crossing a Field Reserved for Javelin-Throwing

D. 9.2.9.4 (Ulpianus, libro octavo decimo ad Edictum)

Sed si per lusum iaculantibus servus fuerit occisus, Aquiliae locus est: sed si cum alii in campo iacularentur, servus per eum locum transierit, Aquilia cessat, quia non debuit per campum iaculatorium iter intempestive facere. qui tamen data opera in eum iaculatus est, utique Aquilia tenebitur.

D. 9.2.10 (Paulus, libro vicensimo secundo ad Edictum)

nam lusus quoque noxius in culpa est.

(Ulpian in the eighteenth book on the Edict)
But if, when persons were throwing javelins in sport, a slave was killed, the Aquilian action lies. However if, while others were throwing javelins in a field, the slave crossed through this area, the Aquilian action fails, since he ought not to have passed inopportunely through a field reserved for javelin-throwing. To be sure, if someone deliberately tossed a javelin at him, he will of course be liable in an Aquilian action,

(Paul in the twenty-second book on the Edict)
for a harmful game is also counted as *culpa*.

Discussion:

1. What duty of care do the javelin-throwers have? Under what circumstances do they become liable for killing a slave with a misthrown javelin? What is "a field reserved for javelin-throwing" — one reserved by law for this purpose, or one just normally used in this way?

2. Paul (D. 50.17.203) elsewhere remarks that: "When someone suffers loss because of his own *culpa*, he is not construed to suffer loss." Is this principle adequate to explain why the slave's owner can recover nothing at all? What if the slave's fault was comparatively small in relation to that of the javelin-throwers?

3. Does the theory of contributory negligence imply that people have a duty of care to look out for the safety of themselves and their property, so that others do not inflict loss? If so, how broad is this duty? How does contributory negligence differ from assumption of risk? Is it that, in contributory negligence, the defendant's carelessness helps to cause the loss that he or she sustains? See also Case 20.

4. If the javelin-throwers spot the slave crossing their field, what duty of care do they have regarding him? Is it enough to say just that they must not aim at the slave? Should they also have to stop their game until the slave has crossed, or at least to shout a warning? Here and elsewhere, the strict dis-

tinction that the jurists draw between deliberate *dolus* and non-deliberate *culpa* may seem excessively artificial; should *dolus* at least include reckless or grossly careless behavior with regard to another's person or property? The context of Paul's appended remark ("for a harmful game is also counted as *culpa*") is unclear, but it suggests some possible answers to these questions. (See also Celsus, D. 16.3.32, writing not of delict but of contract: "Nerva's statement that grosser *culpa* is *dolus* displeased Proculus, but seems exactly right to me.")

5. There are at least two ways of looking at the problem of the javelin-thrower who deliberately aims at a careless slave. One approach is to argue that the javelin-thrower's *dolus* is not commensurable with the slave's *culpa*; although the slave was negligent, the javelin-thrower's deliberate act makes the slave's negligence irrelevant. This argument approaches the problem through an analysis of fault; contributory negligence is not accepted as a defense to an act of *dolus*, because *culpa* is "incommensurable" with *dolus*. But we can also look at the case in terms of causation; the javelin-thrower's *dolus* sets off a wholly new chain of causation, which is independent of the prior fault of the slave. The jurists do not clearly distinguish between these two approaches; but which seems more in accord with their usual reasoning? Which is more satisfactory in solving the problem raised by the previous question? This difficulty will return in later Cases as well.

6. Suppose the following case: X deliberately sets a trap in order to injure Y, who then walks into the trap because of her carelessness. Which of the two approaches discussed in the previous question yields the most satisfactory result for this hypothetical case?

7. It is worth noting the curious way in which the jurists treat slaves not only in this Case but in many others. On the one hand, the slave is a moral agent who is expected to exercise due prudence in his or her conduct, so as to avoid exposure to obvious risks of injury; on the other hand, the slave is a piece of property, for the wrongful slaying of which an Aquilian action lies. To what extent does this illustrate the contradictions of law in a slave-holding society?

Case 61: A Barber Cuts a Slave's Throat

D. 9.2.11 pr. (Ulpianus, libro octavo decimo ad Edictum)

Item Mela scribit, si, cum pila quidam luderent, vehementius quis pila percussa in tonsoris manus eam deiecerit et sic servi, quem tonsor radebat, gula sit praecisa adiecto cultello: in quocumque eorum culpa sit, eum lege Aquilia teneri. Proculus in tonsore esse culpam: et sane si ibi tondebat, ubi ex consuetudine ludebatur vel ubi transitus frequens erat, est quod ei imputetur: quamvis nec illud male dicatur, si in loco periculoso sellam habenti tonsori se quis commiserit, ipsum de se queri debere.

(Ulpian in the eighteenth book on the Edict)

Again, Mela writes that if some persons were playing ball and one of them, hitting the' ball quite hard, knocked it against a barber's hands, and in this way the throat of a slave, whom the barber was shaving, was cut by a razor pressed against it, then the person with whom the *culpa* lay is liable under the Lex Aquilia. Proculus (says) that the *culpa* lies with the barber; and indeed, if he was shaving at a place where games were normally played or where traffic was heavy, there is reason to fault him. But it would not be badly held that if someone entrusts himself to a barber who has a chair in a dangerous place, he should have himself to blame.

Discussion:

1. This is a famous hypothetical. Under what circumstances should a *iudex* hold the ballplayer liable? Under what circumstances, the barber? Is it possible that they could both be liable? If so, what can the owner claim from each?

2. Ulpian seems to hold that, if the ballplayer is liable, the action should be statutory rather than *in factum*. Why? Can a statutory action be reconciled with Case 4?

3. Why did Proculus think the barber was likelier to be at fault? Is it that the *culpa* of the barber is likely to be the more immediate ("proximate") cause of the slave's death?

4. Ulpian adds that the slave may also be held responsible for the accident. What is the result if the slave is held responsible? Does the slave's carelessness interrupt the chain of causation between the barber's carelessness and the damage? Or is it that the slave assumed the risk?

5. By chance, there has survived to us a long commentary on this passage from a Byzantine lawyer named Hagiotheodoreta, writing in the twelfth or thirteenth century A.D. The lawyer observes, in part:

   He (Ulpian) says that when both the barber and the person who entrusted himself to such a barber are at fault, the person who was shaved ought to lose and have it said of him that he has only himself to blame, and have no action against the barber. However, in our view

the barber should lose and be liable in an action, for two reasons: first, so that we not thereby harm the slave's master, who was entirely without fault and completely unaware, by depriving him of his double penalty while letting the barber escape, a result that would be unjust; second, even if the person who had his throat cut was not a slave, but free, it is just to prefer removing the greater of two evils rather than punishing the lesser. For if we do not punish the barber, such a person will harm many other people in a similar way. Clearly, this is the greater evil, which ought to be averted, so that a single barber not damage a large number of people even if all of them are inattentive....
But in the case immediately preceding (Case 60), the only person at fault was the one who passed by the place where people were at play in throwing javelins; the javelin-throwers in the field were entirely without fault.

Examine this passage closely. How does this solution differ from the views of Ulpian? What presumptions does the Byzantine lawyer make that differ from those in Roman law? Does the distinction he draws between this Case and Case 60 seem convincing? Do you prefer his solution to Ulpian's?

6. In modern law, the defense of contributory negligence has been widely criticized because of its possible unfairness: the plaintiff recovers nothing if he or she was in any way at fault for causing the loss. Modern legal systems have widely substituted a standard of "comparative negligence" that allows a finder of fact (such as a jury) to determine the relative weight of the plaintiff's and the defendant's fault in bringing about the loss, with the award of damages adjusted accordingly. Does this seem fairer than the Roman view? How can the Roman view nonetheless be defended?

Section 3: Self-Defense and the Aggressor Doctrine

Case 62: Striking the First Blow

D. 9.2.52.1 (Alfenus, libro secundo Digestorum)

Tabernarius in semita noctu supra lapidem lucernam posuerat: quidam praeteriens eam sustulerat: tabernarius eum consecutus lucernam reposcebat et fugientem retinebat: ille flagello, quod in manu habebat, in quo dolo inerat, verberare tabernarium coeperat, ut se mitteret: ex eo maiore rixa facta tabernarius ei, qui lucernam sustulerat, oculum effoderat: consulebat, num damnum iniuria non videtur dedisse, quoniam prior flagello percussus esset. respondi, nisi data opera effodisset oculum, non videri damnum iniuria fecisse, culpam enim penes eum, qui prior flagello percussit, residere: sed si ab eo non prior vapulasset, sed cum ei lucernam eripere vellet, rixatus esset, tabernarii culpa factum videri.

(Alfenus in the second book of his *Digests*)

A storekeeper had placed his lamp at night on a stone in a road. A certain passerby picked it up; the storekeeper followed him demanding the lamp, and held him when he fled. That man, to make him let go, began to beat the storekeeper with a whip he had in his hand, in which there was a spike. As a result the fight grew worse, and the storekeeper put out the eye of the person who had picked up the lamp. He (the storekeeper) asked whether this loss should be held as not wrongfully inflicted, because he had been struck first with the whip.

I responded that unless he deliberately put out the eye, he is not held to have inflicted wrongful loss, for the *culpa* lay with him who struck first with the whip. But if he (the storekeeper) had not first been struck by him, but had started the fight in trying to take the lamp away from him, this is held to have occurred through the storekeeper's *culpa*.

Discussion:

1. Again, a famous Case, this time probably based on a real incident. Reconstruct the incident carefully. Can we assume that the passerby was a slave? Is it entirely clear that the passerby was trying to steal the lamp?

2. Normally speaking, Roman law permits a person to resist force with force, and also to kill a thief caught in the act at night (see Cases 25, 69–70). Why then does Alfenus lay such great emphasis on who struck the first blow? Is it because the circumstances of the incident are so uncertain?

3. Alfenus holds that if the passerby struck first, then the *culpa* lies with him. Why should this be true? Wasn't the passerby provoked? How realistic is the psychology that underlies Alfenus' decision?

4. Even if the passerby struck first, the storekeeper is liable if he deliberately

put out the passerby's eye. Why? How easy is it to determine, in practice, whether an eye was put out deliberately or by chance during a fight?

5. The "aggressor doctrine" holds that, in circumstances such as these, legal fault is determined by deciding which of the two parties was the aggressor. As the Case suggests, escalating the violence level of a fight represents a new aggression. The aggressor is not allowed to recover losses resulting from acts done to repel his aggression. Does this doctrine provide a sound basis for justifying Alfenus' decision?

6. What if it cannot be determined which of two parties was the aggressor? Paul (D. 9.2.45.3) discusses an odd case in which two slaves are jumping over burning straw; they collide, and one of them is burned to death. There is no Aquilian action unless it can be determined that the survivor upset the other slave. Does this make sense? Why doesn't Paul treat this as an unfortunate accident in the course of a game (see Case 58)?

7. The theory of contributory negligence suggests that people have a duty of care to protect themselves and their property from the loss that others may inflict. Does this theory extend so far that people have a general duty to act positively to prevent the infliction of foreseeable damage or injury by others? Most legal systems have been reluctant to impose such a duty, even if the act would be easy and relatively inexpensive for the victim. What explains this reluctance?

Case 63: The Limits of Self-Defense

D. 9.2.5 pr. (Ulpianus, libro octavo decimo ad Edictum)

Sed et si quemcumque alium ferro se petentem quis occiderit, non videbitur iniuria occidisse: et si metu quis mortis furem occiderit, non dubitabitur, quin lege Aquilia non teneatur. sin autem cum posset adprehendere, maluit occidere, magis est ut iniuria fecisse videatur: ergo et Cornelia tenebitur.

(Ulpian in the eighteenth book on the Edict)

But if a person slays someone else who is coming at him with a sword, he will not be held to have slain wrongfully (*iniuria*). Likewise, if someone fearing death kills a thief, there is no doubt that he is not liable under the Lex Aquilia. But if he could have captured him but preferred to slay him, the better view is that he is held to have acted wrongfully (*iniuria*); so he will also be liable under the Lex Cornelia.

Discussion:

1. The first sentence is clearly consistent with the holding of Case 62; but what about the second sentence? This sentence was probably altered by the *Digest*'s compilers; the original version (given below in Case 69) allowed a person to kill a thief if the thief was taken at night, or if he was taken by day and resisted with a weapon. Does this make better sense in terms of Case 62? Under what circumstances could one legitimately fear death upon encountering a thief?

2. The crucial sentence is the last one. What limits does it put on the right of self-defense? In light of Ulpian's rule, can you give a more plausible meaning to Alfenus' holding about the storekeeper who deliberately put out the passerby's eye (Case 62)? Is there also a resemblance between Ulpian's rule and that for athletic contests (Case 59)?

3. The Lex Cornelia (*de sicariis*) of 81/80 B.C. was a criminal statute against murder and poisoning. As the Case indicates, the offender has both civil and criminal liability for his act.

Case 64: Hitting a Bystander

D. 9.2.45.4 (Paulus, libro decimo ad Sabinum)

Qui, cum aliter tueri se non possent, damni quiddam dederint, innoxii sunt: vim enim vi defendere omnes leges omniaque iura permittunt. sed si defendendi mei causa lapidem in adversarium misero, sed non eum, sed praetereuntem percussero, tenebor lege Aquilia: illum enim solum qui vim infert ferire conceditur, et hoc, si tuendi dumtaxat, non etiam ulciscendi causa factum sit.

(Paul in the tenth book on Sabinus)

Those who inflict some loss because they cannot otherwise defend themselves are guiltless; for all statutes and all laws allow one to repel force with force. But if to defend myself I throw a stone at my opponent, but hit not him but a passerby, I will be liable under the Lex Aquilia; for it is permitted to strike only the person who used force, and this only to the extent required to ward him off, not also for revenge.

Discussion:

1. Is this Case generally consistent with the two preceding Cases in the way that it looks at the aggressor doctrine?

2. The new element that Paul adds is the injury to the passerby. If there is no *culpa* in defending oneself against an attacker, why is it wrongful to throw a stone that inadvertently hits a passing slave? Would it make any difference if the stone would have hit the attacker had he not ducked?

3. Is there any similarity between hitting the wrong man carelessly and hitting the right man in revenge? How easy would it be to spot the latter offense?

4. At this point, try to summarize the Roman rules on self-defense. To what extent do they seem to you reasonable? Do the jurists create a formal legal privilege to repel violence with violence, or do they instead rely mainly on an analysis of fault?

Section 4: Necessity

Case 65: Making a Firebreak (Servius' View)

D. 43.24.7.4 (Ulpianus, libro septuagensimo primo ad Edictum)

Est et alia exceptio, de qua Gallus dubitat, an sit obicienda: ut puta si incendii arcendi causa vicini aedes intercidi et quod vi aut clam mecum agatur aut damni iniuria. Gallus enim dubitat, an excipi oporteret: 'quod incendii defendendi causa factum non sit.' Servius autem ait, si id magistratus fecisset, dandam esse, privato non esse idem concedendum: si tamen quid vi aut clam factum sit neque ignis usque eo pervenisset, simpli litem aestimandam: si pervenisset, absolvi eum oportere. idem ait esse, si damni iniuria actum foret, quoniam nullam iniuriam aut damnum dare videtur aeque perituris aedibus. quod si nullo incendio id feceris, deinde postea incendium ortum fuerit, non idem erit dicendum, quia non ex post facto, sed ex praesenti statu, damnum factum sit necne, aestimari oportere Labeo ait.

(Ulpian in the seventy-first book on the Edict)

There is another formal legal defense (*exceptio*), though Gallus doubts it can be interposed: e.g., if in order to ward off a fire I demolish a neighbor's house and he then sues me on the interdict *quod vi aut clam* or for wrongful damage.. For Gallus doubts there is a rightful formal defense "unless this was done to avert a fire." But Servius said that it should be granted if a magistrate had done this, but that it should not be allowed for a private citizen; but if the act was done "by force or stealth" (*vi aut clam*) and the fire had not reached there, the recovery is for simple damages, but if it had reached there, he ought to be absolved. He says it is the same if the action is for wrongful damage, since a person appears to inflict no wrong or loss (*nullam iniuriam aut damnum*) when the building would be destroyed in any case. If you did this when there was no fire but then later a fire arose, the same will not be held, since Labeo says that whether or not loss (*damnum*) was inflicted ought to be evaluated not in hindsight but from the present situation.

The Hypothetical Problem:

A catastrophic fire is spreading through Rome. You fear that unless a firebreak is constructed, the fire will destroy your house. You rush onto a neighbor's property and pull down his house to create a firebreak. Can the neighbor bring an Aquilian action against you?

Discussion:

1. The neighbor can choose to sue you either through an interdict *quod vi aut clam* (seeking damages for "forcible or stealthy" interference with land) or under the Lex Aquilia. This Case applies the same legal theory to both actions.

2. Under what circumstances do you think that it ought to be allowed to use your neighbor's property as a firebreak? Servius holds that it is permissible to tear down the neighbor's house only if the fire has already reached it and it would be destroyed in any case. Why does Servius say that there is "no wrong or loss" (*nullam iniuriam aut damnum*) in this instance? How realistic is his ruling?

3. Maevius tears down Titius' house in order to avert a nonexistent fire; some hours later a real fire arises, which would have destroyed Titius' house in any case. Why does Labeo hold that Titius may still recover damages from Maevius for tearing down the house?

4. Why should one ever be permitted to destroy another's property in order to save one's own? Should this be permitted even if the other person objects?

5. Note that Servius makes an exception for magistrates; why? For more on the privileges of magistrates, see below, Section 6, where limits are imposed.

Case 66: Making a Firebreak (Celsus' View)

D. 9.2.49.1 (Ulpianus, libro nono Disputationum)

Quod dicitur damnum iniuria datum Aquilia persequi, sic erit accipiendum, ut videatur damnum iniuria datum, quod cum damno iniuriam attulerit: nisi magna vi cogente fuerit factum, ut Celsus scribit circa eum, qui incendii arcendi gratia vicinas aedes intercidit: nam hic scribit cessare legis Aquiliae actionem: iusto enim metu ductus, ne ad se ignis perveniret, vicinas aedes intercidit: et sive pervenit ignis sive ante extinctus est, existimat legis Aquiliae actionem cessare.

(Ulpian in the ninth book of his *Disputations*)

As for the view that what is claimed in an Aquilian action is loss inflicted wrongfully (*damnum iniuria datum*), this should be so construed that loss is held to be wrongfully inflicted when it involves wrongfulness (*iniuria*) along with loss (*damnum*), except if a great force compelled it to be inflicted, as Celsus writes concerning a person who demolished a neighbor's house in order to ward off a fire. For he writes that the action under the Lex Aquilia then fails; for, driven by legitimate fear, he demolished the neighbor's house to prevent the fire reaching his own. Whether the fire reached there or was put out first, he thinks that the action under the Lex Aquilia fails.

Discussion:

1. How do Celsus' views differ from those of Servius in the preceding Case? Celsus holds that the defendant must be "driven by legitimate fear." When is fear legitimate? How can a person be said to have a legitimate fear even though the fire does not in fact reach his own property? Can the person who pulled down his neighbor's house assert that he was unusually timorous, and hence that his fear, although unfounded, was still legitimate?

2. Celsus wrote about a century and a half after Servius. How does his conception of the defense of necessity differ from Servius'? Does he seem to be influenced by the development of the doctrine of *culpa*?

Case 67: Freeing a Ship

D. 9.2.29.3 (Ulpianus, libro octavo decimo ad Edictum)

Item Labeo scribit, si, cum vi ventorum navis impulsa esset in funes anchora-
rum alterius et nautae funes praecidissent, si nullo alio modo nisi praecisis fu-
nibus explicare se potuit, nullam actionem dandam. idemque Labeo et Proculus et circa retia piscatorum, in quae navis piscatorum inciderat, aestimarunt.
plane si culpa nautarum id factum esset, lege Aquilia agendum. sed ubi damni
iniuria agitur ob retia, non piscium, qui ideo capti non sunt, fieri aestimationem, cum incertum fuerit, an caperentur. idemque et in venatoribus et in
aucupibus probandum.

(Ulpian in the eighteenth book on the Edict)

Again, Labeo writes that if a ship was driven by the force of wind
into another ship's anchor ropes and the sailors cut the ropes, no
action should be given if it was not able to be freed other than by
cutting the ropes. Labeo and Proculus thought the same also concerning fishermen's nets into which a fishermen's boat fell. Obviously an action should be brought under the Lex Aquilia if this happened because of the sailors' *culpa*. But where there is a suit for
wrongful loss because of the nets, no evaluation is made of the fish
which were therefore not caught, since it was uncertain whether
they would be caught. The same rule holds also for hunters and
birdcatchers.

Discussion:

1. Why are the sailors on the trapped boat allowed to free themselves by doing
   damage to the other boat? What if the other boat, its anchor ropes cut, drifts
   onto rocks and is destroyed?

2. Note that Ulpian allows an Aquilian suit if the sailors' *culpa* causes the entan-
   glement, but not if it occurs because of wind (a form of *vis maior*). Explain
   this distinction. The action is against the sailors, not the shipowner: see D.
   9.2.29.2.

3. Do you agree that evaluating the future catch of a boat and crew is pure
   speculation?

Case 68: A Free Man Acting on Orders

D. 9.2.37 pr. (Javolenus, libro quarto decimo ex Cassio)

Liber homo si iussu alterius manu iniuriam dedit, actio legis Aquiliae cum eo est qui iussit, si modo ius imperandi habuit: quod si non habuit, cum eo agendum est qui fecit.

(Javolenus in the fourteenth book from Cassius)

If a free man inflicted injury by his own hand but on another's orders, the action under the Lex Aquilia lies with the person who ordered, provided he had the right to command. But if he did not have it, the suit must be against the person who acted.

The Hypothetical Problem:

Sempronia ordered Titius to kill a slave belonging to Cassius; Titius obeyed her order and killed the slave. Under what circumstances can Cassius sue Sempronia?

Discussion:

1. Paul (D. 50.17.169 pr.) states that: "A person inflicts loss who orders it to be inflicted; but there is no *culpa* in a person who must obey." Does this adequately explain Javolenus' rule? How convincing is the logic?

2. How wide is the ambit of those who have "the right to command"? Consider the following:
    — a father who commands a son;
    — a guardian who commands a ten-year-old ward;
    — an employer who commands an employee;
    — a magistrate who commands a private citizen;
    — a military officer who commands a soldier.

3. As will emerge below (Chapter III, Part B, Section 2), masters were fully responsible if their slaves gave wrongful loss on their orders or even with their knowledge. Do the persons in the previous question have a position similar to slaves?

4. I order you to kill a slave, although I have no right to order; you obey. Can an Aquilian action be brought against me?

Section 5: Statutory Defenses

Case 69: Slave Caught During a Robbery

Collatio 7.3.2–3 (Ulpianus, libro octavo decimo ad Edictum)

Sed et quemcumque alium ferro se petentem qui occiderit non videbitur iniuria occidisse. proinde si furem nocturnum, quem lex Duodecim Tabularum
omnimodo permittit occidere, aut diurnum quem aeque lex permittit, sed ita
demum si se telo defendat, videamus an lege Aquilia teneatur. et Pomponius
dubitat num haec lex non sit in usu. (3) Et si quis noctu furem occiderit, non
dubitamus, quin lege Aquilia non teneatur; sin autem, cum posset adprehendere, maluit occidere, magis est, ut iniuria fecisse videatur: ergo etiam lege
Cornelia tenebitur.

(Ulpian in the eighteenth book on the Edict)
But if a person slays someone else who is coming at him with a
sword, he will not be held to have slain wrongfully (*iniuria*). Likewise, if someone (slays) a thief by night, whom the Law of the
Twelve Tables allows one to kill in any case, or a thief by day,
whom the Law also allows one to slay provided he defends himself
with a weapon, let us see whether he is liable under the Lex
Aquilia. Pomponius doubts whether this Law (of the Twelve
Tables) is still in force. (4) And if someone slays a thief by night, we
do not doubt that he is not liable under the Lex Aquilia. But if he
could have captured him but preferred to slay him, the better view
is that he is held to have acted wrongfully (*iniuria*); so he will also
be liable under the Lex Cornelia.

Discussion:

1. The *Collatio*, assembled about A.D. 300, gives abbreviated excerpts from
   many classical juristic texts. This text gives the original version of Case 63,
   which the compilers of the *Digest* altered. Is the rule of the Twelve Tables
   (449 B.C.) just a primitive version of the later theory regarding self-defense?
   Why might the Twelve Tables rule have fallen into disuse?

2. Despite Pomponius, Ulpian retains the Law of the Twelve Tables for noctur-
   nal thieves, although he requires that the slave not be killed deliberately if
   it was possible to capture him. Why?

3. By comparing the *Collatio* with Case 63, reconstruct the law as it was under
   Justinian. What explains the evolution?

Case 70: Slave Taken in Adultery

D. 9.2.30 pr. (Paulus, libro vicensimo secundo ad Edictum)

Qui occidit adulterum deprehensum servum alienum, hac lege non tenebitur.

(Paul in the twenty-second book on the Edict)

A person who slew another's slave taken in adultery will not be liable under this law.

Discussion:

1. It is presumed that the slave was engaged in adultery with the wife or daughter of the person who discovered him *in flagrante* and then killed him. The Lex Julia on Adultery (moved by Augustus in 18 B.C.) specifically allowed the killing of both parties to the adultery, although under specific conditions. What motives might Augustus have had for wanting such a rule? Can the rule be justified?

2. Augustus' legislation overrode the protection usually given to property in Roman law, by allowing the killing of a another person's slave, albeit under provocation. Are there other comparable circumstances that might justify killing someone else's slave? Suppose, for instance, that a slave engages in flagrant and highly insulting conduct. Discuss the legal reasons that might determine whether such conduct should or should not be an excuse that justifies killing the slave. In Roman law, it was apparently not an acceptable excuse.

Section 6: *The Privileges of Magistrates*

Case 71: Municipal Magistrates

D. 9.2.29.7 (Ulpianus, libro octavo decimo ad Edictum)

Magistratus municipales, si damnum iniuria dederint, posse Aquilia teneri. nam et cum pecudes aliquis pignori cepisset et fame eas necavisset, dum non patitur te eis cibaria adferre, in factum actio danda est. item si dum putat se ex lege capere pignus, non ex lege ceperit et res tritas corruptasque reddat, dicitur legem Aquiliam locum habere: quod dicendum est et si ex lege pignus cepit. si quid tamen magistratus adversus resistentem violentius fecerit, non tenebitur Aquilia: nam et cum pignori servum cepisset et ille se suspenderit, nulla datur actio.

(Ulpian in the eighteenth book on the Edict)

(A jurist holds) that municipal magistrates can have Aquilian liability if they inflict wrongful loss. For also when a person seized herd animals in execution (of a debt) and killed them by starvation, not allowing you to bring them fodder, an action *in factum* should be given. Likewise if he thinks that he seizes in execution on the basis of a statute, but does not act on the basis of a statute, and returns the objects worn and spoiled, it is held that the Aquilian law applies; and this should be also held if he seizes in execution on the basis of a statute. But if a magistrate uses some force against a resister, he has no Aquilian liability; for also, when he seized a slave in execution and the slave hanged himself, no action is given.

The Hypothetical Problem:

A municipal magistrate has seized a slave or cattle in order to force payment of a debt owed to his city. Under what circumstances is he liable? When is he not liable?

Discussion:

1. Try to abstract from this text the general principles of a magistrate's liability. Is it any different from the liability of Roman citizens generally?

2. Elsewhere (D. 47.10.13.1), Ulpian argues that: "A person who exercises a public right is not construed as doing this to give outrage (*iniuria*); for the execution of a right contains no outrage." This text concerns the delict of outrage (*iniuria*); is the principle the same as in the present Case?

3. Why should magistrates have a degree of immunity from suits for wrongful damage? What are the proper limits on this sort of immunity?

4. A bedmaker has sold some beds to Maevius. Carrying out his contract, the bedmaker hands over possession and ownership of the beds to Maevius, but retains the beds until Maevius can pick them up. Maevius fails to do so, and the bedmaker places the beds on the street outside his shop. A Roman

Aedile, a magistrate who has the responsibility to keep the streets clear of obstructions, orders the beds destroyed. Can Maevius sue the Aedile for wrongful damage? Julian (D. 18.6.14) says yes, if the Aedile acted "without right" (*non iure*). Why?

5. A tax farmer (*publicanus*) is a private citizen who contracts with the State to collect taxes. Suppose that a tax farmer, erroneously believing that I owe back taxes, seizes my cattle; Labeo (in Ulpian, D. 47.8.2.20) holds that I cannot sue him for taking my property by force, but that he does have Aquilian liability if he does not then let them graze. Is this ruling in accord with the present Case? Should we therefore regard tax farmers as equivalent to magistrates?

6. According to Case 65, a magistrate is immune from Aquilian liability if, acting on his own discretion, he orders a house to be pulled down in order to create a firebreak against a catastrophic fire. Is that Case fully consistent with this one?

Chapter III:
Procedural Problems in Aquilian Liability

This chapter deals with some procedural aspects of the Aquilian action. The first section discusses who can bring the action. The Lex Aquilia itself spoke of the "owner" (*erus*, which in the *Digest* was modernized to *dominus*, see Ulpian, D. 9.2.11.6); and normally the owner of the damaged property would in fact be the plaintiff. However, in certain circumstances other persons with a legal interest in the damaged property are given standing to bring an Aquilian action, even though their interest does not amount to a property claim.

It is usually easy to locate the proper defendant; if the offender is a free person, normally he or she is liable for the damage. Problems arise, however, especially in the case of slaves, who cannot themselves be sued; nonetheless, Aquilian liability attaches to them personally. The Lex Aquilia directed that if the slave had acted without the master's knowledge, the plaintiff could bring suit against the owner of the slave; but it also gave the owner a choice: he or she could either surrender the slave to the plaintiff ("noxal surrender") or pay for the plaintiff's loss. This noxal liability in effect limits the extent of damages the slave's owner is responsible for.

Sometimes, of course, the value of the slave may be considerably less than the plaintiff's loss. The Lex Aquilia also provided that the master should be statutorily liable if he or she "knew" of the slave's act. The jurists devised other theories under which the slave's owner could be held statutorily liable for the damage done by the slave; these theories were eventually extended to some acts done by free employees or others acting on command. However, Roman theories of vicarious liability for the acts of third parties are not nearly so far-reaching as the Common Law doctrine of *respondeat superior*, which holds that a master is often liable for the acts of a servant without regard to the master's fault.

In some circumstances, a defendant may incur simultaneous liability not just under the Lex Aquilia, but also, for instance, under a contract or another delict. The Roman theories concerning concurrence of actions are very complex; sometimes the defendant is liable cumulatively in two or more suits, sometimes the plaintiff can succeed in one action only by forgoing the other. It is clear that the jurists disagreed about when to make liability cumulative or exclusive. The jurists' debates about these matters expose some of their uncertainty about how to conceive Aquilian liability.

(Of course, the same act can also give rise, on occasion, to both Aquilian and criminal liabilities; see, for example, Cases 50 and 63. Such liabilities are always cumulative; but the criminal suit must usually be brought first so that it is not pre-judged by the milder civil suit. See, e.g., Ulpian, D. 9.2.23.9: "If a slave is deliberately killed, it is agreed that the owner may also sue by the Lex Cornelia [against murder]; but if he sues under the Lex Aquilia, no pre-judgment should be made for the Lex Cornelia.")

Part A: The Plaintiff

Section 1: The Owner

Case 72: A Neighbor Destroys Bees

Collatio 12.7.10 (Ulpianus, libro octavo decimo ad Edictum)

Item Celsus libro xxvII Digestorum scribit: si cum apes meae ad tuas advolassent, tu eas exusseris, quosdam negare competere legis Aquiliae actionem, inter quos et Proculum, quasi apes dominii mei non fuerint. sed id falsum esse Celsus ait, cum apes revenire soleant et fructui mihi sint. sed Proculus eo movetur, quod nec mansuetae nec ita clausae fuerint. ipse autem Celsus ait nihil inter has et columbas interesse, quae, si manum refugiunt, domi tamen fugiunt.

(Ulpian in the eighteenth book on the Edict)

Likewise Celsus, in the twenty-seventh book of his *Digests*, writes that if my bees fly over onto your (property) and you burn them up, some jurists deny that the action under the Lex Aquilia lies; among them is Proculus, on the theory that the bees are not my property. But Celsus says that this is false, since the bees are accustomed to return and are a source of profit for me. But Proculus was swayed by the fact that they are neither domesticated nor sufficiently enclosed. Still, Celsus himself says that there is no difference between them and doves, which, if they escape the hand, still fly home.

Discussion:

1. The question in this text revolves around whether a beekeeper retains ownership of bees when they are not enclosed in a hive, but flying off in search of pollen. In Roman law, the owner of wild animals normally loses both ownership and possession when they escape from his or her control. Why does this present a problem in an Aquilian action?

2. Why did Proculus deny that the neighbor was liable for having burned up the bees? How does Celsus counter his arguments? Is Celsus mainly concerned about the analytical problem, or about practicality? Or does he see practical needs as interlinked with legal reasoning?

Case 73: Slave Held by Good Faith Possessor Is Injured

D. 9.2.38 (Javolenus, libro nono Epistularum)

Si eo tempore, quo tibi meus servus quem bona fide emisti serviebat, ipse a servo tuo vulneratus est, placuit omnimodo me tecum recte lege Aquilia experiri.

(Javolenus in the ninth book of his *Letters*)
If my slave, whom you bought in good faith, was serving you, and during that time he was wounded by your slave, in the prevailing view I can in any case rightly sue you under the Lex Aquilia.

The Hypothetical Problem:

You bought a slave and thought that you owned him; the slave was then wounded by another of your slaves. It is later discovered that I own the injured slave. Can I bring an Aquilian action against you?

Discussion:

1. A good faith possessor is a person who purchases and takes control of property, but does not have good title to it; thus he or she may lose the property if the true owner brings a property claim. The good faith possessor does not realize this, however. In this Case a slave, possessed in good faith, is injured by another slave belonging to the good faith possessor. What problem does this present with regard to Aquilian liability?

2. How convincing do you find Javolenus' solution to this problem? Compare closely Case 30, in which Paul upholds Aquilian liability when a person kills a slave whom he thinks to be free. What interests are the jurists seeking to protect? What problems are there with their solution?

3. When the slave of a good faith possessor is injured or slain, the good faith possessor can bring an Aquilian action against the offender (Ulpian, D. 9.2.11.8), and this is true even if the offender actually owns the slave (see Case 81). Are these holdings consistent with the present Case? See below, Section 3.

Case 74: Co-Owned Slave Injured or Killed by Third Party

D. 9.2.19 (Ulpianus, libro octavo decimo ad Edictum)

Sed si communem servum occiderit quis, Aquilia teneri eum Celsus ait: idem est et si vulneraverit:

D. 9.2.20 (Ulpianus, libro quadragensimo secundo ad Sabinum)

scilicet pro ea parte, pro qua dominus est qui agat.

(Ulpian in the eighteenth book on the Edict)
But if someone slays a co-owned slave, Celsus says that he is liable in an Aquilian action; likewise if he wounds him;
(Ulpian in the forty-second book on Sabinus)
that is, in proportion to the share that the plaintiff owns.

The Hypothetical Problem:

Titius and I own Stichus. Stichus is killed by Seia. Can Titius and I each bring an Aquilian action against Seia, and if so, for what?

Discussion:

1. Note that the co-owners may bring suit separately, and that the verdict in one suit does not settle the question of liability in the other suit; thus it is even possible that one owner could win and the other lose. This case illustrates the rather cumbersome nature of Roman formulary procedure. By the end of the classical period, it was probably possible (but not necessary) for plaintiffs who shared the same claim to sue together. What advantages does this have?

2. What results if a co-owned slave is injured by one owner?

3. What if a co-owned slave is killed by a slave belonging to a third party? Ulpian (D. 9.2.27.2) reports Celsus' view: each owner may sue to recover his or her share of the loss; the third party may make use of noxal surrender (Case 84) by surrendering the offending slave to one co-owner, who can then be obliged to share ownership with the other (see Paul, D. 9.4.19 pr.). Does this seem in accord with the present Case?

Case 75: Non-Citizens

Gaius, *Institutiones* 4.37

Item civitas Romana peregrino fingitur, si eo nomine agat aut cum eo agatur, quo nomine nostris legibus actio constituta est, si modo iustum sit eam actionem etiam ad peregrinum extendi, veluti si furti agat peregrinus aut cum eo agatur.... similiter, si ex lege Aquilia peregrinus damni iniuriae agat aut cum eo agatur, ficta civitate Romana iudicium datur.

(Gaius in the fourth book of his *Institutes*)

Likewise, if a non-citizen sues or is sued on a cause for which our statutes establish an action, he is fictitiously treated as a Roman citizen, provided that it is just that this action be extended also to a non-citizen; for instance, if a non-citizen sues or is sued for theft (*furtum*).... Likewise, if under the Lex Aquilia a non-citizen sues or is sued for wrongful damage, a suit is granted with the fiction of Roman citizenship.

Discussion:

1. The legal fiction that Gaius discusses involves a phrase inserted into the formula for the trial; the phrase orders the *iudex* to give judgment as if the alien were a Roman citizen. Thus Roman law is extended to non-Romans. Fictions of this sort are widely used in Roman law, especially to extend the scope of legal protections.

2. Gaius indicates that Roman law is extended only if it is "just" to do so. Why is it "just" to extend the Lex Aquilia in this way?

3. Should an Aquilian action brought by an alien be statutory or *in factum*?

Case 76: Inheritability of Standing

D. 9.2.23.8 (Ulpianus, libro octavo decimo ad Edictum)

Hanc actionem et heredi ceterisque successoribus dari constat: sed in heredem vel ceteros haec actio non dabitur, cum sit poenalis, nisi forte ex damno locupletior heres factus sit.

(Ulpian in the eighteenth book on the Edict)

It is agreed that this action is granted both to the heir and to other successors. But this action will not be granted against the heir or others, since it is penal, unless perchance the heir became wealthier as a result of the loss.

Discussion:

1. This Case involves a principle of Roman inheritance law: the heir "succeeds" into the legal position of the deceased person, assuming (in principle) not only the property but also all the rights and duties of that person. In delict, however, there are some exceptions to this principle of "universal succession." Under the Lex Aquilia, the original plaintiff's standing can be inherited; that is, if loss is inflicted on a person, that person's heir can sue the offender. Why?

2. By contrast, the heir of the offender cannot be sued, so that if the defendant dies before suit is brought, Aquilian liability is lost. What does Gaius' explanation illustrate about the juristic understanding of Aquilian liability? Does it suggest that the jurists understood Aquilian liability as punitive, and for this reason not inheritable?

3. Can you give an example of a case in which the heir might be enriched by the delict of the person from whom he or she inherits? Case 46 may suggest a possible case. Suppose that Maevius erases an account record that established Titius' debt to me; before I can sue Maevius, he dies leaving Titius as his heir. Without the account record, I cannot successfully sue Titius on the original debt, so that he is to this extent enriched; but after he has inherited, I may be able to sue him on the delict. Why does enrichment make the heir liable under the Lex Aquilia? Would the heir be liable even before the death of the person who was the offender?

Section 2: Heirs

Case 77: Damage to an Inheritance

D. 9.2.43 (Pomponius, libro nono decimo ad Sabinum)

Ob id, quod ante quam hereditatem adires damnum admissum in res here-ditarias est, legis Aquiliae actionem habes, quod post mortem eius, cui heres sis, acciderit: dominum enim lex Aquilia appellat non utique eum, qui tunc fuerit, cum damnum daretur: nam isto modo ne ab eo quidem, cui heres quis erit, transire ad eum ea actio poterit: neque ob id, quod tum commissum fuerit, cum in hostium potestate esses, agere postliminio reversus poteris: et hoc aliter constitui sine magna captione postumorum liberorum, qui parentibus heredes erunt, non poterit....

(Pomponius in the nineteenth book on Sabinus)

As to loss an estate suffered before you took up an inheritance, you have an action under the Lex Aquilia for what happened after the death of the person from whom you inherited. For the Lex Aquilia does not name as "owner" only the person who owned when the loss was given, since if that were true, the action could not even pass from the dead person to his heir, nor could you sue, by right of *postliminium* after your return, for (loss) that was in-flicted while you were in the hands of enemies; and this issue cannot be differently decided without great disadvantage to post-humous children who inherit from their parents....

Discussion:

1. The problem Pomponius discusses concerns the ambiguous state of an in-heritance after the death of its owner, but before the heir has accepted; during this period the estate is said to "lie open." How does Pomponius solve this problem? How convincing is his invocation of the rule in Case 76?

2. Pomponius also compares the position of a person who has lost citizen rights because he has been captured by enemies, but regains these rights upon his return to Roman soil (a theory called *postliminium*); and also the position of a posthumous child born some months after the death of its father. How are their cases like that of the heir in the main case?

Case 78: Slave in Inheritance Is Killed

D. 9.2.13.2–3 (Ulpianus, libro octavo decimo ad Edictum)

Si servus hereditarius occidatur, quaeritur, quis Aquilia agat, cum dominus nullus sit huius servi. et ait Celsus legem domino damna salva esse voluisse: dominus ergo hereditas habebitur. quare adita hereditate heres poterit experiri. (3) Si servus legatus post aditam hereditatem sit occisus, competere legis Aquiliae actionem legatario, si non post mortem servi adgnovit legatum; quod si repudiavit, consequens esse ait Iulianus dicere heredi competere.

(Ulpian in the eighteenth book on the Edict)

If a slave in an inheritance is slain, a question arises as to who has the Aquilian action, since there is no owner of this slave. Celsus says that the statute wanted the owner's losses to be compensated; therefore the inheritance is regarded as the owner. Hence the heir can sue when the inheritance is accepted. (3) If a legated slave was slain after the inheritance is accepted, (a jurist says) that the action under the Lex Aquilia goes to the legatee unless he accepted the legacy (only) after the slave's death; but if he rejected it, Julian says the logical consequence is that it goes to the heir.

Discussion:

1. The problem arises because the inheritance has no owner until the heir decides to accept it. Celsus attempts to construe the Lex Aquilia so as to give the heir standing; is his interpretation plausible? What other way can you find for reaching this result?

2. After the heir accepts the inheritance, he or she must distribute the legacies that the deceased person has made to legatees. Does Julian's decision make sense? What if the heir himself kills the slave? See Paul, D. 9.2.14.

3. What would happen if the legated slave was killed before the heir accepted the estate? Ulpian (D. 9.2.15 pr.) holds that the heir keeps the action if the slave is slain; but if the slave is wounded, the heir should cede the action to the legatee. Ulpian asserts that this rule follows from the rule in the present Case. Do you see how?

Section 3: Others with Interests in Property

Case 79: A Usufructuary

D. 9.2.11.10 (Ulpianus, libro octavo decimo ad Edictum)

An fructuarius vel usuarius legis Aquiliae actionem haberet, Iulianus tractat: et ego puto melius utile iudicium ex hac causa dandum.

D. 9.2.12 (Paulus, libro decimo ad Sabinum)

Sed et si proprietatis dominus vulneraverit servum vel occiderit, in quo usus fructus meus est, danda est mihi ad exemplum legis Aquiliae actio in eum pro portione usus fructus, ut etiam ea pars anni in aestimationem veniat, qua nondum usus fructus meus fuit.

(Ulpian in the eighteenth book on the Edict)
Julian considers whether a person who holds a usufruct or a right of use has the action under the Lex Aquilia. I think the better solution is that an analogous action (*utile iudicium*) should be given in these circumstances.

(Paul in the tenth book on Sabinus)
But also if the owner of the property wounds or slays a slave in whom I have a usufruct, I should be granted an action against him, on the model of the Lex Aquilia, in proportion to the usufruct, (but) so that the part of the year is also evaluated in which I did not yet have the usufruct.

Discussion:

1. A usufruct (*usus fructus*) is a property right to enjoy and profit from prop- erty for a term not to exceed the lifetime of the beneficiary; it is usually cre- ated as a legacy in a will, when the testator makes one person the heir but legates the usufruct of some property to another person. The heir has own- ership and possession of the property, but the usufructuary has the right to exploit it. Why does Ulpian grant to the usufructuary an analogous action rather than a statutory one? What would the measure of damages be? Would the claim of the owner be reduced by this amount?

2. Ulpian says that this is the "better solution," which indicates that Julian prob- ably gave the usufructuary a statutory action. Can a statutory action be justi- fied?

3. Paul grants the usufructuary an analogous action against the owner if the owner damages the property. How does he think damages should be meas- ured?

4. The right to use (*usus*) is similar to a usufruct, but involves only personal use of property, not also the exploitation of it; for example, the holder of a usufruct in a farm may live on the farm and take profit from its produce,

while the holder of a right to use can only live on the farm. With respect to the Aquilian action, should the holder of a usufruct be in a stronger position to be plaintiff than the holder of a right to use?

Case 80: A Pledgor and a Pledgee

D. 9.2.30.1 (Paulus, libro vicensimo secundo ad Edictum)

Pignori datus servus si occisus sit, debitori actio competit. sed an et creditori danda sit utilis, quia potest interesse eius, quod debitor solvendo non sit aut quod litem tempore amisit, quaeritur. sed hic iniquum est et domino et creditori eum teneri. nisi quis putaverit nullam in ea re debitorem iniuriam passurum, cum prosit ei ad debiti quantitatem et quod sit amplius consecuturus sit ab eo, vel ab initio in id, quod amplius sit quam in debito, debitori dandam actionem: et ideo in his casibus, in quibus creditori danda est actio propter inopiam debitoris vel quod litem amisit, creditor quidem usque ad modum debiti habebit Aquiliae actionem, ut prosit hoc debitori, ipsi autem debitori in id quod debitum excedit competit Aquiliae actio.

(Paul in the twenty-second book on the Edict)

If a slave was given as a pledge (*pignus*) and then slain, the debtor has the action. But question is raised whether an analogous action (*actio utilis*) should also be granted to the creditor, since he may have an interest because the debtor is insolvent or his suit on the debt is barred by lapse of time. But here it is unfair that he (the defendant) be liable to both the debtor and creditor. Unless one thinks that the debtor will suffer no wrong in this matter, since he is advantaged as regards the amount of the debt and will recover the surplus from him; or that the debtor should from the start be granted an action for the surplus over and above the debt. And so in these cases where the action should be granted to the creditor because of the debtor's insolvency or because action is barred, the creditor will have an Aquilian action up to the amount of the debt so as to benefit the debtor, but the debtor has the Aquilian action for the excess over the debt.

The Hypothetical Problem:

Maevius owes 7,000 to Seius; in order to secure payment of this debt, Maevius gives his slave Stichus, who is worth 10,000, as a pledge (*pignus*) to Seius. This means that if Maevius does not pay what he owes, Seius can sell Stichus, returning any excess to Maevius; but until this sale, Maevius remains the owner of Stichus. Before the debt is paid or Stichus is sold, a third party kills Stichus. Is the third party liable to Maevius, or to Seius, or to both?

Discussion:

1. As Paul says, if Stichus is killed by a third party, ordinarily Maevius alone has the Aquilian action. Why?

2. Paul, however, recognizes two exceptions: Maevius may be insolvent, in which case Seius may be unable to collect all or part of the debt; or Seius' suit may be barred by lapse of time, although the security interest in Stichus remained. In both these cases, Seius is allowed to sue the third party for the

extent of his interest in Stichus (i.e., 7,000), and Maevius can sue for the remainder (i.e., 3,000). Do you understand why Paul reaches this result?

3. This passage has probably been reworked by the compilers of the *Digest*, and it is not entirely clear what the classical law was. However, Marcellus (D. 20.1.27) discusses a case in which a debtor, who had given a slave in pledge, put out the slave's eye, thereby reducing the slave's value; Marcellus unhesitatingly allows the creditor to bring an Aquilian action against the debtor if the creditor suffers material loss as a consequence of the slave's blinding. Note that here an owner is being sued for damage he has done to his own slave; compare Case 81.

4. In the text of this Case as it survives, the rule is supposed to "benefit" the debtor, obviously because the debt is satisfied when the creditor realizes the value of the pledge. But at least in the case of an insolvent debtor, the rule actually benefits the creditor, since he or she gains a preferred status against the debtor's other creditors. Do you see why?

5. Why does the creditor have an analogous and not a statutory action? See also the following Case.

Case 81: A Good Faith Possessor

D. 9.2.17 (Ulpianus, libro octavo decimo ad Edictum)

Si dominus servum suum occiderit, bonae fidei possessori vel ei qui pignori accepit in factum actione tenebitur.

(Ulpian in the eighteenth book on the Edict)

If an owner slays his own slave, he will be liable through an *in factum* action to a good faith possessor or to a person who received (the object) as a pledge.

Discussion:

1. On good faith possessors, see Case 73 above; they hold property that belongs to another person, who can reclaim that property at any time. Why can the good faith possessor of a slave bring an *in factum* Aquilian action against the owner who wrongfully damages the slave?

2. What can the good faith possessor obtain from the owner in an Aquilian action? Note that in many circumstances a good faith possessor can keep property unless the owner compensates the possessor for expenses on the object. Is this the full extent of possible recovery?

3. To what extent is a good faith possessor in a position comparable to that of a person who accepts a pledge?

4. In Case 48, Ulpian says that the owner has an Aquilian action if a fugitive slave is injured. Is that Case entirely consistent with this one?

Case 82: A Borrower

D. 9.2.11.9 (Ulpianus, libro octavo decimo ad Edictum)

Eum, cui vestimenta commodata sunt, non posse, si scissa fuerint, lege Aquilia agere Iulianus ait, sed domino eam competere.

D. 13.6.19 (Iulianus, libro primo Digestorum)

Ad eos, qui servandum aliquid conducunt aut utendum accipiunt, damnum iniuria ab alio datum non pertinere procul dubio est: qua enim cura aut diligentia consequi possumus, ne aliquis damnum nobis iniuria det?

(Ulpian in the eighteenth book on the Edict)

Julian says that a person who is lent clothing cannot sue under the Lex Aquilia if it is torn, but that the owner has the action.

(Julian in the first book of his *Digests*)

It is beyond doubt that those who undertake to guard something (for pay) or who receive its (gratuitous) use are not liable for wrongful loss inflicted by a third party. For what care or diligence of ours can prevent someone from inflicting wrongful loss on us?

Discussion:

1. In Roman law, a person who receives the gratuitous use of an object, or who is hired to guard it, is held to a very high standard of care called *custodia*; he or she is usually liable on the contract if the object is lost or damaged except through irresistible force (*vis maior*). Julian, however, denies that the borrower or employee is contractually liable for damage done by others. What legal consequences flow from this ruling?

2. If the borrower were contractually liable to the lender for loss wrongfully inflicted by a third party, would he or she be able to bring an Aquilian action against the wrongdoer?

3. How convincing do you find Julian's reasoning? Marcellus (D. 19.2.41), answering Julian, says a person employed to guard property should be liable on the contract if he or she failed to guard against the risk of possible loss or set a watchman who inflicted the loss. Does this seem to you more persuasive than Julian's view?

4. Tenants could also have an analogous Aquilian action in some instances (Case 9).

Part B: The Defendant

Section 1: Multiple Defendants

Case 83: Several Attackers

D. 9.2.11.1–2 (Ulpianus, libro octavo decimo ad Edictum)

Si alius tenuit, alius interemit, is qui tenuit, quasi causam mortis praebuit, in factum actione tenetur. (2) Sed si plures servum percusserint, utrum omnes quasi occiderint teneantur, videamus. et si quidem apparet cuius ictu perierit, ille quasi occiderit tenetur: quod si non apparet, omnes quasi occiderint teneri Iulianus ait, et si cum uno agatur, ceteri non liberantur: nam ex lege Aquilia quod alius praestitit, alium non relevat, cum sit poena.

(Ulpian in the eighteenth book on the Edict)

If he (the victim) was held by one person and killed by another, the person who held is liable in an *in factum* action for furnishing the cause of death. (2) But if several persons struck a slave, let us see whether all are liable for slaying him. If indeed it is clear who struck the fatal blow, that person is liable for slaying; but if it is unclear, Julian says that all are liable for slaying, and the rest are not released if one is sued. For under the Lex Aquilia what one person pays does not release another, since it is a penalty.

Discussion:

1. In the first hypothetical, why is the person who held the victim liable *in factum* and not in a statutory action? Is the slayer liable in a statutory action? In the second hypothetical, how convincing is Ulpian's explanation for Julian's rule? The actual killer cannot be identified; does it follow that all the assailants are killers? How similar are these two hypotheticals?

2. Julian (Case 56) attributes the rule concerning multiple wrongdoers to the Republican jurists; he may have revived it. To what extent does it seem archaic? The same rule was used when several persons dropped a heavy beam and killed a slave (Ulpian, D. 9.2.11.4); how does that situation differ from the one above?

3. Titius leads a slave into an ambush, where Seia kills him; is Titius liable *in factum*? See Ulpian, D. 9.2.9.3.

Section 2: Vicarious and Noxal Liability

Case 84: Noxal Liability

D. 9.4.2 pr. (Ulpianus, libro octavo decimo ad Edictum)

Si servus sciente domino occidit, in solidum dominum obligat, ipse enim videtur dominus occidisse: si autem insciente, noxalis est, nec enim debuit ex maleficio servi in plus teneri, quam ut noxae eum dedat.

(Ulpian in the eighteenth book on the Edict)

If a slave slays with his master's knowledge, he obligates the master in full, for the master himself is considered to have slain; but if with him unaware, there is a noxal action, since on his slave's wrongdoing he ought not to be liable for more than noxal surrender.

Discussion:

1. In the noxal form of the Aquilian action, the master could escape liability for the slave's act by surrendering the slave to the plaintiff. Ulpian justifies this by arguing that the master, if he or she was unaware of what the slave was doing, ought not to be liable for an amount higher than the slave's actual worth. How convincing do you find this argument? On what presuppositions does it seem to rest?

2. Liability follows the slave to the extent that the present owner of the slave is liable in a similar way for wrongful damage done by the slave prior to acquisition; and the slave is also personally liable after manumission (Paul, D. 9.4.6). Do these rules suggest a different way to explain noxal liability? Note that the seller of a slave usually had a legal obligation to inform the buyer if the slave was subject to a noxal liability.

3. A *paterfamilias* also has noxal liability for wrongful loss inflicted by free persons in his power; the father can surrender the offender into a form of debt-bondage called *mancipium*. The offender must then work off the debt, after which the plaintiff can be forced to free him back into the power of the *paterfamilias*. (See Papinian, *Coll.* 2.3.1.) Why are slaves not treated similarly?

4. The situation changes dramatically when a slave's master knows of the slave's act; see Case 88 below.

Case 85: Slaves Act Together

D. 9.2.32 pr. (Gaius, libro septimo ad Edictum Provinciale)

Illud quaesitum est, an quod Proconsul in furto observat quod a familia factum sit (id est ut non in singulos detur poenae persecutio, sed sufficeret id praestari, quod praestandum foret, si id furtum unus liber fecisset), debeat et in actione damni iniuriae observari. sed magis visum est idem esse observandum, et merito: cum enim circa furti actionem haec ratio sit, ne ex uno delicto tota familia dominus careat eaque ratio similiter et in actionem damni iniuriae interveniat, sequitur ut idem debeat aestimari, praesertim cum interdum levior sit haec causa delicti, veluti si culpa et non dolo damnum daretur.

(Gaius in the seventh book on the Provincial Edict)

It was asked whether the rule used by Proconsuls for theft (*furtum*) committed by a household of slaves — namely, that pursuit of the penalty not be granted against individual slaves, but that it suffice if payment is made of what would be owed if one free person had committed the theft — ought also to be followed in the action for wrongful loss. But it seemed preferable that the same rule be followed, and deservedly. For the reasoning in the action on theft is that the owner not lose his whole household because of one delict; this reasoning has similar force in the action for wrongful damages. It follows that the same evaluation should be made, especially since this form of delict is sometimes less serious, e.g., if loss is inflicted by *culpa* and not by *dolus*.

Discussion:

1. The rule for theft, which Gaius quotes from the Provincial Edict, was first established by the Urban Praetor (Ulpian, D. 47.6.1 pr.). How convincing is Gaius' attempt to apply this rule also in Aquilian actions?

2. Does this rule undermine the punitive basis of Aquilian liability (see Case 83)? Why might the jurists have wanted to apply a different rule to slaves than to free persons?

Case 86: Slave Held by Good Faith Possessor; Fugitive Slave

D. 9.2.27.3 (Ulpianus, libro octavo decimo ad Edictum)

Servi autem occidentis nomine dominus tenetur, is vero cui bona fide servit non tenetur. sed an is, qui servum in fuga habet, teneatur nomine eius Aquiliae actione, quaeritur: et ait Iulianus teneri et est verissimum: cui et Marcellus consentit.

(Ulpian in the eighteenth book on the Edict)

The owner is liable in the name of a slave who slays, but a person whom he (the slave) serves in good faith is not liable. But the question is raised whether the owner is liable in an Aquilian action for a fugitive slave. Julian says that he is liable, and this is quite correct; Marcellus also agrees on this.

Discussion:

1. Can you think of a good practical reason why a person who possesses a slave, without realizing that the slave belongs to another, should have no Aquilian liability for damage done by the slave? Why should the true owner be liable?

2. On what theory is a fugitive slave's owner held liable for wrongful damage done by the slave? Ulpian indicates that Julian's position was controversial; what alternative views are possible?

Case 87: Co-Owned Slave Inflicts Loss on One Owner

D. 9.2.27.1 (Ulpianus, libro octavo decimo ad Edictum)

Si servus communis, id est meus et tuus, servum meum occiderit, legi Aquiliae locus est adversus te, si tua voluntate fecit: et ita Proculum existimasse Urseius refert. quod si non voluntate tua fecit, cessare noxalem actionem, ne sit in potestate servi, ut tibi soli serviat: quod puto verum esse.

(Ulpian in the eighteenth book on the Edict)

If a co-owned slave, i.e., one belonging to me and you, slays my slave, the Lex Aquilia applies against you if he did it by your will; Urseius reports that Proculus also thought this. But if he did not act by your will, (Proculus adds that) the noxal action fails, lest the slave have it in his power to serve you alone. I consider this view correct.

Discussion:

1. The first of Ulpian's hypotheticals is a straightforward application of the rule in Case 84; but the second hypothetical is much more difficult. If a slave belonging to you and me kills my slave, and he did not act by your will, why is no noxal action available? The text might make more sense if changed to read: "lest the slave have it in his power to serve *me* alone"; but what would the reasoning be? Why should it make any difference that I might end up as sole owner of the offending slave, who would have brought this about by his own action? In any event, Ulpian also held (D. 9.2.27.2) that noxal surrender of part of a slave was not possible.

2. In general, the jurists prefer that these questions be settled in an action for dividing common property, where account can be taken of complicating liabilities. Julian (D. 9.4.41) explains:

    When a co-owned slave inflicts wrongful loss on one of his owners, there is no action under the Lex Aquilia for this. Otherwise, if he had given loss to a third party, either owner could bring suit against the other under the Lex Aquilia for the entire amount. Likewise, when a co-owned slave commits theft, one owner cannot sue the other on the theft, but can sue for division of common property.

    How, if at all, does Julian's explanation help?

Case 88: Slave Acts with Master's Knowledge

D. 9.2.44.1 (Ulpianus, libro quadragensimo secundo ad Sabinum)

Quotiens sciente domino servus vulnerat vel occidit, Aquilia dominum teneri dubium non est.

D. 9.2.45 pr. (Paulus, libro decimo ad Sabinum)

Scientiam hic pro patientia accipimus, ut qui prohibere potuit teneatur, si non fecerit.

(Ulpian in the forty-second book on Sabinus)

Whenever a slave wounds or slays with his master's knowledge, there is no doubt that the master has Aquilian liability.

(Paul in the tenth book on Sabinus)

We construe knowledge here to mean sufferance, so that a person who could prevent is liable if he does not do so.

Discussion:

1. The slave's owner is liable for all of the wrongful loss inflicted by the slave, and there is no noxal liability unless the plaintiff prefers this. What theory can be used to justify the master's liability?

2. Is the owner liable in a statutory or in an *in factum* action? The jurists give a statutory Aquilian action, provided the other criteria for such an action are present. Why?

3. How plausible is the jurists' interpretation of "knowledge" as allowing the slave's act to occur when one could have prevented it? Is the master liable because he or she failed in a duty of care owed to third parties when supervising slaves?

4. Does the slave also have Aquilian liability if he or she inflicts loss with the master's knowledge? Ulpian (D. 9.4.2.1) reports a lengthy discussion of Celsus, who holds that the slave has no liability if the master ordered the act (see Case 68), and the master remains solely liable even if he or she ceases to own the slave. If the master merely did not forbid the act, Celsus also assigns sole liability to the master; but Julian holds that in this case both slave and master are liable, so that the plaintiff can bring either a noxal suit directed toward the slave, or a suit against the master in his own right. Ulpian prefers Julian's view; do you?

Case 89: A Dangerous Fire

D. 9.2.27.9 (Ulpianus, libro octavo decimo ad Edictum)

Si fornacarius servus coloni ad fornacem obdormisset et villa fuerit exusta, Neratius scribit ex locato conventum praestare debere, si neglegens in eligendis ministeriis fuit: ceterum si alius ignem subiecerit fornaci, alius neglegenter custodierit, an tenebitur qui subiecerit? nam qui custodit, nihil fecit, qui recte ignem subiecit, non peccavit: quid ergo est? puto utilem competere actionem tam in eum qui ad fornacem obdormivit quam in eum qui neglegenter custodit, nec quisquam dixerit in eo qui obdormivit rem humanam et naturalem passum, cum deberet vel ignem extinguere vel ita munire, ne evagetur.

(Ulpian in the eighteenth book on the Edict)

If a tenant farmer's slave, a furnaceman, fell asleep at a furnace and the farmhouse burnt down, Neratius writes that (the tenant) must fulfill his obligation under the contract of lease (and so must pay for the loss) if he was careless in choosing his servants.

But if one person set the fire in the furnace and another carelessly guarded it, will the one who set it be liable? For the one who watched did nothing, and the one who correctly set the fire did nothing wrong; so what outcome? I think that an analogous (Aquilian) action lies against the man who fell asleep at the furnace, just as it does against one who watches carelessly. Nor, in the case of the man who fell asleep, should one say that he did something human and natural, since he should either have extinguished the fire or banked it to prevent its escape.

The Hypothetical Problems:

1) A tenant farmer sets a slave furnaceman to watch a fire in a farmhouse; after the slave falls asleep, the fire escapes and burns down the farmhouse. Is the tenant liable to the farm's owner, and if so, how?

2) One person sets a fire in a furnace; another then undertakes to watch it. The second person is careless in watching the fire, which escapes and does damage. Is the second person liable under the Lex Aquilia?

Discussion:

1. This is a confusing but important Case; it was plainly abbreviated, although the parallel version in the *Collatio* (12.7.7) shows that much of the damage occurred very early. A fire escaped from a furnace and burned down a rented farmhouse. The loss is therefore very high, undoubtedly much higher than the value of the slave who was tending the furnace. The question arises: on what theory can the tenant farmer be held liable for the full value of the farmhouse?

2. In the first sentence, Neratius suggests one answer: If the tenant farmer's

slave fell asleep at the furnace, the tenant farmer is liable on the lease if he was himself careless in choosing the slave (e.g., the slave was inexperienced, or obviously tired). How has the tenant violated the contract with the landlord?

3. The remainder of the text goes off on a somewhat different problem associated with Aquilian liability. Ulpian raises a query about whether a person commits *culpa* by falling asleep beside a dangerous fire. If the person set the fire and then did not watch it properly, then he or she is similar to a doctor who fails to provide care after surgery (see Case 24); as the *Collatio* shows, Ulpian originally compared the doctor directly. What is the force of this comparison?

4. But what if one person set the fire, and another, who undertook to watch it, then fell asleep? Here the person who set the fire did nothing wrong, that is, committed no *culpa*; accordingly, he or she has no Aquilian liability. The person who fell asleep is in a more ambiguous position, since he or she did nothing: no positive act, such as is normally required for Aquilian liability. But Ulpian finally holds that the obviously dangerous character of a fire requires that the person tending it not fall asleep without making sure that it will be safe in the meantime. Is Ulpian arguing that because the person who fell asleep had assumed responsibility for control of a dangerous object, he or she has a duty of care even for acts of omission in guarding the object? To what extent would this theory extend the normal duty of care?

5. While Ulpian's theory is sufficient if the furnaceman is to be made liable, it does not solve the central problem in Aquilian actions if the furnaceman is also a slave. In that case, the tenant may very well be content with noxal surrender; but the landlord may want more. This problem is discussed in the two Cases that follow.

Case 90: A Rented Muleteer

D. 9.2.27.34 (Ulpianus, libro octavo decimo ad Edictum)

Si quis servum conductum ad mulum regendum commendaverit ei, mulum ille ad pollicem suum eum alligaverit de loro et mulus eruperit sic ut et pollicem avelleret servo et se praecipitaret, Mela scribit, si pro perito imperitus locatus sit, ex conducto agendum cum domino ob mulum ruptum vel debilitatum, sed si ictu aut terrore mulus turbatus sit, tum dominum eius, id est muli, et servi cum eo qui turbavit habiturum legis Aquiliae actionem. mihi autem videtur et eo casu, quo ex locato actio est, competere etiam Aquiliae.

(Ulpian in the eighteenth book on the Edict)

Someone puts a rented slave in charge of driving a mule, and he (the slave) ties the mule by its rein to his thumb; the mule breaks away, thereby ripping off the slave's thumb and rushing headlong. Mela writes that if an unskilled slave was leased as a skilled one, the (slave's) owner may be sued on the lease because the mule was rent or lamed; but if the mule was scared by a blow or a fear, then both the mule's owner and the slave's will have an action under the Lex Aquilia against the person who disturbed it. But I think that in this case as well, if the action on the lease lies, so does the Aquilian.

Discussion:

1. The text is disturbed, but the sense is clear enough. The rented slave tied the mule's rein to his thumb — a foolish thing to do. The mule bolted, ripping off the slave's thumb and then injuring itself. If the mule was struck by a third party, there is little doubt that both the owner of the mule and the owner of the slave have an Aquilian action, normally *in factum*; Ulpian (D. 9.2.9.3) gives a comparable case, in which someone startles a horse on which my slave is riding, and the slave is thrown into a river and drowns. (But see also Cases 60–61, on contributory negligence.)

2. The more difficult case is when no third party is involved. If the slave's owner had represented the slave as an experienced muleteer, Mela let the mule's owner sue him on the contract; Ulpian accords the Aquilian action as well, obviously for the full loss. What is the theory justifying Aquilian liability? Is it that the slave's owner, in leasing the slave, has a duty of care with respect to losses the lessee may suffer if the slave is unqualified?

Case 91: A Tenant's Slaves Burn Down a Farmhouse

D. 9.2.27.11 (Ulpianus, libro octavo decimo ad Edictum)

Proculus ait, cum coloni servi villam exussissent, colonum vel ex locato vel lege Aquilia teneri, ita ut colonus possit servos noxae dedere, et si uno iudicio res esset iudicata, altero amplius non agendum. sed haec ita, si culpa colonus careret: ceterum si noxios servos habuit, damni eum iniuria teneri, cur tales habuit. idem servandum et circa inquilinorum insulae personas scribit: quae sententia habet rationem.

(Ulpian in the eighteenth book on the Edict)
Proculus says that when a tenant farmer's slaves burned down a farmhouse, the tenant is liable either on the lease or under the Lex Aquilia, such that the tenant can make noxal surrender of the slaves; and if the matter is adjudged in one action, there can be no further suit by the other. But this is so if the tenant lacks *culpa*; but if he had guilty slaves, he is liable for wrongful loss for having such persons. He writes that the same rule should be observed also for persons who are tenants of an apartment house; this view makes sense.

Discussion:

1. In the first part of this text (of which there is a different version in *Collatio* 12.7.9), Proculus extends the option of noxal surrender from the Aquilian action to the action on lease. There is no parallel for this extension. What is the underlying theory? Why should a tenant be liable in contract for the acts of his or her slaves?

2. Much more difficult is the second half of this text, which was undoubtedly heavily rewritten by the compilers of the *Digest*. As the text stands, Ulpian allows the landlord to sue the tenant for full damages "if he had culpable slaves"; this act is construed as the tenant's *culpa*, and thus the tenant would presumably be personally liable. Ulpian seems to hold that the landlord could bring an Aquilian action. What is the theory? See also Ulpian, D. 19.2.11 pr., a companion text that also concerns the guests of tenants.

3. On concurrent actions in delict and contract, see Cases 94–95. This Case applies the usual rule, that a judgment in one action precludes the bringing of the other.

Part C: Concurrence of Actions

Case 92: Action on Outrage

D. 47.10.15.46 (Ulpianus, libro quinquagensimo septimo ad Edictum)

Si quis servo verberato iniuriarum egerit, deinde postea damni iniuriae agat, Labeo scribit eandem rem non esse, quia altera actio ad damnum pertineret culpa datum, altera ad contumeliam.

(Ulpian in the fifty-seventh book on the Edict)

If a person, whose slave was thrashed, sues for outrage (*iniuria*) and then later for wrongful damage, Labeo writes that this is not the same cause of action, since the second action concerns loss inflicted by *culpa*, while the first concerns insult (to the slave's master).

Discussion:

1. This is the regular rule, which Ulpian gives also in D. 9.2.5.1 (Case 27). What theory does Labeo use to explain the rule?

2. The Praetor's Edict provided that if one person thrashed another person's slave, the slave's master could sue for outrage (*iniuria*); the provision is quoted below in the ·discussion on Case 133. In what sense is thrashing a slave an insult to the slave's owner?

3. In general, the jurists allow cumulation of punitive actions. A good example is Papinian, D. 48.5.6 pr.: A person who seduces another's female slave is liable in an Aquilian action (what is the loss?), an action on the outrage, and an action for corrupting a slave. Papinian reasons: "One accused of this sort of thing should not be spared (simply) because several charges (are available)." How convincing is this logic?

Case 93: Action on Outrage (A Dissent)

D. 44.7.34 pr. (Paulus, libro singulari de Concurrentibus Actionibus)

Qui servum alienum iniuriose verberat, ex uno facto incidit et in Aquiliam et in actionem iniuriarum: iniuria enim ex affectu fit, damnum ex culpa et ideo possunt utraeque competere. sed quidam altera elec ta alteram consumi. alii per legis Aquiliae actionem iniuriarum consumi, quoniam desiit bonum et aequum esse condemnari eum, qui aestimationem praestitit: sed si ante iniuriarum actum esset, teneri eum ex lege Aquilia. sed et haec sententia per Praetorem inhibenda est, nisi in id, quod amplius ex lege Aquilia competit, agatur. rationabilius itaque est eam admitti sententiam, ut liceat ei quam voluerit actionem prius exercere, quod autem amplius in altera est, etiam hoc exsequi.

(Paul in his monograph on *Concurrent Actions*)
A person who wrongfully beats another's slave is liable from one act both to the Aquilian action and to the action on outrage (*iniuria*); for the *iniuria* arises from intent, the loss from *culpa*, and so both can lie. But some (hold) that if one action is chosen, the other is consumed. Others (hold) that the action on outrage is consumed by that under the Lex Aquilia, since it ceased to be good and fair that a person be condemned who had (already) proffered the evaluation (of the loss); but if action is brought first on the outrage, he is liable under the Lex Aquilia. But this view should be restricted by the Praetor unless suit is brought (only) for the excess over what is due under the Lex Aquilia. And so it is more reasonable that this view be accepted, that he be permitted to bring first the action he prefers, and then also to recover the excess in the other action.

Discussion:

1. List and justify the various views that Paul discusses. Contrast the majority view expressed in the preceding Case.

2. How does Paul's understanding of the problem of concurrent actions differ from the majority view?

Case 94: Contract Actions

D. 13.6.18.1 (Gaius, libro nono ad Edictum Provinciale)

Sive autem pignus sive commodata res sive deposita deterior ab eo qui acceperit facta sit, non solum istae sunt actiones, de quibus loquimur, verum etiam legis Aquiliae: sed si qua earum actum fuerit, aliae tolluntur.

(Gaius in the ninth book on the Provincial Edict)

If an object that has been pledged or loaned or deposited is made worse by the person who takes it, not only do those (contract) actions under discussion lie, but also the action under the Lex Aquilia. But if suit is brought on any of these actions, the rest are eliminated.

Discussion:

1. Again, this is the normal rule. Whereas the Aquilian action can be cumulated with a purely punitive action (such as that on outrage), it cannot be cumulated with a contract action. Why should this be true?

2. The jurists vary in describing how a plaintiff is prevented from cumulating actions; sometimes the *iudex* in the first trial refuses to condemn the defendant unless the plaintiff formally renounces further actions, sometimes the Praetor refuses to give a second action.

3. The rule is the same when an Aquilian action overlaps with a property claim, as for instance when a true owner claims property that has been damaged by its possessor. The *iudex* in a vindication can award the amount of the loss, but only if the plaintiff forswears the Aquilian action; see Ulpian, D. 6.1.13. What underlying principle links this situation with the one described in the main Case?

Case 95: Contract Actions (A Dissent)

D. 44.7.34.2 (Paulus, libro singulari de Concurrentibus Actionibus)

... et hoc in legis Aquiliae actione dicitur, si tibi commodavero vestimenta et tu ea ruperis: utraeque enim actiones rei persecutionem continent. et quidem post legis Aquiliae actionem utique commodati finietur: post commodati an Aquiliae remaneat in eo, quod in repetitione triginta dierum amplius est, dubitatur: sed verius est remanere, quia simplo accedit: et simplo subducto locum non habet.

(Paul in his monograph on *Concurrent Actions*)

... This is also held with regard to the action under the Lex Aquilia, if I lend (*commodavero*) clothes to you and you rend (*ruperis*) them; for both actions involve recovery of (compensation for) a thing. Indeed, after an action under the Lex Aquilia, that on loan (*commodatum*) will always be ended. But there is doubt whether, after one on loan, the Aquilian remains for any excess in recovery for the thirty-day period. But the more correct view is that it remains, since it goes beyond the simple value; but it does not lie when the simple value is subtracted.

Discussion:

1. In this Case, Paul continues the discussion in Case 93. Suppose that I lend you clothes worth 100, and you damage them so that they are worth 60. The loss in value can normally be recovered either in an action on loan (*commodatum*), or in an Aquilian action. To what extent does Paul's view represent any real departure from Case 94?

2. Paul says that the Aquilian action normally cannot be cumulated with the action on loan because "both actions involve recovery of a thing." The Latin is *persecutio rei*, i.e., the focus of the lawsuit is on recovery or compensation and not on a penalty. Is this really true for the Aquilian action?

Chapter IV: Liability for Animals

The owners of animals were usually not liable under the Lex Aquilia for the damage that their animals caused if the owners were not themselves at fault for this loss. Instead, they were more normally held liable under the action on *pauperies* (literally, "impoverishment"), which was created by the Twelve Tables and later included in the Praetor's Edict. This liability is in principle a strict liability in that it is imposed without regard to the owner's fault: but the owner can escape liability by surrendering the animal (noxal surrender), and the extent of the owner's responsibility is also limited in other ways by the jurists. Otherwise, however, many of the fundamental principles of Aquilian liability are carried over and applied to domestic animals. Particularly curious is the way in which the liability is said to follow the animal, rather in the fashion that liability follows a slave.

The action on *pauperies* is not available in the case of naturally wild animals, such as bears and lions, when they escape from their owner's control. However, the Curule Aediles, who had a general policing function in Rome, established a separate basis of liability for certain dangerous animals.

Part A: Four-Footed Animals (The *Actio de Pauperie*)

Case 96: The *Actio de Pauperie*

D. 9.1.1 pr.–3 (Ulpianus, libro octavo decimo ad Edictum)

Si quadrupes pauperiem fecisse dicetur, actio ex lege Duodecim Tabularum descendit: quae lex voluit aut dari id quod nocuit, id est id animal quod noxiam commisit, aut aestimationem noxiae offerri. (1) Noxia autem est ipsum delictum. (2) Quae actio ad omnes quadrupedes pertinet. (3) Ait Praetor 'pauperiem fecisse.' pauperies est damnum sine iniuria facientis datum: nec enim potest animal iniuria fecisse, quod sensu caret.

(Ulpian in the eighteenth book on the Edict)

If a quadruped is said to have inflicted impoverishment (*pauperies*), an action derives from the Twelve Tables; this statute provided that either that which did harm — i.e., the animal that inflicted the harm — be surrendered, or that an evaluation of the harm be provided. (1) The harm is the delict itself. (2) This action pertains to all quadrupeds. (3) The Praetor says: "to have inflicted *pauperies.*" *Pauperies* is loss given without the doer's wrongfulness (*iniuria*); for an animal cannot have acted wrongfully, since it lacks understanding.

Discussion:

1. How does liability under the action on *pauperies* differ from the liability of a slave's owner under the Lex Aquilia? What is meant by: "The harm is the delict itself"? Why is the owner liable for the actual loss (and not for double) if he or she fails to surrender the animal?

2. Is it correct to claim that animals lack understanding altogether? Note that the jurists used this action as an analogy in denying the Aquilian liability of young children and madmen; see Case 35.

3. Paul (D. 9.1.4) grants an analogous action on *pauperies* in the case of loss caused by non-quadrupeds (such as geese). Why did the original action single out quadrupeds? Does the action also apply to naturally wild animals, such as bears? See Case 103.

Case 97: The Wildness of the Animal

D. 9.1.1.4–6 (Ulpianus, libro octavo decimo ad Edictum)

Itaque, ut Servius scribit, tunc haec actio locum habet, cum commota feritate nocuit quadrupes, puta si equus calcitrosus calce percusserit, aut bos cornu petere solitus petierit, aut mulae propter nimiam ferociam: quod si propter loci iniquitatem aut propter culpam mulionis, aut si plus iusto onerata quadrupes in aliquem onus everterit, haec actio cessabit damnique iniuriae agetur. (5) Sed et si canis, cum duceretur ab aliquo, asperitate sua evaserit et alicui damnum dederit: si contineri firmius ab alio poterit vel si per eum locum induci non debuit, haec actio cessabit et tenebitur qui canem tenebat. (6) Sed et si instigatu alterius fera damnum dederit, cessabit haec actio.

(Ulpian in the eighteenth book on the Edict)

And so, as Servius writes, this action lies when a quadruped does harm because its wildness is stirred, for example if a horse prone to kicking strikes with its hoof, or an ox prone to goring gores, or mules (kick) because of excessive high spirits; but if (this happens) because of the place's steepness or the muleteer's *culpa*, or if an overloaded quadruped upsets its load on someone, this action fails and the suit should be for wrongful loss. (5) But also if a dog being led by somebody breaks loose because of its fierceness and inflicts loss on someone else, if it could be better restrained by another person or if it ought not to be led through that place, this action fails and the person who held the dog is liable. (6) But also if a wild animal inflicted loss at a third party's instigation, this action fails.

Discussion:

1. The action on *pauperies* lies when the animal's "wildness is stirred"; as Justinian puts it (*Inst.* 4.9 pr.), the action covers loss caused by the animal's "wantonness, passion, or wildness." Ulpian (D. 9.1.1.7) states that when a horse kicks someone who is stroking it, the action on *pauperies* lies. Why? The jurists seem to concentrate mainly on animals that can be aggressive or ferocious; is this concentration justified by the terms of the action?

2. On the action on *pauperies*, see also Case 51: mules are pulling a cart up a steep incline; they shy at something, and the muleteers abandon the cart from fear that they will be crushed. Does the action on *pauperies* lie? Alfenus says that it does; why?

3. You are riding a horse, which inadvertently treads on the foot of a passing slave; the slave's foot is broken. Neither you nor the slave is at fault. Does the action on *pauperies* lie? Why or why not? Does the result seem right?

4. Section (6) of this Case suggests that the action was also applied to naturally wild animals (see Case 103); does this make sense?

5. This Case also sets out the boundaries between the action on *pauperies* and the Aquilian action. Generally speaking, the latter is preferred whenever a particular defendant's *culpa* can be established; why? What general principles emerge from this Case as to the circumstances in which one or the other action is appropriate?

6. Ofilius (cited by Ulpian, D. 9.2.9.3) proposes this problem: A slave is riding on a horse; you scare the horse, which rears and throws its rider into a river; the slave drowns. What result?

7. Javolenus (D. 9.2.57) gives another case: I lend you a horse; while you are riding with other people, another rider bumps into you; the horse throws you and in the ensuing tumult breaks its legs. Who should be liable? Javolenus holds that if the other rider acted with *culpa*, he can be sued on the Lex Aquilia; but in any case neither I nor you can sue the owner of the other horse. Why not?

8. Ulpian (D. 4.3.7.6) discusses a case in which a quadruped gives loss to me because of the *dolus* of a third party. (An example might be maliciously opening the door of a cowshed and letting out a savage bull, which gores me.) What is interesting about the answer Ulpian gives is that he seems to assume that the animal's owner would be subject to an action on *pauperies*. Why would this be true?

9. Alfenus (D. 9.1.5) puts the following case: A groom leads a horse into an inn; the horse sniffs at a mule, which kicks out and breaks the groom's leg. Can the groom sue the mule's owner through the action on *pauperies*? Alfenus answers yes, but does not explain his reasoning. Could it be argued, against Alfenus, that the groom ought to have prevented the horse from annoying other animals, so that he is responsible for the injury to himself?

Case 98: A Dog Attacks a Trespasser

D. 9.1.2.1 (Paulus, libro vicensimo secundo ad Edictum)

Si quis aliquem evitans, magistratum forte, in taberna proxima se immississet ibique a cane feroce laesus esset, non posse agi canis nomine quidam putant: at si solutus fuisset, contra.

(Paul in the twenty-second book on the Edict)

If a person who was avoiding somebody — e.g., a magistrate — had hid in a nearby shop and was there wounded by a ferocious dog, some think that there can be no suit in the name of the dog; but if it had been off the leash, the reverse.

Discussion:

1. Does Paul suppose that the person had no right to be in the shop? Why would this make a difference?

2. Why should it matter whether or not the dog was on a leash? Owners were required to keep savage dogs on the leash during daylight hours in public streets and squares (Paul, *Sent.* 1.15.1a); why should the storekeeper have a similar responsibility in his shop?

3. This Case speaks of a "ferocious dog"; how would one know whether a dog was "ferocious"? Is the bite itself proof of its ferocity? Do you have Aquilian liability if you fail to keep an apparently mild-mannered dog on the leash, and the dog bites someone? See also section (5) of the preceding Case. In general, Roman law displays a fairly hostile attitude to dogs; see also Case 104.

4. Ulpian (D. 9.2.11.5) discusses a case in which the owner incites a dog to bite someone; Proculus held that the victim had a statutory action under the Lex Aquilia against the owner, while Julian gave a statutory action if the dog was being held, but an action *in factum* if the dog was not. Would the shopkeeper be similarly liable if he sicked the dog on the trespasser?

Case 99: An Ox Upsets a Cart

D. 9.1.1.9 (Ulpianus, libro octavo decimo ad Edictum)

Sive autem corpore suo pauperiem quadrupes dedit, sive per aliam rem, quam tetigit quadrupes, haec actio locum habebit: ut puta si plaustro bos obtrivit aliquem vel alia re deiecta.

(Ulpian in the eighteenth book on the Edict)
Whether the quadruped inflicts *pauperies* with its own body or through something else that the quadruped touches, this action lies; for example, if an ox crushes someone with a cart or something else it upset.

Discussion:

1. The issue in this case is how direct the chain of causation must be between the animal and the damage inflicted. Suppose, for instance, that a teamster swerved his cart in order to avoid running into a horse that was bucking wildly, and as a result the cart went into a ditch and was destroyed. What result from this Case?

2. The problem of causation is also discussed in Chapter II, Part D; does the answer in this Case differ significantly from the jurists' handling of causation in Aquilian liability?

Case 100: The Aggressor Doctrine

D. 9.1.1.8, 11 (Ulpianus, libro octavo decimo ad Edictum)

(8) Et si alia quadrupes aliam concitavit ut damnum daret, eius quae concitavit nomine agendum erit.... (11) Cum arietes vel boves commississent et alter alterum occidit, Quintus Mucius distinxit, ut si quidem is perisset qui adgressus erat, cessaret actio, si is, qui non provocaverat, competeret actio: quamobrem eum sibi aut noxam sarcire aut in noxam dedere oportere.

(Ulpian in the eighteenth book on the Edict)

(8) Also, if one quadruped provokes another to inflict loss, an action will lie in regard to the one provoking.... (11) When rams or oxen had fought and one slew the other, Quintus Mucius distinguished: if the one who was the aggressor died, the action fails; but if the one who had not provoked, the action lies. Wherefore he (the owner) ought either to recompense the injury or make noxal surrender.

Discussion:

1. How realistic is it to attempt to determine which of two animals provoked a fight? What is the outcome if it cannot be determined which was the aggressor?

2. On the aggressor doctrine in Aquilian liability, see above Cases 62–64. How similar is the doctrine for the action on *pauperies*? Does this seem to be a mechanical transfer of a legal doctrine from one area of the law to another?

Case 101: Noxal Surrender

D. 9.1.1.12–13 (Ulpianus, libro octavo decimo ad Edictum)

Et cum etiam in quadrupedibus noxa caput sequitur, adversus dominum haec actio datur, non cuius fuerit quadrupes, cum noceret, sed cuius nunc est. (13) Plane si ante litem contestatam decesserit animal, extincta erit actio.

(Ulpian in the eighteenth book on the Edict)

And since also with quadrupeds liability follows the doer, this action is given against the present owner, not the owner at the time the damage occurred. (13) Obviously, should the animal have died before the issue is joined, the action will be extinguished.

Discussion:

1. Although an animal cannot commit a wrong (Case 96), the liability follows it, just as with a slave (see Case 84); the current owner is liable in the action on *pauperies* for the damage done by the animal in the past, and the action is extinguished if the animal dies. Why might the Romans have wanted this rule? Note that sellers of animals were normally obliged to indicate if an animal had caused loss for which the buyer might be held liable.

2. The owner could also be held fully liable if before the Praetor he or she falsely denied ownership of the animal (Ulpian, D. 9.1.1.15). Why?

3. After joinder of issue (*litis contestatio*; completion of the initial stage of the trial before the Praetor), the owner must pay full damages if the animal dies, thus making noxal surrender impossible. If a third party kills the animal, will he or she have Aquilian liability for whatever the owner must pay? See Javolenus, D. 9.2.37.1; Ulpian, D. 9.1.1.16 (both answering yes). For the theory, see Case 43.

Case 102: Measure of Damages

D. 9.1.3 (Gaius, libro septimo ad Edictum Provinciale)

Ex hac lege iam non dubitatur etiam liberarum personarum nomine agi posse, forte si patrem familias aut filium familias vulneraverit quadrupes: scilicet ut non deformitatis ratio habeatur, cum liberum corpus aestimationem non recipiat, sed impensarum in curationem factarum et operarum amissarum quasque amissurus quis esset inutilis factus.

(Gaius in the seventh book on the Provincial Edict)

On the basis of this law it is not now doubted that action can be brought with respect to free persons, e.g., if a quadruped wounds a *paterfamilias* or a son in his father's power; obviously, not that account be taken of disfigurement, since a free person's body does not admit of evaluation, but rather of medical expenses and of lost pay or what he will lose by being disabled.

Discussion:

1. Compare this Case with Cases 47–48, on the Lex Aquilia. Gaius allows recovery of consequential dsamages for an injured freeperson, regardless of whether he or she was in the power of a *paterfamilias*. It is doubtful that injury to free persons was treated differently under the action on *pauperies* than under the Lex Aquilia; still, the action on *pauperies* was compensatory, not punitive. Why might this have made a difference?

2. If an ox gores a free person, as a consequence of which he or she is left physically unimpaired but so badly scarred that normal social life is impossible, why should there be no recovery except for medical expenses and lost wages? Does Gaius' explanation seem adequate?

Part B: Wild Animals

Case 103: A Bear Escapes

D. 9.1.1.10 (Ulpianus, libro octavo decimo ad Edictum)

In bestiis autem propter naturalem feritatem haec actio locum non habet: et ideo si ursus fugit et sic nocuit, non potest quondam dominus conveniri, quia desinit dominus esse, ubi fera evasit: et ideo et si eum occidi, meum corpus est.

(Ulpian in the eighteenth book on the Edict)

In the case of wild animals, because of their natural wildness, this action does not lie. So, if a bear escapes and thereby does harm, the former owner cannot be sued, since he ceases to be owner when the wild animal escaped. And so if I slew it, the body belongs to me.

Discussion:

1. Wild animals remain our property so long as they are in our physical control (see Case 72). How does this explain Ulpian's ruling in the case of the escaped bear?

2. What if physical control remains? Suppose, for example, that a caged bear reaches out of its cage and mauls a passerby. The first sentence of this Case says that the owner of a wild animal is not liable under the action on *pauperies* at all. Most scholars believe that this sentence does not reflect classical Roman law, but was added by the compilers to reflect later Byzantine law; see Justinian, *Inst.* 4.9 pr.:

   [T]he action (on *pauperies*) does not lie unless in causing the damage the animal is acting contrary to its natural disposition; if its nature is to be savage, this remedy is not available.

   Justinian here contradicts Ulpian's statements in D. 9.1.1.2 (Case 96) and 6 (Case 97); also, the first sentence of this Case is inconsistent with the example that Ulpian then gives in the second sentence. The first sentence therefore seems to misstate classical law. Does the classical position seem preferable to Justinian's rule?

Case 104: The Edict of the Curule Aediles

D. 21.1.40.1, 42 (Ulpianus, libro secundo ad Edictum Aedilium Curulium)

(40.1) Deinde aiunt Aediles: 'ne quis canem, verrem vel minorem aprum, lupum, ursum, pantheram, leonem,... (42) qua vulgo iter fiet, ita habuisse velit, ut cuiquam nocere damnumve dare possit. si adversus ea factum erit et homo liber ex ea re perierit, solidi ducenti, si nocitum homini libero esse dicetur, quanti bonum aequum iudici videbitur, condemnetur, ceterarum rerum, quanti damnum datum factumve sit, dupli.'

(Ulpian in the second book on the Curule Aediles' Edict)
(40.1) Then the (Curule) Aediles say: "Let no one seek to have had a dog, a boar or a smaller wild pig, a wolf, a bear, a panther, or a lion... (42) in a place of common traffic, in such a way that it can do harm or give loss to anyone. If this rule is contravened and a free man dies as a result, (the penalty is) two hundred *solidi*; if a free man is allegedly harmed, let condemnation be for as much as seems good and fair to a *iudex*; for other things, (the penalty is) double the loss that was inflicted or caused."

Discussion:

1. Does this seem a better way to handle the problem of wild animals than the action on *pauperies*? The fine would presumably be claimed in most cases by the victim or an heir.

2. The fine for the death of a freeman is given in the *Digest* as two hundred *solidi*; the original fine may have been 200,000 sesterces, a sum of money equal to about two hundred times the annual wage of an unskilled workman at Rome. Does this seem excessive? When a freeperson is killed by something dropped from a window, the praetorian fine is 50,000 sesterces (Ulpian, D. 9.3.1 pr., 5; see Case 163). How would you compare the gravity of the two offenses?

3. Is it reasonable to conjecture that the Aediles acted because of problems caused by imported circus animals? Note that the action lies for keeping the animal in such a way that it can inflict loss; would it also lie if the animal escaped? Is the fact that the animal gave loss proof in itself that it was not being adequately kept?

Chapter V: Other Major Delicts

This chapter deals more briefly with the two other major delicts in Roman private law: theft (*furtum*) and outrage (*iniuria*). The Cases concentrate on the definition and content of these two delicts, which differ from Aquilian liability in that a defendant is liable only for deliberate misconduct (*dolus*), not also for unintentional carelessness (*culpa*). Further, the actions resulting from these delicts are purely punitive, not "mixed" like the Aquilian action (see Case 15); the actions on theft and outrage aim primarily to punish the defendant, not to compensate the plaintiff for a loss.

However, the actions on theft and outrage otherwise share many characteristics with Aquilian liability: the liability of a wrongdoer does not pass to the wrongdoer's heir (passive intransmissibility, see Case 76); joint perpetrators are each liable fully (cumulative concurrence, see Cases 56, 83); as punitive actions, the actions on theft and outrage can be brought along with actions for recovery of compensation (see Cases 92–93); and, above all, noxal surrender is possible when the actual wrongdoer is a slave or a child in the power of a *paterfamilias* (see esp. Case 84). Since these characteristics of delictual actions have already been discussed in earlier chapters, they are not further dealt with here.

In many respects, theft and outrage are more typical of Roman delicts than is Aquilian liability, especially in their stark emphasis on social control through punishment of offenders. They are also interesting for the jurists' attempts to define them both quite broadly, so as to bring the greatest possible number of offenses under them. At times, the juristic definitions seem to be so broad that it is difficult to determine the boundaries between one delict and another.

Part A: Theft (*Furtum*)

In modern law, we normally think that theft should be punished through criminal law; the State prosecutes accused thieves, and upon their conviction it exacts sanctions. By the end of the classical period, this was also largely true in Roman law (see Case 116). But in archaic Roman law theft (*furtum*) was regarded primarily as an affront to another's property rights, an affront that warranted private redress. Under the influence of this archaic understanding, classical law allowed the victim of theft to sue the thief not only for return of the stolen object or its value (the *condictio furtiva*), but also, through the delictual action on theft (*actio furti*), for a multiple of the object's value. This delictual action is the subject of the Cases that follow.

The multiplier was determined by the degree to which the theft was aggravated by special circumstances. Ordinary theft (*furtum nec manifestum*) subjected the thief to a liability for double the object's worth. But if the thief was caught more or less in the act (*furtum manifestum*), the liability was for quadruple. Other special actions applied if the occupant of a house prevented another from searching the premises for stolen property (*furtum prohibitum*; quadruple), or if the occupant permitted a search and the stolen goods were found (*furtum conceptum*; triple); in the latter case the actual thief was liable to the occupant for the same amount (*furtum oblatum*). These complex distinctions, which derive at least ultimately from the Twelve Tables, are of little modern interest and are not further dealt with in this chapter; but Gaius, *Inst.* 3.183–194, discusses at length the various categories and the general history of *furtum*.

Of greater interest are the jurists' attempts to define *furtum*. The jurists seem to require two things: "handling" of another's property against his or her will (*contrectatio*), especially if the defendant profits or expects to profit from the act; and also the deliberate intent to steal (*animus furandi*). Both of these requirements are so broadly conceived as to be rather nebulous. They reach even to include a person who aids and abets theft by another, or who conceals a thief and a stolen object, or who appropriates an object that was lawfully in his or her control (embezzlement). The jurists also define very broadly the property rights that are protected by the *actio furti*.

Theft aggravated by violence is robbery (*rapina*). Two provisions of the Praetor's Edict provided a quadruple penalty against forms of robbery.

Section 1: The Components of Theft

Case 105: Intent and "Handling"

Gaius, *Institutiones* 3.195–197

Furtum autem fit non solum cum quis intercipiendi causa rem alienam amovet, sed generaliter cum quis rem alienam invito domino contrectat. (196) Itaque, si quis re quae apud eum deposita sit utatur, furtum committit. et si quis utendam rem acceperit eamque in alium usum transtulerit, furti obligatur, veluti si quis argentum utendum acceperit, quasi amicos ad cenam invitaturus, et id peregre secum tulerit, aut si quis equum gestandi gratia commodatum longius aliquo duxerit, quod veteres scripserunt de eo qui in aciem perduxisset. (197) Placuit tamen eos qui rebus commodatis aliter uterentur quam utendas accepissent, ita furtum committere, si intellegant id se invito domino facere, eumque, si intellexisset, non permissurum; at si permissurum credant, extra furti crimen videri; optima sane distinctione, quod furtum sine dolo malo non committitur.

(Gaius in the third book of his *Institutes*)

Theft (*furtum*) occurs not only when someone removes another's property in order to appropriate it, but generally when someone handles (*contrectat*) another's property against the owner's will. (196) Thus, if someone uses an object that was deposited with him, he commits theft. Also, if someone receives use of an object and turns it to another use, he is obligated for theft, e.g., if he receives the use of silver on the pretext of inviting friends to dinner and then takes it abroad with him, or if he borrows a horse for a ride and takes it somewhat further (than was agreed); the Republican jurists wrote this of one who took it into battle. (197) But it is agreed that those who use borrowed objects other than for what they had borrowed them commit theft if they realize that they do this against the owner's will, and that he would not permit it if he knew. But if they believe he would permit it, this is not construed as theft, by a very sound distinction, since theft is not committed without *dolus malus*.

Discussion:

1. In section (195), Gaius distinguishes between removing an object ("asportation") and handling it (*contrectatio*). The examples that follow in (196–197) are variants of a single situation: one person's property is with another person as a result of a contract (either a deposit, *depositum*, or a loan for use, *commodatum*), and that person makes use of it beyond the limits agreed upon. How do these examples illustrate the distinction in (195)? See also below, Section 3, on "theft of use" (*furtum usus*).

2. What is "handling" (*contrectatio*)? Suppose that I pick up your vase and decide to steal it at the first opportunity. Have I already stolen it in Roman

law? The verb *contrectare* often seems to have the sense, not just of "handling," but also of "appropriating" by treating the object as one's own. Note that the word *furtum* itself seems to derive from the verb *ferre* ("to carry off"); why do the jurists insist on a broader concept? See also Case 120 for one odd result of their emphasis on "handling."

3. In a famous fragment, Paul (D. 47.2.1.3) defines *furtum* as "the fraudulent handling (*contrectatio*) of an object with the intent to make a profit either from the thing itself or from its use or possession." How does this definition differ from Gaius'? Is it more adequate? Keep Paul's definition in mind as you examine the cases below.

4. Compare also Sabinus' definition of *furtum* in the early classical period: "A person who handled another's property, when he ought to judge that he does this against the owner's will, is liable for *furtum*" (Gellius, *Attic Nights* 11.18.20). Sabinus also held (21): "A person who, to profit from it, took away another's property that was lying about, is obligated for *furtum* whether or not he knew whose it was." (Cf. Case 115 below.) Is this latter example consistent with Sabinus' definition of *furtum*?

5. How widely should "theftuous intent" be understood? Some curious and contradictory texts deal with persons who abduct slave women in order to have sexual relations. Paul (*Sent.* 2.31.12; D. 47.2.83.2) holds that it is theft to do this, whether or not the slave woman is by trade a prostitute; but Ulpian (D. 47.2.39) emphatically holds that this is not theft at least when the woman is a prostitute. "For," says Ulpian, "it is not the act that is examined, but the cause of the act; but the cause of the act was lust, not theft." Do you agree? Would Ulpian hold differently if the woman were not a prostitute?

Case 106: Intent Alone

D. 47.2.1.1–2 (Paulus, libro trigensimo nono ad Edictum)

Inde sola cogitatio furti faciendi non facit furem. (2) Sic is, qui depositum abnegat, non statim etiam furti tenetur, sed ita, si id intercipiendi causa occultaverit.

(Paul in the thirty-ninth book on the Edict)

Thus the mere plan to commit theft (*furtum*) does not make one a thief. (2) So a person who denies (the existence of) a deposit is not at once liable for theft, but only if he conceals it in order to steal it.

The Hypothetical Problem:

I leave a silver table with you for safekeeping. When I later come to you and demand the table back, you deny that you have it. Are you liable for theft?

Discussion:

1. Why does Roman law not punish the intent to steal?

2. What is the logic of section (2)? Suppose that I deposit an object with you, and when I reclaim it, you deny that a deposit is made. What might your reason be, other than to steal the object? If you deny the deposit, and also intend to steal the deposited object, are you then a thief? (The answer is not necessarily; you may simply forget that you have the object, even though you intend to steal it.)

3. Ulpian (D. 47.2.52.19) writes: "No one commits theft by speech or writing; for our law is that theft is not committed without handling." What sort of a case might he be thinking of? Suppose that I falsely persuade you that you owe me 50,000 sesterces, and you undertake to pay this amount. At what point do I become a thief?

Case 107: Embezzlement

D. 47.2.52.7 (Ulpianus, libro trigensimo septimo ad Edictum)

Eum creditorem, qui post solutam pecuniam pignus non reddat, teneri furti Mela ait, si celandi animo retineat: quod verum esse arbitror.

(Ulpian in the thirty-seventh book on the Edict)

Mela says that when a creditor does not return a pledged object (*pignus*) after the money is paid, he is liable for *furtum* if he retains it with the intent to conceal it. I think this view is correct.

Discussion:

1. We ordinarily think of theft as larceny, taking an object from the owner against his or her will and with the intent to deprive the owner of its use. Here, however, the owner has voluntarily consigned the object to his or her creditor as security for a debt; by this consignment, the creditor obtained lawful possession of the object. All that the creditor then did was to conceal it from the debtor. Mela holds that this too is *furtum*. Do you see any difficulties in his view? Do instances such as this help to explain why the jurists insist on "handling" (rather than "asportation" or "conversion") as the crucial element of theft?

2. Modern Anglo-American criminal law tends to merge the crimes of larceny (the taking of another's property) and embezzlement (the fraudulent use of another's property lawfully in one's possession) into an overarching offense committed by one "who dishonestly appropriates the property of another," in the words of the British Theft Act of 1968 (chap. 60, sec. 1). "Appropriation" is defined as "any assumption by a person of the rights of an owner" (chap. 60, sec. 3(1)). In the United States, the Model Penal Code (sec. 223.1) reaches a broadly similar result. The overarching offense somewhat resembles in its sweep the Roman delict of *furtum*. In general, modern law has tried to consolidate various formerly separate crimes against property, including larceny, embezzlement, obtaining property by false pretenses, receipt of stolen property, and even extortion. What reasons might underlie this consolidation? To what extent might similar reasons underlie the broad Roman definition of *furtum*? Should the penalties be the same for all these types of offenses?

Case 108: Taking Advantage of Another's Mistake

D. 13.1.18 (Scaevola, libro quarto Quaestionum)

Quoniam furtum fit, cum quis indebitos nummos sciens acceperit, videndum, si procurator suos nummos solvat, an ipsi furtum fiat. et Pomponius Epistularum libro octavo ipsum condicere ait ex causa furtiva: sed et me condicere, si ratum habeam quod indebitum datum sit. sed altera condictione altera tollitur.

(Scaevola in the fourth book of *Questions*)
Since theft (*furtum*) is committed when someone knowingly accepts unowed money, we must examine whether theft is committed against a procurator if he pays his own coins. Pomponius, in the eighth book of his *Letters*, says that there is a suit for recovery on the basis of theft (*condictio ex causa furtiva*), but that I too can sue for recovery if I ratified the payment of what was not owed. But the one suit for recovery is excluded by the other.

Discussion:

1. Why is it *furtum* when someone accepts money that he or she is not owed? How does this type of *furtum* differ from those discussed in the Cases above?

2. My procurator (a sort of general manager) uses his own money to pay a debt that I do not owe; the recipient is aware of the non-existence of the debt. As this Case indicates, the procurator can sue for recovery of the money (by the *condictio furtiva*) if I do not ratify the transaction; if I do ratify it, both of us can sue for recovery, but one suit excludes the other. Do you follow the logic? There would also be a suit on the delict of theft against the recipient.

3. Would it be theft if I paid you unowed money when I knew that I did not owe it?

Case 109: False Pretenses

D. 47.2.52.15 (Ulpianus, libro trigensimo septimo ad Edictum)

Servus, qui se liberum adfirmavit, ut sibi pecunia crederetur, furtum non facit: namque hic nihil amplius quam idoneum se debitorem adfirmat. idem est et in eo, qui se patrem familias finxit, cum esset filius familias, ut sibi promptius pecunia crederetur.

(Ulpian in the thirty-seventh book on the Edict)

A slave who stated that he was free so that he could get a loan of money does not commit *furtum*; for he states no more than that he is a suitable debtor. The same is true also for one who pretended to be a *paterfamilias* when he was a son-in-power, in order that money be advanced to him more readily.

Discussion:

1. What is the difference between fraudulently accepting an unowed debt (Case 108) and deliberately misrepresenting one's legal status in order to obtain a loan?

2. Although the person in this Case may escape liability for theft, he is probably liable for the praetorian delict of *dolus*; see Chapter VI, Part A. Ulpian (D. 47.2.43.3) holds:

   If someone did not lie regarding his status, but used words fraudulently, he deceives more than commits a *furtum*; e.g., if he said that he was wealthy, or would use for trade the money he received, or would give suitable guarantors or would repay the money at once. In all these situations he deceives more than commits *furtum*, and so he is not liable for *furtum*. But because he acts with *dolus*, an action will be given on *dolus* unless there is another available against him.

   Is this a better way to handle such cases?

3. However, other sources hold it is theft to misrepresent oneself as another's business manager (procurator) and receive money from that person's debtor; see, e.g., Papinian, D. 47.2.81.6. But Ulpian (D. 47.2.43.1) reports a distinction drawn by Neratius: if the debtor intended that the money be conveyed to the principal and the false procurator appropriated it, then the false procurator is liable for theft; but if the debtor intended that the money belong to the procurator, the procurator "does not commit theft by receiving coins with their owner's consent." Is this distinction reconcilable with other Cases?

Case 110: Aiding and Abetting a Theft

Gaius, *Institutiones* 3.202

Interdum furti tenetur qui ipse furtum non feçerit, qualis est cuius ope consilio furtum factum est. in quo numero est qui nummos tibi excussit ut eos alius
subriperet, vel obstitit tibi ut alius subriperet, aut oves aut boves tuas fugavit ut
alius eas exciperet. et hoc veteres scripserunt de eo qui panno rubro fugavit
armentum. sed si quid per lasciviam, et non data opera ut furtum committere-
tur, factum sit, videbimus an utilis actio dari debeat, cum per legem Aquiliam,
quae de damno lata est, etiam culpa puniatur.

(Gaius in the third book of his *Institutes*)
Sometimes a person is liable for *furtum* when he does not commit
the *furtum* himself; for instance, someone by whose aid and advice
a *furtum* is committed. In this category is a person who knocks
coins away from you so that someone else may steal them, or ob-
structs you so that another may steal, or puts to flight your sheep
or cattle for another to catch. So the Republican jurists wrote of a
person who stampeded a herd with a red flag. But if this is done as
a prank, and not as a deliberate effort to commit a *furtum*, we will
see whether an analogous (Aquilian) action should be given, since
under the Lex Aquilia, which concerns loss, *culpa* too is punished.

Discussion:

1. Must the defendant be cooperating with the real thief? See Ulpian, D.
   47.2.50.3: "A person is held to give advice if he persuades, directs, and facili-
   tates with advice for committing the theft; a person lends aid if he provides
   help and assistance for taking the object." Why is this person as much a thief
   as the actual taker? Is the accomplice liable even if the attempted theft is unsuccessful?

2. With this Case, compare closely Case 22 ("Causing a Stampede"). Try to define the boundary between *furtum* and Aquilian liability. Could both actions
   sometimes lie?

3. Paul (D. 50.16.53.2) holds "that no one is held to have given aid unless he also
   has hostile intent, nor is it wrong to have hostile intent unless an act also followed." Is this theory consistently applied by the jurists?

Case 111: Bad Counsel

D. 47.2.36 pr. (Ulpianus, libro quadragensimo primo ad Sabinum)

Qui servo persuasit, ut fugeret, fur non est: nec enim qui alicui malum consilium dedit, furtum facit, non magis quam si ei persuasit, ut se praecipitet aut manus sibi inferret: haec enim furti non admittunt actionem. sed si alius ei fugam persuaserit, ut ab alio subripiatur, furti tenebitur is qui persuasit, quasi ope consilio eius furtum factum sit. plus Pomponius scripsit eum, qui persuasit, quamvis interim furti non teneretur, tunc tamen incipere teneri, cum quis fugitivi fur esse coeperit, quasi videatur ope consilio eius furtum factum.

(Ulpian in the forty-first book on Sabinus)

Someone who persuaded a slave to run away is not a thief; for a person who gave bad advice to someone does not commit *furtum*, no more than if he persuaded him to jump off a height or kill himself. For these things do not give rise to the action on *furtum*. But if one person persuades him to flee in order that he be stolen by another, the one who persuaded will be liable for *furtum* on the theory that the *furtum* was committed with his aid and advice. Pomponius wrote further that the one who persuaded, although he is not liable for *furtum* in the meantime, still does become liable when someone steals the fugitive slave, it being held that the *furtum* was committed with his aid and advice.

The Hypothetical Problem:

Titius persuades Cassia's slave to run away, and the slave does so. Is Titius liable to Cassia for theft of the slave?

Discussion:

1. Why is it not theft to persuade someone else's slave to run away? How does the theft committed by the second party change the situation?

2. According to Africanus (D. 47.2.61), "Just as a fugitive slave woman is regarded as committing *furtum* of herself, so too by 'handling' she makes her child stolen." Although this odd theory is not consistently adopted in classical law, does it suggest how someone who advises flight could be regarded as a thief?

3. Pomponius appears to hold that if you persuade a slave to run away, and the slave is then stolen by a third party, you are a thief even if you were not cooperating with the third party. Can this extremely harsh view be justified? Pomponius (cited by Ulpian, D. 47.2.36.2) also held that if the fugitive slave stole anything from the master, the persuader is liable on theft for this. What social considerations may motivate his decisions?

4. Is it theft to harbor a fugitive slave? Ulpian (D. 47.2.48.3) holds that harboring is theft if the person acts both against the owner's will and with the intent to conceal; if either requirement is not met, there is no *furtum*. Is this a straightforward application of ordinary theft doctrine?

5. Is it theft to release a chained slave? Ulpian (D. 4.3.7.7) preserves a curious opinion apparently from the high classical jurist Venuleius, who holds that: "If you did not do this for motives of pity, you are liable for *furtum*; if for pity, an action *in factum* should be given." In the latter case, there is no intent to steal; but is the intent clear in the first case?

Case 112: Summoning a Muleteer into Court

D. 47.2.67.2 (Paulus, libro septimo ad Plautium)

Eum, qui mulionem dolo malo in ius vocasset, si interea mulae perissent, furti teneri veteres responderunt.

(Paul in the seventh book on Plautius)

The Republican jurists responded that a person was liable for *furtum* when he deceitfully (*dolo malo*) summoned a muleteer into court and the mules were lost in the meantime.

Discussion:

1. This Case is a very difficult one. What does Paul mean by "deceitfully (*dolo malo*) summon[ing] a muleteer into court": that the lawsuit was not seriously intended in itself, or rather that it was brought to get the muleteer away from his mules so that they could be stolen? In sum, is it necessary to assume that the deceitful plaintiff was cooperating with the actual thief? If we do not assume this, in what sense can the deceitful plaintiff be said to have "handled" the mules? Unfortunately, the jurists do not provide clear answers to these questions, nor to those that follow. What do you think the answers should be?

2. Pomponius (D. 47.2.37) sets the following case: "If my tame peacock escaped from my house, and you pursued it until it was lost, I will be able to sue you for *furtum* provided that someone eventually took it." What fact situation does Pomponius appear to presuppose? Is his decision any less difficult than the case of the muleteer?

3. I assure you that Titius is a good credit risk, and others tell you the same; I then bring forward someone else who I falsely claim is Titius, and you lend that person money. Have the other person and I committed *furtum*? Paul (D. 47.2.67.4) holds that if the other person and I are both aware of the deception, then we are both liable for theft (why?); but if he is not aware, then neither he nor I is liable for theft, but an action *in factum* for theft lies against me. Does this ruling make sense? The critical part of the ruling is Paul's holding that I am not liable as an accomplice in situations where the actual recipient is not himself liable as a thief. Do you see the logic? Can it be applied to the cases discussed above?

Case 113: False Weights

D. 47.2.52.22 (Ulpianus, libro trigensimo septimo ad Edictum)

Maiora quis pondera tibi commodavit, cum emeres ad pondus: furti eum venditori teneri Mela scribit: te quoque, si scisti: nam non ex voluntate venditoris accipis, cum erret in pondere.

(Ulpian in the thirty-seventh book on the Edict)
You were buying by weight, and someone lent you weights that were heavier (than correct ones); Mela writes that he is liable to the seller for *furtum*, and that you also are liable if you knew. For you do not acquire by the seller's will when he is mistaken about the weight.

The Hypothetical Problem:

You purchase a large quantity of wheat from me at two sesterces per pound; in order to determine the price, the wheat must be weighed. Titius lends you weights that are supposed to be scaled in pounds, but are in fact heavier. As a result I lose money on the sale. Can I sue Titius for theft?

Discussion:

1. If Titius and you were both aware that the weights were too heavy, you are both liable for *furtum*; this case presents few difficulties. Much harder is the situation where only Titius is aware. Mela and Ulpian hold that Titius is liable for *furtum*; why? Did Titius "handle" the wheat? Did Titius necessarily intend to profit from the transaction?

2. You owe me money; you persuade my slave to erase your name from my record of the debt, so that the debt cannot be recovered. Ulpian (D. 47.2.52.23), following Mela, holds that you are liable to me for *furtum*. Note that in this case the basic components of *furtum* are attenuated almost beyond recognition, since no property is "handled" at all. Can any theory be found to justify this decision? (Note that erasure of documents can also result in Aquilian liability, see Case 46; does it make more sense to treat erasure in this way rather than as a case of *furtum*?)

3. In light of this Case and the preceding one, is there any coherent way to define *furtum*? Consider, for instance, the following definition: "intentional and secret appropriation of a thing which belongs to another." Does this cover all the cases discussed above?

Case 114: The Owner's Consent

D. 47.2.46.7–8 (Ulpianus, libro quadragensimo secundo ad Sabinum)

Recte dictum est, qui putavit se domini voluntate rem attingere, non esse furem: quid enim dolo facit, qui putat dominum consensurum fuisse, sive falso id sive vere putet? is ergo solus fur est, qui adtrectavit, quod invito domino se facere scivit. (8) Per contrarium quaeritur, si ego me invito domino facere putarem, cum dominus vellet, an furti actio sit. et ait Pomponius furtum me facere: verum tamen est, ut, cum ego velim eum uti, licet ignoret, ne furti sit obligatus.

(Ulpian in the forty-second book on Sabinus)

It is correctly held that a person is not a thief when he thought he handled the thing with its owner's consent; for how does he act with *dolus* if he thinks that the owner would consent, whether he thinks this wrongly or rightly? Therefore he alone is a thief who handled what he knew he did against the owner's will. (8) Conversely it is asked whether there is an action on *furtum* if I think I act against the owner's will, and the owner is (in fact) willing. Pomponius says that I commit *furtum*; but the correct view is that since I wish him to use it, although he is unaware (of this), he is not obligated for *furtum*.

Discussion:

1. What does this Case require in order for an act to be theft?

2. The rule in section (7) is wider than the text suggests. For instance, Gaius (*Inst.* 2.50) holds that it is not *furtum* if an heir sells or gives away property that the deceased had borrowed or leased, provided that the heir believes that this property belongs to the estate; "for *furtum* is not committed without the intent to steal." For further applications, see Section 3 below.

3. In section (8), why does Ulpian hold, against Pomponius, that theftuous intent is a necessary but not a sufficient requirement for *furtum*? Do you agree? See also the next Case.

Case 115: A Found Object

D. 47.2.43.5–9 (Ulpianus, libro quadragensimo primo ad Sabinum)

Quod si dominus id dereliquit, furtum non fit eius, etiamsi ego furandi animum habuero: nec enim furtum fit, nisi sit cui fiat: in proposito autem nulli fit, quippe cum placeat Sabini et Cassii sententia existimantium statim nostram esse desinere rem, quam derelinquimus. (6) Sed si non fuit derelictum, putavit tamen derelictum, furti non tenetur. (7) Sed si neque fuit neque putavit, iacens tamen tulit, non ut lucretur, sed redditurus ei cuius fuit, non tenetur furti. (8) Proinde videamus, si nescit cuius esset, sic tamen tulit quasi redditurus ei qui desiderasset vel qui ostendisset rem suam, an furti obligetur. et non puto obligari eum. solent plerique etiam hoc facere, ut libellum proponant continentem invenisse se et redditurum ei qui desideraverit: hi ergo ostendunt non furandi animo se fecisse. (9) Quid ergo, si *euretra* quae dicunt petat? nec hic videtur furtum facere, etsi non probe petat aliquid.

(Ulpian in the forty-first book on Sabinus)
Therefore if the owner abandoned it, there is no *furtum* of it even if I had the intent to steal. For no *furtum* is committed unless it is done to someone, but in this case it is done to no one; for, indeed, the prevailing view is that of Sabinus and Cassius, who think that an object we abandon ceases at once to be ours. (6) But if it was not abandoned, but he (the finder) thought it was abandoned, he is not liable for *furtum*. (7) But if it was neither (abandoned) nor did he think it to be, but he took it (while it was) lying about (with the intention) not to profit but to return it to its owner, he is not liable for *furtum*. (8) So let us examine whether he is obligated for *furtum* if he does not know whose it is, but takes it as if to return it to anyone who claimed it or showed that it was his. I do not think he is obligated. For many persons commonly do this in order to post a notice that they have found it and will return it to the claimant; so they show that they did not act with the intent to steal. (9) But what if he asks for what they call (in Greek) a finder's fee? He too is not held to commit *furtum*, although he is not right to ask for something.

The Hypothetical Problem:

You find a wallet lying on a path. What should you do?

Discussion:

1. Describe the legal consequences of the various courses of action you can take. Does Roman law seem sufficiently realistic in dealing with these various acts?

2. A ballplayer tosses his jacket down at the edge of a playing field, and then forgets to pick it up before going home. The next morning you find the jacket. Has the owner abandoned it? Are you entitled to assume that the

jacket has been abandoned? Would it be different if you found the jacket in a trash can?

3. Is a finder legally obliged to advertise for the owner, even if he or she assumes that the object was abandoned? What legal risks does the finder run if no notice is posted? Why can the finder not demand a reward? Can he or she at least demand repayment of expenses on advertising?

4. Particularly difficult problems are created by the jettison of cargo from foundering ships. For instance, Ulpian (D. 47.2.43.11) holds that if the owner, in jettisoning the cargo, assumes it will be permanently lost (and this, says Ulpian, is the usual assumption), then it belongs to the finder. But if he assumes that it will still belong to him, then he can claim it from the finder. In the latter case, the finder is liable for *furtum* if he or she had theftuous intent, but not for a mistaken belief that the cargo had been abandoned. How realistic is this decision?

Case 116: Crime and Delict

D. 47.2.93 (Ulpianus, libro trigensimo octavo ad Edictum)

Meminisse oportebit nunc furti plerumque criminaliter agi et eum qui agit in crimen subscribere, non quasi publicum sit iudicium, sed quia visum est temeritatem agentium etiam extraordinaria animadversione coercendam. non ideo tamen minus, si qui velit, poterit civiliter agere.

(Ulpian in the thirty-eighth book on the Edict)

It must be remembered that criminal proceedings for *furtum* are at present frequent, and the plaintiff brings the complaint for the crime, not on the theory that this is a public trial, but because it seemed proper that the boldness of offenders be also sanctioned by punishment in proceedings *extra ordinem*. But still, if someone wishes, he can bring a civil suit.

Discussion:

1. As this text indicates, by the late classical period many instances of *furtum* were normally dealt with outside private law (*extra ordinem*), and criminal sanctions were inflicted on convicted defendants. What advantages does this system have over the earlier system of private remedies? Remember that many thieves will have no assets with which to pay a judgment.

2. Julian (D. 47.2.57.1) says that a victim who uses the criminal action loses the private action on theft; why?

3. The process whereby *furtum* came to be recognized as primarily a crime is little known. Already in the late Republic and early Empire, certain aggravated types of theft, especially those associated with violence, were handled through criminal law. Gradually this criminal law was extended, although still in Ulpian's day many common thefts were still normally just private delicts. Thus, Ulpian (*Collatio* 7.4.1) says: "Daytime thieves should be remitted to private law, but nighttime thieves should be investigated *extra ordinem* and, when the case has been heard, punished." On the ancient distinction between theft at night and by day, see Case 68.

4. In view of the very wide definition that the jurists gave to the private delict of *furtum*, would you favor treating all instances of the private delict as crimes? Consider, for instance, the borrower who uses silverware beyond the agreement with the lender (Case 105).

Section 2: The Object of Theft

Case 117: Theft of One's Own Property

Gaius, *Institutiones* 3.200

Aliquando etiam suae rei quisque furtum committit, veluti si debitor rem quam creditori pignori dedit subtraxerit, vel si bonae fidei possessori rem meam possidenti subripuerim. unde placuit eum qui servum suum, quem alius bona fide possidebat, ad se reversum celaverit, furtum committere.

(Gaius in the third book of his *Institutes*)

Sometimes a person commits *furtum* even of his own property, e.g., if a debtor steals a thing that he gave to a creditor as a pledge (*pignus*), or if I steal from someone who possesses my property in good faith. Hence the prevailing view is that a person commits *furtum* if a slave, whom another possessed in good faith, returned to his owner and was concealed by him.

Discussion:

1. With this Case, compare Cases 80–81 on Aquilian liability. A pledgor is a person who gives a pledge (*pignus*) to a creditor in order to secure payment of a debt; a good faith possessor is someone who takes possession of an object without realizing that another owns it. Are their positions strictly comparable? On what theory does the owner "steal" his or her own property in these cases? See further below, Section 4 (especially Case 123).

2. My slave comes into the hands of a good faith possessor; the slave escapes and returns to me; I take in the slave and conceal him from the good faith possessor. In what sense am I a thief? Does Gaius presume that I know the good faith possessor is looking for the slave? See also above, Case 111.

3. If someone can steal property that belongs to him or her, then what is the crucial property interest protected by the delict of *furtum*? Is it possession?

Case 118: Theft of Land?

Aulus Gellius, *Noctes Atticae* 11.18.13

In quo id quoque scriptum est, quod volgo inopinatum est, non hominum tantum neque rerum moventium, quae auferri occulte et subripi possunt, sed fundi quoque et aedium fieri furtum; condemnatum quoque furti colonum, qui fundo, quem conduxerat, vendito possessione eius dominum intervertisset.

(Aulus Gellius in the eleventh book of his *Attic Nights*)
In this (Sabinus' monograph on *furtum*) it is also written — what is not commonly suspected — that *furtum* is committed not just of slaves and movable objects that can be secretly taken away and stolen, but also of a farm and buildings; a tenant farmer, who sold the farm he had leased and (thereby) defrauded the owner of its possession, was condemned for *furtum*.

Discussion:

1. Sabinus' view that land can be stolen was rejected in later classical law; as Gaius (*Inst.* 2.51) says, "the opinion of those who think that a farm can be an object of theft has been disapproved." Given the very wide classical definition of *furtum*, why did the jurists draw the line at movable objects? Is it that land cannot be "handled" in the way that movable objects can?

2. Usucapion is a means of acquiring ownership of another's property by possessing it for a legally prescribed length of time. By law, it is not possible to usucapt stolen property. One consequence of limiting theft to movables is that if a person takes possession of land in good faith, and holds this possession for two years, he or she acquires ownership through usucapion. Does this relatively narrow time-frame provide an argument for accepting Sabinus' view?

3. Although land cannot be stolen, it is possible to steal things by separating them from land. Ulpian (D. 47.2.25.2) gives as examples trees, stones, gravel, and fruits.

Case 119: Theft of Free Persons

Gaius, *Institutiones* 3.199

Interdum autem etiam liberorum hominum furtum fit, veluti si quis liberorum nostrorum qui in potestate nostra sint, sive etiam uxor quae in manu nostra sit, sive etiam iudicatus vel auctoratus meus subreptus fuerit.

(Gaius in the third book of his *Institutes*)

Sometimes there is *furtum* even of free persons, e.g., if one of our children who are in our power was stolen, or also a wife who is in our *manus*, or also my judgment debtor or my sworn gladiator.

Discussion:

1. This is perhaps the most extraordinary extension of the delict of *furtum*; other sources leave no doubt that this rule was accepted in classical law. Children in the power of their *paterfamilias*, like wives in the old-fashioned form of *manus*-marriage, are dependents of the *paterfamilias*. A judgment debtor has been condemned in a lawsuit and then "adjudged" to the plaintiff in order to work off the debt; a sworn gladiator (*auctoratus*) has hired himself out as a gladiator and is regarded as entirely dependent on his employer. In what sense is it possible to "steal" such persons from someone?

2. What is the measure of damages in a trial on *furtum* for theft of a free person?

3. Paul (D. 47.2.38.1) notes that although it is possible to sue on *furtum* for theft of free persons, it is not possible to bring an action for their recovery (*condictio furtiva*). Is this logical? However, a *paterfamilias* does have an action that requires the person holding them to produce children in his power.

Case 120: Theft of a Part

D. 47.2.21 pr. (Ulpianus, libro quadragensimo ad Sabinum)

Volgaris est quaestio, an is, qui ex acervo frumenti modium sustulit, totius rei furtum faciat an vero eius tantum quod abstulit. Ofilius totius acervi furem esse putat: nam et qui aurem alicuius tetigit, inquit Trebatius totum eum videri tetigisse: proinde et qui dolium aperuit et inde parvum vini abstulit, non tantum eius quod abstulit, verum totius videtur fur esse. sed verum est in tantum eos furti actione teneri, quantum abstulerunt....

(Ulpian in the fortieth book on Sabinus)

It is a commonly raised question whether a person who took a bushel from a pile of grain commits *furtum* of the entire object or only of as much as he removed. Ofilius thinks that he steals the whole pile; for Trebatius also says that a person who touched someone's ear is held to have touched the entire person. Hence also someone who opened a container and took from it a small amount of wine is considered to steal not just what he took, but all of it. But the correct view is that they are liable in an action on *furtum* for only as much as they took....

Discussion:

1. The jurists seem to have found this question very difficult. What is the underlying problem? When a person "breaks bulk" by opening a container, he or she might be thought to "handle" the entire contents of the container, even though only some of the contents are actually taken. This could explain the vat of wine; is the pile of grain essentially similar? Do you prefer Ulpian's solution to that of the late Republican jurists whom he cites? Why?

2. Ulpian (D. 47.2.21.8) sets the following case: A person opens a cupboard that is too heavy for him to move, and handles its contents. Ulpian holds him liable only for what he takes. But Ulpian goes on to say that if he could have moved the container, he is liable for the theft of it and all its contents, even though he only takes some objects. What logic supports this odd ruling? Does the ruling depend on the jurists' use of "handling," rather than asportation, as the basic criterion for defining *furtum*?

Section 3: Theft of Use (Furtum Usus)

Case 121: Riding a Borrowed Horse

D. 47.2.40 (Paulus, libro nono ad Sabinum)

Qui iumenta sibi commodata longius duxerit alienave re invito domino usus sit, furtum facit.

(Paul in the ninth book on Sabinus)
A person who borrowed horses and took them further (than was agreed), or who used another's property against the owner's will, commits *furtum*.

The Hypothetical Problem:

You borrow my horse in order to ride to the neighboring town; you then ride it to the town next further. Are you liable to me for theft?

Discussion:

1. You have plainly violated our agreement. Why is your violation handled as *furtum*, rather than through contract law? You might begin to answer this question by thinking about what measurable loss I suffer as a result of your act.

2. Modern scholars believe that the problem of "theft of use" was what led the Roman jurists to insist on "handling," rather than asportation, as the crucial criterion of *furtum*; see Case 105 above. Do you follow the logic?

3. The term *furtum usus* ("theft of use") is modern, and misleading to the extent that it suggests that the use itself is being stolen. Rather, it is the object that is stolen through use of it, and accordingly the plaintiff sues for a multiple of the object's value, not for a multiple of the value of the use. Aulus Gellius (*Attic Nights* 7.15.1) reports Labeo's view that this was unduly punitive; do you agree?

4. In order to avoid excessive harshness, classical jurists require that the offender act in the conscious belief that the owner would not consent to the act; see, e.g., Gaius, *Inst.* 3.197 (= Case 105); Pomponius, D. 47.2.77 pr. If he or she believes that the owner would assent, the act is not theft. Why should the offender be allowed to assume such consent without expressly obtaining it?

Case 122: Lending a Borrowed Object

D. 47.2.55.1 (Gaius, libro tertio decimo ad Edictum Provinciale)

Eum, qui quod utendum accepit ipse alii commodaverit, furti obligari responsum est. ex quo satis apparet furtum fieri et si quis usum alienae rei in suum lucrum convertat. nec movere quem debet, quasi nihil lucri sui gratia faciat: species enim lucri est ex alieno largiri et beneficii debitorem sibi adquirere. unde et is furti tenetur, qui ideo rem amovet, ut eam alii donet.

(Gaius in the thirteenth book on the Provincial Edict)
It was responded that a person who received the use of an object and lent it to another person (for his gratuitous use) is obligated for *furtum.* Hence it appears that *furtum* is committed also if someone appropriates for his own profit (*lucrum*) the use of another's property. Nor should it sway anyone that he seemingly does nothing for his own profit; for it is a kind of profit to bestow another's property and gain for oneself a debtor from the benefit. Hence also a person is liable for *furtum* who removes property in order to give it to someone else (for free).

The Hypothetical Problem:

You borrow a set of table silver from me, and you then lend it to Cassia. Are you liable to me for theft?

Discussion:

1. What concept of "profit" (*lucrum*) does Gaius rely on in order to reach his decision? Does this concept seem too large?

2. Ulpian (D. 47.2.48.4) puts the following case: I give you my clothing for cleaning; you lend it to Titius from whom it is stolen. Because you are liable for the safekeeping of the clothing (see Case 124), I can sue you for theft; but you can also sue the thief for theft. As Ulpian comments, "Thus there will be a case in which a thief can sue for *furtum.*" Does this result seem plausible?

Section 4: The Plaintiff

Case 123: "Interest"

Gaius, *Institutiones* 3.203–204

Furti autem actio ei competit cuius interest rem salvam esse, licet dominus non sit. itaque nec domino aliter competit quam si eius intersit rem non perire. (204) Unde constat creditorem de pignore subrepto furti agere posse, adeo quidem ut quamvis ipse dominus, id est ipse debitor, eam rem subripuerit nihilo minus creditori competat actio furti.

(Gaius in the third book of his *Institutes*)
The action on *furtum* belongs to the person who has an interest in the object being safe, even if he is not the owner. So it (the action) does not belong to the owner unless he has an interest in the thing not being lost. (204) Hence it is agreed that a creditor can sue on *furtum* regarding a stolen pledge (*pignus*), to such an extent that even though the object is stolen by its owner, i.e. the debtor, nonetheless the creditor has the action on *furtum*.

Discussion:

1. This Case explains the theory underlying Case 117. How clear is the concept of "interest"?

2. What exactly is the creditor's interest? Paul (D. 47.2.15 pr.) holds that, if a third party steals the object, only the creditor can sue, but that the debtor can bring an action on pledge against the creditor in order to recover any excess over the value of the debt. This would appear to mean that the creditor's interest is defined as the full value of the pledged object. What theory might justify this rule? The Romans seem to uphold the rule even if the debtor retains possession of the pledge (see Gaius, D. 47.2.49 pr.).

3. Those with limited property rights, such as usufructuaries and good faith possessors, also have the action on theft even against the owner. But Julian (D. 47.2.54.4) denied the action to a good faith possessor against the owner unless the possessor had a financial interest in retaining the object. Does this seem more sensible?

Case 124: Fullers and Tailors

Gaius, *Institutiones* 3.205–207

Item, si fullo polienda curandave aut sarcinator sarcienda vestimenta mercede certa acceperit eaque furto amiserit, ipse furti habet actionem, non dominus, quia domini nihil interest ea non periisse, cum iudicio locati a fullone aut sarcinatore suum consequi possit, si modo is fullo aut sarcinator rei praestandae sufficiat; nam si solvendo non est, tunc quia ab eo dominus suum consequi non potest, ipsi furti actio competit, quia hoc casu ipsius interest rem salvam esse. (206) Quae de fullone aut sarcinatore diximus, eadem transferemus et ad eum cui rem commodavimus. nam ut illi mercedem capiendo custodiam praestant, ita hic quoque utendi commodum percipiendo similiter necesse habet custodiam praestare. (207) Sed is apud quem res deposita est custodiam non praestat, tantumque in eo obnoxius est, si quid ipse dolo malo fecerit. qua de causa si res ei subrepta fuerit, quia restituendae eius nomine depositi non tenetur nec ob id eius interest rem salvam esse, furti agere non potest, sed ea actio domino competit.

(Gaius in the third book of his *Institutes*)

Likewise, if for a fixed fee a fuller receives clothes for smoothing or cleaning, or a tailor for mending, and he loses them by *furtum*, he has the action on *furtum*, and not the owner, since the owner has no interest in their not being lost; for in an action on hire he can recover from the fuller or tailor, provided that the fuller or tailor has sufficient means to pay. For if he is insolvent, then, because the owner cannot recover from him, he (the owner) has the action on theft, since in this case he has an interest in the object being safe. (206) What I said about the fuller or tailor I will apply also to the borrower. For as they are liable for safekeeping (*custodia*) by receiving a fee, so too he (the borrower), by receiving the benefit of use, must similarly be liable for *custodia*. (207) But a person who receives a deposit is not liable for *custodia*, and is liable only if he acts with *dolus malus*. Accordingly, if the object is stolen from him, since he is not liable to restore it on the basis of the deposit and therefore has no interest in its being safe, he cannot sue on *furtum*, but the owner has the action.

Discussion:

1. This Case depends on the liabilities that are created through contract. A liability for safekeeping (*custodia*) means that a person is liable for the loss of an object except when it occurs through an irresistible force (*vis maior*). As Gaius indicates, fullers and tailors have such a liability for clothing that they receive; so too do borrowers who receive property gratuitously (under the contract of *commodatum*) for their own use. Why does the existence of this liability mean that it is they, and not the owner, who have the action on theft? What concept of "interest" are the jurists employing?

2. On the other hand, if they are insolvent, the owner still has the action on *furtum*. Why?

3. What if a fuller conspires with the thief? Ulpian (D. 47.2.12.1) holds that, although the fuller still has an interest in the object's not being stolen (in the sense that he must pay the customer for the object), his bad faith results in his not having the action on theft. Does the owner then have it?

4. Like the fuller or the borrower, an innkeeper has liability for *custodia* in the case of property received from guests; see Chapter VII, Part B. The innkeeper therefore also has the action on theft; see Ulpian, D. 47.5.1.4.

5. A depositary gratuitously receives an object (under the contract of *depositum*) and watches it for the owner. Why is the depositary not liable to the owner if the object is stolen? How is this related to the rule that the owner, and not the depositary, has the action on theft?

Case 125: Pledgor Throws Pledge Out Window

D. 13.7.3 (Pomponius, libro octavo decimo ad Sabinum)

Si quasi recepturus a debitore tuo comminus pecuniam reddidisti ei pignus isque per fenestram id misit excepturo eo, quem de industria ad id posuerit, Labeo ait furti te agere cum debitore posse et ad exhibendum: et, si agente te contraria pigneraticia excipiat debitor de pignore sibi reddito, replicabitur de dolo et fraude, per quam nec redditum, sed per fallaciam ablatum id intellegitur.

(Pomponius in the eighteenth book on Sabinus)

If you, believing that you were about to receive payment from your debtor, returned a pledge (*pignus*) to him, and he threw it out a window to be taken by a person he had deliberately positioned for this purpose, Labeo says that you can sue the debtor for *furtum* and also for production of the object (*ad exhibendum*). If you bring the countersuit on pledge, and the debtor raises a defense (*exceptio*) that the object was returned to him, there will be a counterdefense of *dolus* and fraud, (based on the assertion) that the object is not understood as returned, but as taken away by a trick.

The Hypothetical Case:

Cassia owes money to Titius, and has given him an object as a pledge (*pignus*) for payment. Cassia comes to Titius pretending that she is going to pay; Titius hands back the pledge, and Cassia throws it out the window. Is she a thief?

Discussion:

1. The creditor has two actions: one for production of the object (*ad exhibendum*), and one on theft. Why might there have been doubt about the availability of the action on theft?

2. The second sentence of the Case describes some complex rules under formulary procedure. When the creditor brings an action on theft, the debtor inserts into the formula a defense (*exceptio*) that there was no theft because the creditor voluntarily returned the object; the creditor inserts a counterdefense (*replicatio*) that the "voluntary return" resulted from deceit (*dolus*). The litigants had to make sure that their conflicting claims were in the formula, or they might lose the right to plead them before the *iudex*.

Section 5: Violent Theft

Case 126: Violence

Gaius, *Institutiones* 3.209

Qui res alienas rapit, tenetur etiam furti. quis enim magis alienam rem invito domino contrectat quam qui vi rapit? itaque recte dictum est eum improbum furem esse. sed propriam actionem eius delicti nomine Praetor introduxit, quae appellatur vi bonorum raptorum, et est intra annum quadrupli, post annum simpli. quae actio utilis est, etsi quis unam rem, licet minimam, rapuerit.

(Gaius in the third book of his *Institutes*)
A person who violently steals another's property is also liable for *furtum*. For who more truly handles (*contrectat*) another's property against the owner's will than one who violently steals it? So it is rightly held that he is a shameless thief. But the Praetor introduced a separate action for this delict, which is called (the action) for property that was violently robbed, which lies for quadruple (the value of the stolen object) within one year and for simple value thereafter. This action is available even if someone violently steals a single object, even one of minimal value.

Discussion:

1. As in our law, the Romans distinguished robbery (*rapina*) from theft; robbery is associated with overt violence, theft with stealth. The Praetorian action was introduced, in a somewhat different form, during the unsettled late Republic. Note that it too is a private remedy, although a criminal sanction was also usually available.

2. What is the difference between robbery and manifest theft?

Part B: Outrage (*Iniuria*)

The history of the delict of outrage (*iniuria*) is complex. In the classical period, the Praetor's Edict contained a "general" provision making *iniuria* a source of delictual obligation, but also several provisions on specific types of *iniuria*. Modern scholars believe that the "general" edict was based on the Twelve Tables and originally concerned only deliberate physical injury or battery (especially to free persons); at a later date, however, the concept of *iniuria* was widened until it came to include almost any intentional offense to another's personality. But the "special" types of *iniuria* remained in the Edict, alongside the "general" provision.

Iniuria is interesting because it helps to indicate what the Romans viewed as insulting conduct. *Iniuria* may result from assault and battery, trespass to land, defamation, misuse of legal procedure, interference with family relations, preventing the exercise of ordinary citizen rights, and (to a more limited extent) invasion of privacy and interference with economic relations — in short, from a wide variety of offenses to another's dignity and personal well-being, so long as these offenses are deliberate. *Iniuria* thus serves to protect the individual by creating a legally defensible perimeter for his or her personal life. Further, in many instances not only the immediate victim but also his or her family members can sue the offender, on the theory that they too have been outraged by an insult to a relative.

In the action on *iniuria*, the plaintiff claims a monetary sum that estimates the extent of the "outrage" caused by the defendant's conduct; the *iudex* can fix the judgment at this or a lower figure. The judgment is treated as a penalty (*poena*) for the defendant's conduct, rather than as compensation to the victim. If the *iniuria* is aggravated by special circumstances, the judgment can be appreciably higher than for ordinary *iniuria*, and the Praetor sets the amount.

Because of the highly personal nature of *iniuria*, the victim must actually be "outraged" by the conduct in question. Further, he or she must bring action within a year (after which, it is presumed, the sense of outrage is effectively gone); the plaintiff's standing is also not inheritable, since outrage is a personal feeling.

In examining the Cases below, consider how the personal nature of *iniuria* interacts with the secondary function of the delict in maintaining more general standards of social decency and order. On Common Law, compare J.G. Fleming, *An Introduction to the Law of Torts* (2d ed. 1985) 192: "Increasing sophistication has, with the advance of civilization, fostered demands for extending legal protection to nonmaterial interests of personality like self-respect, reputation, and privacy. In actual fact the common law's entry into this field (like the Roman Law's) occurred remarkably early, not so much because it felt any singular tenderness for such claims, but because they happened to become identified with the early law's unremitting concern with public order."

Section 1: The Scope of the Action

Case 127: Types of *Iniuria*

Gaius, *Institutiones* 3.220

Iniuria autem committitur non solum cum quis pugno puta aut fuste percussus vel etiam verberatus erit, sed etiam si cui convicium factum fuerit, sive
quis bona alicuius quasi debitoris, sciens eum nihil sibi debere, proscripserit,
sive quis ad infamiam alicuius libellum aut carmen scripserit, sive quis matrem
familias aut praetextatum adsectatus fuerit, et denique aliis pluribus modis.

(Gaius in the third book of his *Institutes*)

Outrage (*iniuria*) is committed not only by beating someone
with, e.g., a fist or a stick, or even thrashing him, but also by raising a clamor against him, or if someone, knowing that another
owes nothing to him, advertises his estate for sale as a debtor's, or
if he writes a pamphlet or song to defame another, or if he pursues
a matron or a youth, and in short in many other ways.

Discussion:

1. What is the common feature of the various forms of *iniuria* described by
   Gaius?

2. Gaius lays special stress on physical battery. Recall that originally, under the
   Lex Aquilia, free persons could not recover for personal injuries. The action
   on *iniuria* provides recovery under a different theory; even a person who
   was not injured at all can recover from an assailant, provided the battery was
   deliberate. Is this an adequate way of handling the problem?

3. Ulpian (D. 47.10.1.2), following Labeo, distinguishes between three types of
   iniuria: to the body (e.g., striking someone), to the dignity (e.g., abducting
   a woman's chaperon), and to the reputation (e.g., assaulting a woman's
   chastity). Is this classification useful?

4. How is the word *iniuria* differently defined for this action than for the
   Aquilian action? See Case 27.

Case 128: Basis of the Action

Paulus, *Sententiae* 5.4.6–8

Iniuriarum actio aut lege aut more aut mixto iure introducta est. lege Duo-decim Tabularum de famosis carminibus, membris ruptis et ossibus fractis. (7) Moribus, quotiens factum pro qualitate sui arbitrio iudicis aestimatur, congru-entis poenae supplicio vindicatur. (8) Mixto iure actio iniuriarum ex lege Cor-nelia constituitur, quotiens quis pulsatur, vel cuius domus introitur ab his, qui vulgo derectarii appellantur. in quos extra ordinem animadvertitur, ita ut prius ingruentis consilium pro modo commentae fraudis poena vindicetur exilii aut metalli aut operis publici.

(Paul in the fifth book of *Sentences*)

The action on *iniuria* was introduced either by statute or by mo-rality or by mixed law; by the Law of the Twelve Tables, concerning defamatory poems, broken limbs, and broken bones. (7) By moral-ity, when conduct is evaluated in accord with its character through the judgment of a *iudex*, and is avenged by a punishment of appro-priate penalty. (8) By mixed law, an action on *iniuria* is established under the Lex Cornelia when someone is beaten, or his house is en-tered by those who are commonly called "burglars." Against them there is punishment *extra ordinem*, so that the previous intent of the assailant is punished by the penalty of exile or the mines or public works, depending on the degree of the offense committed.

Discussion:

1. This Case (excerpted from a postclassical abridgement of Paul's writings) describes, in rather summary fashion, the three sources of liability for *in-iuria*. The Law of the Twelve Tables (449 B.C.) established liability for physi-cal injury to both free persons and slaves; it also established liability for bat-tery less than mayhem, such as hitting another person's face with one's fist. This latter liability, which the Twelve Tables simply called "outrage" (*iniuria*), was later gradually expanded to form the classical delict of *iniuria*. The Twelve Tables also contained a provision against "evil songs" (*mala carmina*); the provision originally referred to magical spells, but later it was interpreted to mean defamatory poems, which became yet another form of *iniuria*.

2. What is more important is Paul's recognition that the expansion of the origi-nal liability in the Twelve Tables resulted from common morality (*mores*); this suggests the underlying social basis of the classical delict. In examining the Cases that follow, try to determine why each type of *iniuria* is given legal sanction.

3. The Lex Cornelia *de iniuriis*, a statute of 81/80 B.C., provided for criminal penalties in at least three specific cases: beating another person, thrashing him or her, and forcibly entering another person's home. All of these acts were also instances of *iniuria*, so that a defendant was subject to both civil

and criminal liability; under the Lex Cornelia, the defendant had to pay a fine to the offended party. By Paul's time, however, the criminal trial was normally held *extra ordinem*, under an imperial judge; the earlier fines had been replaced by the stiffer sanctions that Paul describes. Why are these three cases deserving of special legal sanction?

4. As with *furtum* (Case 116), *iniuria* in all its forms also eventually came to be treated as a crime, although not until after the classical period of Roman law. The postclassical jurist Hermogenianus (D. 47.10.45) reports:

> With regard to *iniuria*, it is now usual to determine it *extra ordinem* in accord with the case and the person. Slaves are thrashed with whips and returned to their owners; free persons of low rank are subjected to cudgels; and all others are punished either by exile for a term or by forfeiture of specified property.

This text, which dates ca. A.D. 300, reflects the much harsher and more class-oriented temperament of late imperial law.

Case 129: Declaiming Against Someone

D. 47.10.15.2–3, 5–6, 8, 12 (Ulpianus, libro quinquagensimo septimo ad Edictum)

Ait Praetor: 'qui adversus bonos mores convicium cui fecisse cuiusve opera factum esse dicetur, quo adversus bonos mores convicium fieret: in eum iudicium dabo.' (3) Convicium iniuriam esse Labeo ait.... (5) Sed quod adicitur a Praetore 'adversus bonos mores' ostendit non omnem in unum collatam vociferationem Praetorem notare, sed eam, quae bonis moribus improbatur quaeque ad infamiam vel invidiam alicuius spectaret. (6) Idem ait 'adversus bonos mores' sic accipiendum non eius qui fecit, sed generaliter accipiendum adversus bonos mores huius civitatis.... (8) Fecisse convicium non tantum is videtur, qui vociferatus est, verum is quoque, qui concitavit ad vociferationem alios vel qui summisit ut vociferentur.... (11) Ex his apparet non omne maledictum convicium esse: (12) sed id solum, quod cum vociferatione dictum est, sive unus sive plures dixerint, quod in coetu dictum est, convicium est: quod autem non in coetu nec vociferatione dicitur, convicium non proprie dicitur, sed infamandi causa dictum.

(Ulpian in the fifty-seventh book on the Edict)

The Praetor says: "I will give a trial against a person who allegedly raised a clamor (*convicium*) against someone contrary to good morals, or by whose help it allegedly occurred that a clamor was raised contrary to good morals." (3) Labeo says that a clamor is an *iniuria*.... (5) But the Praetor's qualification "contrary to good morals" shows that the Praetor does not censure every outcry directed at a person, but (only) one that offends against good morals and looks to someone's disgrace or odium. (6) He (Labeo) also says that "contrary to good morals" should be interpreted not with respect to (the morals of) the offender, but generally: contrary to the morals of this community.... (8) Not just the person who cried out is held to have raised a clamor, but also a person who roused others to cry out, or who brought about the outcry.... (11) From this it is clear that not all abusive language is a clamor; (12) a clamor is only something that was uttered loudly — whether one person said it or many — and was said in a group. If something is not said in a group nor loudly, it is not properly called a clamor, but (rather) defamatory speech.

Discussion:

1. The Praetor's Edict contained a special provision on the form of *iniuria* called a "clamor" (*convicium*). On the basis of this Case, try to define a "clamor"; what elements must be present? How is a clamor different from defamatory speech in general? Is a *convicium* just an aggravated form of *iniuria*? Why might the Praetor have wished to provide a special remedy for *convicium*?

2. What did Labeo mean by holding (see section 6) that "'contrary to good morals' should be interpreted not with respect to (the morals of) the offender, but generally: contrary to the morals of this community"?

3. The Praetor's Edict also had a special provision against intentionally defamatory accusations when the offender does not proclaim them, but writes or publishes them, or even acts in such a way that disrepute results. Ulpian (D. 47.10.15.27, 31–32) gives some examples: to wear mourning or filthy clothes, or to let one's beard grow (these acts may carry the suggestion that one has been unjustly wronged); to write or post or sing a satirical lampoon; to post for sale a pledged object or to seize another's property (implying that the person's credit is bad). What is the common element underlying these various examples?

4. Is it a defense that the accusation is true? Paul (D. 47.10.18 pr.) says that "it is improper that a person be condemned for defaming a guilty person, since it is proper and beneficial that the faults of the guilty be known." Is this entirely convincing?

5. In modern Anglo-American law, a distinction is drawn between defamation of character (blackening someone's reputation) and invasion of privacy (including, e.g., drawing public attention to facts about someone that he or she would prefer remain secret). Are both these offenses covered by the law of *iniuria*?

Case 130: Accosting a Woman

D. 47.10.15.15, 20–22 (Ulpianus, libro quinquagensimo septimo ad Edictum)

Si quis virgines appellasset, si tamen ancillari veste vestitas, minus peccare videtur: multo minus, si meretricia veste feminae, non matrum familiarum vestitae fuissent. si igitur non matronali habitu femina fuerit et quis eam appellavit vel ei comitem abduxit, iniuriarum tenetur.... (20) Appellare est blanda oratione alterius pudicitiam adtemptare: hoc enim non est convicium, sed adversus bonos mores adtemptare. (21) Qui turpibus verbis utitur, non temptat pudicitiam, sed iniuriarum tenetur. (22) Aliud est appellare, aliud adsectari: appellat enim, qui sermone pudicitiam adtemptat, adsectatur, qui tacitus frequenter sequitur: adsidua enim frequentia quasi praebet nonnullam infamiam.

(Ulpian in the fifty-seventh book on the Edict)
If someone had accosted maidens, provided they were dressed in a slave woman's clothing, the offense seems small; and smaller still if the women were dressed in prostitute's clothing and not in that of matrons. Therefore if a woman was not in a matron's dress, and someone accosted her or abducted her chaperon, he is liable for *iniuria*.... (20) To accost is to assault another's chastity with smooth talk. This is not clamor (*convicium*), but to make an assault contrary to good morals. (21) One who uses foul language does not assault chastity, but is liable for *iniuria*. (22) It is one thing to accost and another to pursue. One accosts by using speech to assault chastity; one pursues by often following in silence. For (a pursuer's) constant presence virtually ensures considerable disrepute.

Discussion:

1. This Case is part of Ulpian's commentary on another special provision of the Praetor's Edict, which makes it an offense "to abduct the chaperon of a matron or a young person of either sex, or to accost or pursue him or her contrary to good morals." Reconstruct the nature of the offense. What social purpose is served by this edictal provision?

2. Is it a defense to this action if one argues that the victim was already unchaste? See Paul, D. 47.10.10 (yes).

3. In section (15), Ulpian admits that the outrage is minor if a woman is accosted when she is dressed in clothing beneath her station, particularly in the clothing of a prostitute. Why does he nonetheless grant an action on *iniuria*? Is he presuming that the defendant knew or should have known the woman's true status?

4. Why is it also an offense to abduct a chaperon? Ulpian (D. 47.10.15.16) quotes Labeo's definition of a chaperon as one "who is appointed to follow someone for companionship in public or private." Ulpian adds that this includes slaves who take children to school (*paedagogi*). "Abducting" means successfully forcing or persuading the chaperon to leave the side of the intended target.

5. What is the difference (if any) between accosting or pursuing another, and simply trying to make friends (perhaps with amorous intent)? Ulpian (D. 47.10.15.23) notes that the offense must be "contrary to good morals"; what considerations might be used to decide whether a particular case met this criterion?

6. Why is it *iniuria* to use foul language in the presence of a matron?

7. This Case may lead you to reflect on the status of women in the Roman world. While women are protected from sexual advances by men, the reverse is not true unless the man is an adolescent. What is the apparent social function of extending such protection to women, and what social image of women does the law seem to presuppose?

Case 131: Preventing Exercise of a Right

D. 47.10.13.7 (Ulpianus, libro quinquagensimo septimo ad Edictum)

Si quis me prohibeat in mari piscari vel everriculum (quod Graece *sagene* dicitur) ducere, an iniuriarum iudicio possim eum convenire? sunt qui putent iniuriarum me posse agere: et ita Pomponius. et plerique esse huic similem eum, qui in publicum lavare vel in cavea publica sedere vel in quo alio loco agere sedere conversari non patiatur, aut si quis re mea uti me non permittat: nam et hic iniuriarum conveniri potest.... si quem tamen ante aedes meas vel ante praetorium meum piscari prohibeam, quid dicendum est? me iniuriarum iudicio teneri an non? et quidem mare commune omnium est et litora, sicuti aer, et est saepissime rescriptum non posse quem piscari prohiberi: sed nec aucupari, nisi quod ingredi quis agrum alienum prohiberi potest. usurpatum tamen et hoc est, tametsi nullo iure, ut quis prohiberi possit ante aedes meas vel praetorium meum piscari: quare si quis prohibeatur, adhuc iniuriarum agi potest. in lacu tamen, qui mei dominii est, utique piscari aliquem prohibere possum.

(Ulpian in the fifty-seventh book on the Edict)

If someone forbids me from fishing in the sea or dragging a net (which in Greek is called a *sagene*), can I sue him for *iniuria*? Some think that I can sue for *iniuria*; and so Pomponius. And many (hold) that he is like a person who does not allow (me) to use a public bath, or to sit in a public theater, or to conduct business or sit or talk in some other place, or does not permit me to use my property; for he can be sued for *iniuria*.... But what should be ruled if I forbid someone from fishing in front of my house or my villa? Am I liable in an action for *iniuria*, or not? And indeed the sea and its shores are, like the air, common to all; and imperial rescripts have often held that a person cannot be forbidden from fishing, no more than from birdcatching, except if he is forbidden to enter another's land. But people have claimed, although without legal right (to do so), that someone can be forbidden from fishing in front of my house or my villa; hence if someone is forbidden, the suit on *iniuria* can lie for this. However, I can at any rate forbid someone from fishing in a lake that I own.

The Hypothetical Problem:

I am standing on the shore in front of your villa and casting a fishing line into the sea; you order me to stop. Can I sue you for *iniuria*?

Discussion:

1. Reconstruct what this Case holds about the right of persons to act on public and common property, or on their own property. Why is it *iniuria* to prevent use of such rights?

2. I incorrectly believe that I have the right to prevent you from fishing in front of my house, and I do prevent you. Why is this *iniuria*? Do I intend to insult or degrade you? Or does the outrage rather stem from my assertion of a right that I do not have, in order to prevent you exercising a right that you do have?

3. I prevent you from selling your own slave. Is this *iniuria*? See Ulpian, D. 47.10.24.

4. You are in pursuit of a fox on public land; I intercept and kill the fox before you can catch it. Under what circumstances would I be liable for *iniuria*?

5. What larger social interests are being protected by this type of *iniuria*?

Case 132: Trespass

D. 47.10.23 (Paulus, libro quarto ad Edictum)

Qui in domum alienam invito domino introiret, quamvis in ius vocat, actionem iniuriarum in eum competere Ofilius ait.

(Paul in the fourth book on the Edict)

If someone enters another person's house when the owner is unwilling, even to summon (that person) to court, Ofilius says that the action on *iniuria* lies against him.

Discussion:

1. Where does the *iniuria* lie in this Case? Would it also be *iniuria* to enter another person's land when that person is unwilling? (See the preceding Case.)

2. What is meant by "when the owner is unwilling"? Is it that the owner has forbidden entry, or that he or she has not extended an invitation to enter? Does the prohibition have to be specifically directed at the defendant, or can it be general (a "No Trespassing" sign)?

3. Why is no exception made even when the intruder seeks to summon the householder to court?

Case 133: Outrage Against Another's Slave

Gaius, *Institutiones* 3.222

Servo autem ipsi quidem nulla iniuria intellegitur fieri, sed domino per eum fieri videtur, non tamen iisdem modis quibus etiam per liberos nostros vel uxores iniuriam pati videmur, sed ita cum quid atrocius commissum fuerit, quod aperte in contumeliam domini fieri videtur, veluti si quis alienum servum verberaverit; et in hunc casum formula proponitur. at si quis servo convicium fecerit vel pugno eum percusserit, non proponitur ulla formula, nec temere petenti datur.

(Gaius in the third book of his *Institutes*)
No *iniuria* is held to be done to a slave himself, but it is held to be inflicted on the master through him, although not in the same way as we are held to suffer *iniuria* through our children or wives, but only when something quite serious is inflicted that is regarded as obviously done to insult the master, e.g., if someone thrashes another's slave; a formula is published (in the Praetor's Edict) for this case. But if someone raises a clamor against a slave or strikes him with a fist, no formula is published, nor is one lightly given to a plaintiff.

Discussion:

1. The provision in the Edict read: "I will give an action against one who allegedly thrashed another's slave contrary to good morals, or who submitted him to questioning (under torture) without the owner's order. Likewise, if anything other is alleged to have been done, I will grant an action after considering the case." To what extent does Gaius interpret this provision?

2. If a clamor is raised against a slave (e.g., that the slave is a thief), should the Praetor consider the slave's character before granting an action? Ulpian, D. 47.10.15.44, says yes; "for it matters greatly what kind of slave he is: honest, a supervisor or steward, or instead common or middling or whatever." Why does this matter? Isn't the insult to the master what is important?

3. I beat a slave who I think belongs to Titius; I would not have beaten him had I known he belonged to you. Am I liable to you? See Ulpian, D. 47.10.15.45 (no).

Case 134: Multiple Outrages

D. 47.10.7.5 (Ulpianus, libro quinquagensimo septimo ad Edictum)

Si mihi plures iniurias feceris, puta turba et coetu facto domum alicuius introeas et hoc facto efficiatur, ut simul et convicium patiar et verberer: an possim separatim tecum experiri de singulis iniuriis, quaeritur. et Marcellus secundum Neratii sententiam hoc probat cogendum iniurias, quas simul passus est, coniungere.

(Ulpian in the fifty-seventh book on the Edict)

If you inflict several (simultaneous) outrages on me, e.g., after gathering a throng and crowd, you enter someone's home and thereby bring it about that I simultaneously endure a clamor and am thrashed, it is asked whether I can sue you separately on each *iniuria*. Marcellus, following Neratius' view, holds that (the plaintiff) should be forced to join (in a single lawsuit) the outrages he suffered simultaneously.

Discussion:

1. Reconstruct the incident on which this holding is based.

2. Why do the jurists hold that the various outrages must be joined together in a single suit on *iniuria*, so that the plaintiff cannot sue on each of them separately? Consider this issue both from the practical side (clogging the courts, the risk of inconsistent verdicts) and from the analytical side (can simultaneous outrages be separated from one another?). You may find it helpful to review the Cases on concurrence of actions (Chapter III, Part C).

Case 135: Disrespect

D. 47.10.13.3–4 (Ulpianus, libro quinquagensimo septimo ad Edictum)

Si quis per iniuriam ad tribunal alicuius me interpellaverit vexandi mei causa, potero iniuriarum experiri. (4) Si quis de honoribus decernendis alicuius passus non sit decerni ut puta imaginem alicui vel quid aliud tale: an iniuriarum teneatur? et ait Labeo non teneri, quamvis hoc contumeliae causa faciet: etenim multum interest, inquit, contumeliae causa quid fiat an vero fieri quid in honorem alicuius quis non patiatur.

(Ulpian in the fifty-seventh book on the Edict)

If, to annoy me, a person interrupts me with an insult before someone's tribunal, I will be able to sue on *iniuria*. (4) If, with regard to decreeing honors for someone, a person did not allow that, for instance, a statue or something similar be decreed in someone's honor, should he be liable for *iniuria*? Labeo says he is not liable, even though he did this to be insulting. For, he says, there is a great difference between what is done to insult and what someone does not allow to be done to honor another.

The Hypothetical Problem:

The Senate is voting on a motion to erect a statue in my honor. You prevent the motion from being adopted. Can I sue you for *iniuria*?

Discussion:

1. This Case touches on some of the difficulties of *iniuria* in areas that are today associated with free speech. To what extent does the delict of *iniuria* tend to discourage free exchange of opinion?

2. What is the "great difference" of which Labeo speaks? Can you phrase his point more exactly?

3. If a magistrate, in performing his functions, gives offense to someone, is there an action on *iniuria*? See Ulpian, D. 47.10.13.5–6.

Case 136: Aggravated *Iniuria*

Gaius, *Institutiones* 3.224–225

Sed nunc alio iure utimur. permittitur enim nobis a Praetore ipsis iniuriam aestimare, et iudex vel tanti condemnat quanti nos aestimaverimus, vel minoris, prout illi visum fuerit. sed cum atrocem iniuriam Praetor aestimare soleat, si simul constituerit quantae pecuniae eo nomine fieri debeat vadimonium, hac ipsa quantitate taxamus formulam, et iudex, quamvis possit vel minoris damnare, plerumque tamen propter ipsius Praetoris auctoritatem non audet minuere condemnationem. (225) Atrox autem iniuria aestimatur vel ex facto, veluti si quis ab aliquo vulneratus aut verberatus fustibusve caesus fuerit, vel ex loco, veluti si cui in theatro aut in foro iniuria facta sit, vel ex persona, veluti si magistratus iniuriam passus fuerit, vel senatori ab humili persona facta sit iniuria.

(Gaius in the third book of his *Institutes*)

But we now use another rule (for estimating the penalty). The Praetor allows us (as plaintiffs) to evaluate the *iniuria* ourselves, and the *iudex* condemns for either the value we set or less, as seems right to him. But since the Praetor usually evaluates a serious *iniuria* simultaneously with determining the amount of the bond for reappearance (*vadimonium*), we limit the formula to this amount, and the *iudex*, although he can condemn also for less, normally does not dare to lessen the judgment because of the Praetor's authority. (225) An *iniuria* is evaluated as serious either from the act, e.g., if someone is wounded or thrashed or slain with cudgels by another; or from the place, e.g., if *iniuria* is inflicted on someone in the theater or in the forum; or from the person, e.g., if a magistrate suffers *iniuria*, or *iniuria* is inflicted on a Senator by one of low degree.

Discussion:

1. Reconstruct the process for assessing the penalty paid for an *iniuria*. How does it relate to the delict's purposes?

2. What is the nature of "serious outrage" (*atrox iniuria*)? Why is it handled more drastically than ordinary *iniuria*? *Vadimonium* is a formal promise by the defendant guaranteeing his or her reappearance in court.

Section 2: Intent

Case 137: The Wrongdoer's Intent

D. 47.10.3 pr.–3 (Ulpianus, libro quinquagensimo sexto ad Edictum)

Illud relatum peraeque est eos, qui iniuriam pati possunt, et facere posse. (1) Sane sunt quidam, qui facere non possunt, ut puta furiosus et inpubes, qui doli capax non est: namque hi pati iniuriam solent, non facere. cum enim iniuria ex affectu facientis consistat, consequens erit dicere hos, sive pulsent sive convicium dicant, iniuriam fecisse non videri. (2) Itaque pati quis iniuriam, etiamsi non sentiat, potest, facere nemo, nisi qui scit se iniuriam facere, etiamsi nesciat cui faciat. (3) Quare si quis per iocum percutiat aut dum certat, iniuriarum non tenetur.

(Ulpian in the fifty-sixth book on the Edict)

It is equally held that those who can suffer *iniuria* can also inflict it. (1) To be sure, there are some who cannot inflict it, e.g., a lunatic and a minor not capable of *dolus*; for these persons may suffer *iniuria*, not inflict it. For since *iniuria* arises from the offender's intent (*affectus*), the logical consequence is that they (lunatics and minors) are not held to inflict *iniuria*, whether they strike (another) or raise a clamor. (2) And so a person can suffer *iniuria* even if he does not feel it, but no one can do it except a person who knows that he inflicts *iniuria*, even if the one to whom it is done is unaware. (3) Therefore if someone strikes (another) as a joke or during a contest, he is not liable for *iniuria*.

Discussion:

1. Why can a mad person suffer *iniuria*, but not inflict it? Compare closely Case 35, on the Lex Aquilia. To what extent does this Case represent an exception to the rule discussed below in Case 140?

2. How does the rule in section (3) follow from the discussion above? Does this rule seem to you correct?

3. Is it *iniuria* accidentally or carelessly to injure the feelings of another person? Should it be?

Case 138: Knowing Who the Victim Is

D. 47.10.18.3–5 (Paulus, libro quinquagensimo quinto ad Edictum)

Si iniuria mihi fiat ab eo, cui sim ignotus, aut si quis putet me Lucium Titium esse, cum sim Gaius Seius: praevalet, quod principale est, iniuriam eum mihi facere velle: nam certus ego sum, licet ille putet me alium esse quam sum, et ideo iniuriarum habeo. (4) At cum aliquis filium familias patrem familias putat, non potest videri iniuriam patri facere, non magis quam viro, si mulierem viduam esse credat, quia neque in personam eorum confertur iniuria nec transferri personae putationem ex persona filiorum ad eos potest, cum affectus iniuriam facientis in hunc tamquam in patrem familias consistat. (5) Quod si scisset filium familias esse, tametsi nescisset, cuius filius esset, dicerem, inquit, patrem suo nomine iniuriarum agere posse: nec minus virum, si ille nuptam esse sciret: nam qui haec non ignorat, cuicumque patri, cuicumque marito per filium, per uxorem vult facere iniuriam.

(Paul in the fifty-fifth book on the Edict)

If an *iniuria* is done to me by a person to whom I am unknown, or if someone thinks I am Lucius Titius when I am Gaius Seius, the prevailing view in principle is that he wishes to inflict an *iniuria* on me; for I am a definite person, although he thinks me other than I am, and so I have the action on *iniuria*. (4) But when someone thinks a son in (his father's) power is a *paterfamilias*, he cannot be held to inflict *iniuria* on the father, no more than on a husband if he believes a woman to be a widow, since the *iniuria* is not directed to their person, nor can the imputation of the person be transferred from the person of the sons to them; for the intent (*affectus*) of the offender is directed to him (the son) as a *paterfamilias*. (5) But if he had known him to be a son in power, although he did not know whose son he was, I would hold, says (Pomponius), that the father can sue for *iniuria* in his own name; and no less the husband, if he knew her to be married. For one who is unaware of these things (still) wishes to inflict *iniuria* through the son on the father whoever he is, and through the wife on the husband whoever he is.

The Hypothetical Problem:

Sempronia points to me and claims that I am a scoundrel. In fact, she has me confused with Lucius Titius. Can I sue Sempronia for *iniuria*?

Discussion:

1. Discuss the legal reasons for allowing the victim to sue on *iniuria* when the offender is unaware of the victim's true identity. Is the offender being held liable, in effect, for mistaking the identity of the person he or she is insulting?

2. In many circumstances, a family member is allowed to regard an *iniuria* to a relative as simultaneously an *iniuria* to him or herself; thus not only the direct victim, but also the relative can sue. (See Case 142.) How is the logic of section (3) extended to the situations discussed in sections (4–5)? Why is it less serious to think that a son in his father's power is a *paterfamilias* than to know he is a son in power but be mistaken about the identity of his *paterfamilias*?

3. What does this Case suggest about the nature of *iniuria*? Does *iniuria* really involve the intentional insult of one's victim, or rather intentional insulting conduct in general?

4. You beat a free person who you wrongly believe is your slave; are you liable to him for *iniuria*? See Ulpian, D. 47.10.3.4 (no); why?

5. I want to punch my slave; but my punch goes wild and I unwillingly strike you, who are standing nearby. Am I liable to you for *iniuria*? See Paul, D. 47.10.4 (no). Would the same be true if I had wanted to strike someone I knew to be a free person?

Case 139: Aiding and Abetting *Iniuria*

D. 47.10.11 pr. (Ulpianus, libro quinquagensimo septimo ad Edictum)

Non solum is iniuriarum tenetur, qui fecit iniuriam, hoc est qui percussit, verum ille quoque continetur, qui dolo fecit vel qui curavit, ut cui mala pugno percuteretur.

(Ulpian in the fifty-seventh book on the Edict)
Not only is a person liable for *iniuria* if he (himself) inflicted the *iniuria*, i.e., the one who struck (someone else); a person is also included who through *dolus* brings it about, or who procures, that another's cheek be struck with a fist.

The Hypothetical Problem:

Cassius persuades Titia to slap Sempronia. Can Sempronia sue Cassius for *iniuria*?

Discussion:

1. In what sense did Cassius also inflict an *iniuria* on the victim?

2. How active must the person be who aids or abets? Ulpian (D. 47.10.11.4–6) holds such a person liable in three situations: if he gives an order (*mandatum*) to a third party to inflict an *iniuria*, or if he gives an order to his son, or if he hires someone to give the *iniuria*. Does this imply a fairly high degree of involvement in the *iniuria*? What if the second person only suggested the *iniuria*?

Section 3: The Plaintiff

Case 140: The Victim's Outrage

D. 47.10.11.1 (Ulpianus, libro quinquagensimo septimo ad Edictum)

Iniuriarum actio ex bono et aequo est et dissimulatione aboletur. si quis enim iniuriam dereliquerit, hoc est statim passus ad animum suum non revocaverit, postea ex paenitentia remissam iniuriam non poterit recolere. secundum haec ergo aequitas actionis omnem metum eius abolere videtur, ubicumque contra aequum quis venit. proinde et si pactum de iniuria intercessit et si transactum et si iusiurandum exactum erit, actio iniuriarum non tenebit.

(Ulpian in the fifty-seventh book on the Edict)
The action on *iniuria* is based on what is good and fair (*bonum et aequum*), and does not lie if he (the victim) dissembles (about his outrage). For if someone abandons an *iniuria*, that is, if he does not immediately take it to heart after suffering it, he cannot afterwards change his mind and revive the *iniuria* he has let pass. Therefore it follows that fairness is held to eliminate fear of the action (being brought) whenever someone sues contrary to what is fair. So if the parties reach agreement on the *iniuria* or settle out of court, or if an oath is taken (from the defendant that he is not guilty), the action on *iniuria* does not lie.

Discussion:

1. What does this Case suggest about how the jurists conceived *iniuria*? Compare also Case 137, on *iniuria* to madmen and young children. The formula for the action ordered the *iudex* to condemn the defendant for "as much money as will seem good and fair."

2. The Edict required that the action on *iniuria* be brought within one year. Is this requirement related to the necessity that the victim feel actual outrage?

3. I insult you, but you fail to understand what I say and laugh it off, and we part as friends. Later the insult is explained to you. Can you sue me on *iniuria*?

Case 141: Outrage to a Corpse

D. 47.10.1.4 (Ulpianus, libro quinquagensimo sexto ad Edictum)

Et si forte cadaveri defuncti fit iniuria, cui heredes bonorumve possessores exstitimus, iniuriarum nostro nomine habemus actionem: spectat enim ad existimationem nostram, si qua ei fiat iniuria. idemque et si fama eius, cui heredes exstitimus, lacessatur.

(Ulpian in the fifty-sixth book on the Edict)

And if, as it happens, *iniuria* is inflicted on the corpse of a dead person from whom we have inherited or received possession of the estate, we have the action on *iniuria* in our own name; for it concerns our reputation if *iniuria* is inflicted on the corpse. Likewise also if the reputation is attacked of a person from whom we have inherited.

Discussion:

1. For the action on *iniuria*, the victim's standing is not inheritable; that is, if the victim fails to bring suit during his or her lifetime, the victim's heir cannot then sue. (Contrast Aquilian liability, Case 76.) Is this rule related to the "personal" nature of *iniuria*? In this Case, therefore, the outrage to the corpse must be interpreted as an outrage to the heir if there is to be an action.

2. Give examples of how one can insult the corpse or the reputation of a dead person. Why does this represent an *iniuria* to the heir? How would the *iudex* determine the award if, for instance, the dead man was highly honorable but the heir was not, or vice versa?

3. What if the heir has not yet accepted the inheritance? According to Ulpian (D. 47.10.1.6), the inheritance itself acquires the action, which can then be brought by the heir after acceptance; compare Cases 77–78 on the Lex Aquilia. How would this affect the measure of the award?

Case 142: Family Members

Gaius, *Institutiones* 3.221

Pati autem iniuriam videmur non solum per nosmet ipsos, sed etiam per liberos nostros quos in potestate habemus; item per uxores nostras quamvis in manu nostra <non>sint. itaque si filiae meae quae Titio nupta est iniuriam feceris, non solum filiae nomine tecum agi iniuriarum potest, verum etiam meo quoque et Titii nomine.

(Gaius in the third book of his *Institutes*)
We are understood to suffer *iniuria* not only through ourselves, but also through children whom we have in our power; likewise, through our wives even if they are (not) in our *manus*. And so if you inflict an *iniuria* on my daughter who is married to Titius, you can be sued for *iniuria* not only in respect to the daughter, but also in respect to me and Titius.

Discussion:

1. In what sense do I suffer *iniuria* when my daughter or wife is insulted? See also Case 138 for a limitation on this power to sue. In classical law, the action on *iniuria* was not apparently limited to cases where the wife was in *manus*, the archaic form of Roman marriage in which the wife was subordinated to her husband's power (*manus*); the text of Gaius seems to be corrupt at this point.

2. If Titius were a son in his father's power, would Titius' father also have an action for an *iniuria* inflicted on Titius' wife? See Justinian, *Inst.* 4.4.2 (yes).

3. Is an insult to a *paterfamilias* an insult also to his wife and children? Normally not (Justinian, *Inst.* 4.4.2; but for an exception see Case 143). How can this rule be explained? Paul (D. 47.10.2) says, with regard to wives, that "it is right that wives be defended by their husbands, not husbands by their wives." Is this just sexism?

4. A betrothed fiancé (*sponsus*) can also sue in his own name if his bride-to-be is insulted: Ulpian, D. 47.10.15.24.

5. In multiple trials for the same *iniuria*, how should the penalties be assessed? Ulpian (D. 47.10.30.1) indicates that they may differ in each case; what factors would the *iudex* consider in each case?

Case 143: Privileges

D. 47.10.11.7–8 (Ulpianus, libro quinquagensimo septimo ad Edictum)

Quamquam adversus patronum liberto iniuriarum actio non detur, verum marito libertae nomine cum patrono actio competit: maritus enim uxore sua iniuriam passa suo nomine iniuriarum agere videtur. quod et Marcellus admittit. ego autem apud eum notavi non de omni iniuria hoc esse dicendum me putare: levis enim coercitio etiam in nuptam vel convici non impudici dictio cur patrono denegetur? si autem conliberto nupta esset, diceremus omnino iniuriarum marito adversus patronum cessare actionem, et ita multi sentiunt. ex quibus apparet libertos nostros non tantum eas iniurias adversus nos iniuriarum actione exequi non posse, quaecumque fiunt ipsis, sed ne eas quidem, quae eis fiunt, quos eorum interest iniuriam non pati. (8) Plane si forte filius liberti vel uxor velint iniurarum experiri: quia patri maritove non datur, denegandum non erit, quia suo nomine experiuntur.

(Ulpian in the fifty-seventh book on the Edict)

Although no action on *iniuria* is given to a freedman against his patron, the husband of a freedwoman has an action with the patron in her name; for when his wife suffers *iniuria*, the husband is held to sue for *iniuria* in his own name. Marcellus also allows this. But I added a note to his rule that I do not think this should be held for every *iniuria*; for why should the patron be denied (the right to) mild punishment or the raising of a clamor that is not indecent? However, were she married to a co-freedman, we would hold that the husband's action against the patron fails altogether, and many jurists agree. From this it is clear that our freedmen cannot pursue, through an action on *iniuria* against us, not only outrages done to them (by us), but also those done to persons in whose not suffering *iniuria* they have an interest. (8) Clearly, if, by chance, the son or wife of a freedman wishes to sue on *iniuria*, then because no action is given to the father or husband, it should not be denied to them, since they sue in their own name.

Discussion:

1. This Case offers a lively example of the normal relations that Romans had with their freed slaves. Why does Ulpian regard it as not *iniuria* when a patron lightly chastizes or abuses a freed person? This is only one of a large number of instances in which freed persons are legally disadvantaged with respect to theeir former masters.

2. Note that a freed person cannot sue his patron for *iniuria* at all, and his near relatives can sue only for more serious outrages to the freed person. As a rule, the Praetor allowed freed persons to sue their patrons only in exceptional cases, and suit was not permitted at all in cases where the action involved "disgrace" (*infamia*) to the losing defendant; this is so of the action on *iniuria*. Although the patron does not have a positive right to inflict *iniuria*

on a freed person, procedural law in effect creates such a right. How and
why? How does this Case implement the logic of earlier Cases?

3. Section (8) of this Case offers a curious exception to the usual rule that *iniuria* to a man is not *iniuria* also to his child or wife. What is the logic behind
the exception? Do you find it convincing?

Chapter VI: Praetorian Delicts

The major delicts in Roman law all have at least their ultimate origin in statutes, and they all have markedly punitive aspects. Although these delicts were broadly conceived and interpreted, some situations were still not encompassed by them. In order to meet these situations, the Urban Praetor introduced into his Edict new delictual actions of his own devising; these Praetorian delicts are heavily influenced in their form by Roman delictual theory.

The action on deceit (*dolus malus*) was created in the late Republic by the jurist Aquilius Gallus. It provides that, within one year, the plaintiff can recover the simple value of losses suffered through the defendant's deceit; however, the defendant can escape liability by restoring the lost property. This action was available only if the plaintiff had no other action. What the jurists mean by "deceit" is not always clear, but in some Cases it appears that the deceit need not have been self-serving fraud.

The action on duress (*metus*), also probably created in the late Republic, covers cases of extortion. This delict allowed the victim of extortion to be restored to his or her position through recovery of extorted property or its value. The action is for quadruple damages within one year, and for simple damages thereafter; but again, the defendant can escape liability by returning the property. Unlike the action on deceit, the action on duress lies not only against a person who uses extortion, but also against a third party who profits from the extortion of another.

Deceit and duress also can be used as formal defenses (*exceptiones*) against plaintiffs who by suing are taking advantage either of their own deceit or of duress used by themselves or another.

Besides these two supplementary actions, late Republican Praetors established many other minor actions that have a primarily policing function; some provide fixed monetary penalties, while others establish liability ranging from simple to quadruple damages. One especially interesting example of such actions is the suit given to an owner whose slave has been morally corrupted by a third party.

Part A: Deceit (*Dolus*)

Case 144: The Edict on Deceit

D. 4.3.1 pr.–1 (Ulpianus, libro undecimo ad Edictum)

Hoc edicto Praetor adversus varios et dolosos, qui aliis offuerunt calliditate quadam, subvenit, ne vel illis malitia sua sit lucrosa vel istis simplicitas damnosa. (1) Verba autem edicti talia sunt: 'Quae dolo malo facta esse dicentur, si de his rebus alia actio non erit et iusta causa esse videbitur, iudicium dabo.'

(Ulpian in the eleventh book on the Edict)
Through this edict the Praetor gives relief against shifty and deceitful persons who by some craftiness have harmed others, so that their own wickedness not be of gain to them, nor naiveté be harmful to their victims. (1) The edict provides as follows: "I will give a trial concerning things allegedly done with *dolus malus* if there is no other action and the case seems justified."

Discussion:

1. Note the extreme breadth of the edict. Is *dolus malus* itself a delict? Or is the Praetor seeking to remedy only the harmful consequences of deceit?

2. I sell you something for a price that is much higher than the object is worth. Is this *dolus*? Paul (D. 19.2.22.3) writes:

   > Just as in sale the parties are naturally allowed to buy for a lower price an object that is worth more and to sell for a higher price what is worth less, and in this way to cheat one another, so the rule is also the same in lease.

   What is the boundary between such free market thinking and deceit? Compare Ulpian (D. 4.3.9 pr.): "If someone affirms that an estate is of small worth and on this basis buys it from the heir, there is no action on *dolus* since the action on sale suffices." Is this situation different?

3. Why should law protect people who are unusually naive?

4. The action on deceit, which lies for a year after the existence of the deceit is discoverable, allows the plaintiff to recover "as much as the matter will be worth" if the defendant does not make restitution. The measure of damages is the same as in the Lex Aquilia's Third Chapter (Case 2).

Case 145: Availability of Another Action

D. 4.3.7.3 (Ulpianus, libro undecimo ad Edictum)

Non solum autem si alia actio non sit, sed et si dubitetur an alia sit, putat Labeo de dolo dandam actionem et adfert talem speciem. qui servum mihi debebat vel ex venditione vel ex stipulatu, venenum ei dedit et sic eum tradidit: vel fundum, et dum tradit, imposuit ei servitutem vel aedificia diruit, arbores excidit vel extirpavit: ait Labeo, sive cavit de dolo sive non, dandam in eum de dolo actionem, quoniam si cavit, dubium est, an competat ex stipulatu actio. sed est verius, si quidem de dolo cautum est, cessare actionem de dolo, quoniam est ex stipulatu actio: si non est cautum, in ex empto quidem actione cessat de dolo actio, quoniam est ex empto, in ex stipulatu de dolo actio necessaria est.

(Ulpian in the eleventh book on the Edict)
Labeo thinks that not only if there is no other action, but also if there is doubt whether there is another, the action on *dolus* should be granted, and he gives these examples. A person who owed me a slave on the basis of a sale or stipulation gave the slave poison and delivered him thus; or while handing over a farm he imposed a servitude on it, or destroyed buildings, or cut down or dug up trees. Labeo says that whether or not he gave a formal undertaking against *dolus*, an action on *dolus* should be given against him, since if he gave an undertaking, it is doubtful whether the action on stipulation lies. But the more correct view is that if there was an undertaking against *dolus*, the action on *dolus* fails since there is an action on the stipulation. If there was no undertaking, in the case of an action on sale the action on *dolus* fails, since there is one on sale; in that on stipulation the action *dolus* is needed.

The Hypothetical Problem:

Titius is obligated, on the basis of a contract, to deliver a slave to Seia. Before delivery, or in the process of delivery, Titius poisons the slave so that he will eventually die, and he then delivers the slave in this condition. What suit, if any, can Seia bring against Titius?

Discussion:

1. What is Titius' "deceit" in this Case? Does he intend to profit from his misdeed?

2. Labeo discusses two types of contracts. The first is sale, in which the duties of the two parties are defined by *bona fides*. In early classical law, when Labeo wrote, it may still have been unclear that the seller's duty to deliver implied a duty to deliver in good condition; but in late classical law this duty is well established. As Ulpian reasons, since the buyer has the action on sale if the seller commits *dolus* in delivering, she does not need the action on *dolus*.

3. The formal contract of stipulation is more difficult, since in this contract the promissor's duties are interpreted strictly in accordance with the words he or she uses in promising. So if the promissor does not give a formal undertaking (*cautio*) to abstain from *dolus* in making delivery, he does not have this duty under the stipulation. Hence, the action on *dolus* must be granted.

4. However, even if the promissor under a stipulation does undertake to abstain from *dolus*, Labeo was not certain that this promise could be extended to include *dolus* in delivery. What might have been the basis for his doubt? Is it that the promissor's conduct seems to be purely malicious, without any intent to profit from the *dolus*? Ulpian, by contrast, has no difficulty with this situation; he regards the undertaking as sufficient basis for a lawsuit, and so does not give the promissee an action on *dolus*.

5. As this Case suggests, the jurists interpret the Praetor's edict relatively closely. But the Case also shows how Roman law gave increasing protection against deceit by extending the scope of other actions.

Case 146: Defining Deceit

D. 4.3.1.2 (Ulpianus, libro undecimo ad Edictum)

Dolum malum Servius quidem ita definiit machinationem quandam alterius decipiendi causa, cum aliud simulatur et aliud agitur. Labeo autem posse et sine simulatione id agi, ut quis circumveniatur: posse et sine dolo malo aliud agi, aliud simulari, sicuti faciunt, qui per eiusmodi dissimulationem deserviant et tuentur vel sua vel aliena: itaque ipse sic definiit dolum malum esse omnem calliditatem fallaciam machinationem ad circumveniendum fallendum decipiendum alterum adhibitam. Labeonis definitio vera est.

(Ulpian in the eleventh book on the Edict)

Servius defines *dolus malus* as a contrivance to deceive another, when one thing is feigned and another done. But Labeo (says) that it is possible, without feigning, to act so as to cheat someone; also, it is possible, without *dolus malus*, to do one thing and feign something else, as people do when through a pretense of this kind they protect and preserve either their own or others' interests. So he himself defines *dolus malus* as any craftiness, trickery, or contrivance used to cheat, trick, or deceive another. Labeo's definition is correct.

The Hypothetical Problem:

My slave's business is failing. I believe that the slave can save it if you give him a loan of 10,000 sesterces. I tell you that the business is sound, and you then make him the loan. The business fails anyway, and you cannot recover your loan. Have I committed *dolus*?

Discussion:

1. What kinds of cases does Servius' definition exclude and Labeo's include? What cases does Servius include and Labeo exclude? Which definition seems better?

2. A customer means to give a shopkeeper 125 denarii, but inadvertently gives 150. The shopkeeper soon notices the mistake, but does not call it to the customer's attention. Is this theft (see Case 108)? Is it *dolus*?

3. Is it necessary, under Labeo's definition, that the offender seek to profit from the deception him or herself? See the previous Case.

Case 147: Affirming Solvency

D. 4.3.7.10 (Ulpianus, libro undecimo ad Edictum)

Idem Pomponius refert Caecidianum Praetorem non dedisse de dolo actionem adversus eum, qui adfirmaverat idoneum esse eum, cui mutua pecunia dabatur, quod verum est: nam nisi ex magna et evidenti calliditate non debet de dolo actio dari.

D. 4.3.8 (Gaius, libro quarto ad Edictum Provinciale)

Quod si cum scires eum facultatibus labi, tui lucri gratia adfirmasti mihi idoneum esse, merito adversus te, cum mei decipiendi gratia alium falso laudasti, de dolo iudicium dandum est.

(Ulpian in the eleventh book on the Edict)
Pomponius also reports that the Praetor Caecidianus did not give an action on *dolus* against someone who had affirmed that a person, to whom money was lent (by the plaintiff), was solvent. This is correct; for the action *de dolo* should not be given except for great and obvious craftiness.

(Gaius in the fourth book on the Provincial Edict)
But if you knew that he lacked resources, and for your own gain you affirmed to me that he was solvent, a trial on *dolus* should rightly be given against you, since you falsely praised another in order to deceive me.

Discussion:

1. Why does Ulpian hold that falsely affirming another person's solvency is not "great and obvious craftiness"? Is it that the insecurities of a marketplace make such affirmations always a matter of speculation?

2. How might your false affirmation of another's solvency be "for your own gain"? Suppose that you want me to make the loan so that the recipient, who is near insolvency, can repay you; would this be "great and obvious craftiness"?

3. Must I actually profit from the deceit, or is it enough that I intend to profit and that you lose by the deceit?

Case 148: Offering Bad Advice

D. 4.3.9.1 (Ulpianus, libro undecimo ad Edictum)

Si autem mihi persuaseris, ut repudiem hereditatem, quasi minus solvendo sit, vel ut optem servum, quasi melior eo in familia non sit: dico de dolo dandam, si callide hoc feceris.

(Ulpian in the eleventh book on the Edict)
If you persuade me to decline an inheritance on the ground that it is not solvent, or to choose a slave on the ground that he is the best in the household, I rule that an action on *dolus* should be given if you did this craftily.

The Hypothetical Problem:

I have been named heir to an estate; you tell me that I should not accept the estate because it is insolvent. In fact, the estate is solvent. Under what circumstances can you be liable for *dolus* because of this advice?

Discussion:

1. Do I have to act on your advice, and on it alone? Must your advice be clearly and objectively wrong? Must you realize that it is wrong? Ulpian writes that there is liability "if you did this craftily"; does this mean that you expect to gain at my expense if I decline the estate, or that you do in fact gain, or that I lose money by refusing the estate?

2. As a legacy, I have been allowed to pick a slave from a household; I ask your advice, and you persuade me that Stichus is the best slave I could pick. If I then pick Stichus, under what circumstances will you be liable for *dolus*? What responsibility do I have to weigh your advice critically?

3. The obscure jurist Furius Anthianus (D. 4.3.40) gives the converse case: "A person who deceived another into accepting an insolvent inheritance will be liable for *dolus* unless, as it happened, he was the sole creditor (of the estate); for then the defense of deceit (*exceptio doli*) is sufficient against him." After acceptance, the heir is liable for most debts of the deceased. If an insolvent estate has only one creditor who deceives the heir into accepting the estate, Furius' ruling prevents the creditor from bringing a successful lawsuit, so that the action on *dolus* is not needed. Otherwise, the person giving the advice, whether or not he stood to profit from it, is liable for the losses the heir sustains. Why? On the defense of deceit, see Case 150.

Case 149: Malicious Litigation

D. 4.3.33 (Ulpianus, libro quarto Opinionum)

Rei, quam venalem possessor habebat, litem proprietatis adversarius movere coepit et posteaquam oportunitatem emptoris, cui venundari potuit, peremit, destitit: placuit possessori hoc nomine actionem in factum cum sua indemnitate competere.

(Ulpian in the fourth book of *Opinions*)

The possessor of property was selling it. A plaintiff brought suit over ownership; then, after he (the possessor) lost a prospective buyer to whom it could be sold, he (the plaintiff) dropped his suit. It was decided that on this account the possessor can sue *in factum* for his compensation.

Discussion:

1. This Case is less clear than it may seem at first sight. Does Ulpian presume that the plaintiff raised a claim over ownership solely in order to disrupt the proposed sale? Does the plaintiff intend to profit by disrupting the sale? Indeed, does Ulpian even presume that the plaintiff knows of the sale? Note that the sale was never actually concluded; does Ulpian presume that the buyer backed out solely because of the dispute over ownership? Does he also presume that there is no other potential buyer, at least not at the seller's price? In sum, what exactly is the "deceit" committed by the plaintiff? What definition of the delict of *dolus* does Ulpian seem to use?

2. What can the possessor sue for?

3. A defendant who believes that the plaintiff is deliberately bringing a vexatious lawsuit can file a counterclaim for "calumny" (*calumnia*); see Gaius, *Inst.* 4.174–181. The counterclaim is for one-tenth the value of the original claim, and it is valid if the original lawsuit is deliberately vexatious and the plaintiff either loses or abandons the lawsuit (see Ulpian, D. 5.1.10). Since the defendant in this Case evidently failed to raise such a counterclaim, why should he have an action on *dolus*?

Case 150: The Defense of Deceit

Gaius, *Institutiones* 4.119

Omnes autem exceptiones in contrarium concipiuntur quam adfirmat is cum quo agitur. nam si verbi gratia reus dolo malo aliquid actorem facere dicat, qui forte pecuniam petit quam non numeravit, sic exceptio concipitur: 'si in ea re nihil dolo malo Auli Agerii factum sit neque fiat'; item, si dicat contra pactionem pecuniam peti, ita concipitur exceptio: 'si inter Aulum Agerium et Numerium Negidium non convenit ne ea pecunia peteretur'; et denique in ceteris causis similiter concipi solet, ideo scilicet quia omnis exceptio obicitur quidem a reo, sed ita formulae inseritur ut condicionalem faciat condemnationem, id est, ne aliter iudex eum cum quo agitur condemnet, quam si nihil in ea re qua de agitur dolo actoris factum sit; item, ne aliter iudex eum condemnet quam si nullum pactum conventum de non petenda pecunia factum fuerit.

(Gaius in the fourth book of his *Institutes*)

All defenses (*exceptiones*) are formulated to contradict what the plaintiff asserts. For if, e.g., the defendant asserts that the plaintiff acts with *dolus malus* in, for instance, suing to get money that he never paid, the *exceptio* is formulated thus: "if in this matter nothing was done or is being done through the plaintiff's *dolus malus.*" Likewise, if he says that money is sought in violation of an informal agreement, the *exceptio* is formulated thus: "if there was no agreement (*pactum*) between plaintiff and defendant that the money not be sued for." And, in sum, in all other instances the formulation is similar, obviously because every *exceptio* is indeed interposed by the defendant, but is inserted into the formula so as to make condemnation conditional, meaning that the *iudex* should not condemn the defendant unless in this matter nothing was done through the plaintiff's *dolus malus*; likewise, that the *iudex* should not condemn him unless no agreement was made about not seeking the money.

Discussion:

1. In this Case, Gaius is discussing procedural characteristics of *exceptiones*. These are raised at the start of the trial, when the parties appear before the Urban Praetor. After the plaintiff states the cause of action that justifies issuance of a formula, the defendant may then raise a defense (*exceptio*) that bars this action from being effective. Gaius discusses two such defenses: the defense of deceit (*exceptio doli*) and the defense of a pact (*exceptio pacti conventi*). Do you see how they would operate in the two situations he describes?

2. You bring suit against me claiming 10,000 sesterces that you have allegedly loaned me. According to Gaius (*Inst.* 4.41, 43, 49), the formula for the trial (a *condictio*) would read:

"If it appears that the defendant ought to pay HS 10,000 to the plaintiff, [*] let the *iudex* condemn the defendant to the plaintiff for 10,000 sesterces; if it does not appear, let him absolve him."

Suppose that I formally promised by stipulation to pay you this amount; but the stipulation was given in consideration of a loan that I expected to receive from you but never received. If I allow the suit to go forward, I may lose; accordingly, I must demand an *exceptio doli*. This *exceptio* involves inserting into the formula, at the point marked by the asterisk, the words "and if in this matter nothing was done or is being done through the plaintiff's *dolus malus*." According to Gaius, what is the procedural effect of this *exceptio*? Who bears the burden of proving that what it alleges is true?

3. The defense of an agreement (*pactum*) is useful if, for instance, a creditor and a debtor informally agree that the creditor will not sue on an existing debt until a certain date, and the creditor brings suit before that date. Why couldn't a defendant, who alleges that suit is barred by such an agreement between the two parties, use the *exceptio doli* instead of the defense based on a pact? See Case 151.

4. Note the wording of the *exceptio doli*: "if in this matter nothing was done or is being done through the plaintiff's *dolus malus*." What is the difference between a defense based on the assertion that the plaintiff's previous conduct in this matter involves *dolus*, and a defense asserting that the plaintiff is acting deceitfully in bringing suit?

5. Ulpian (D. 44.4.2 pr.) notes that: "It is apparent that this *exceptio* (the defense of deceit) was established for the same reason that the action on *dolus malus* was established." Do you see the connection? In section 1, Ulpian goes on to note that the defense concerns the plaintiff's own deceit, not just deceit in general; how might this point be relevant?

Case 151: Uses of the Defense

D. 44.4.2.3–4 (Ulpianus, libro septuagensimo sexto ad Edictum)

Circa primam speciem, quibus ex causis exceptio haec locum habeat, haec sunt, quae tractari possunt. si quis sine causa ab aliquo fuerit stipulatus, deinde ex ea stipulatione experiatur, exceptio utique doli mali ei nocebit: licet enim eo tempore, quo stipulabatur, nihil dolo malo admiserit, tamen dicendum est eum, cum litem contestatur, dolo facere, qui perseveret ex ea stipulatione petere: et si cum interponeretur, iustam causam habuit, tamen nunc nullam idoneam causam habere videtur. proinde et si crediturus pecuniam stipulatus est nec credidit et si certa fuit causa stipulationis, quae tamen aut non est secuta aut finita est, dicendum erit nocere exceptionem. (4) Item quaeritur, si quis pure stipulatus sit certam quantitatem, quia hoc actum sit, sed post stipulationem interpositam pactus sit, ne interim pecunia usque ad certum diem petatur, an noceat exceptio doli. et quidem et de pacto convento excipi posse nequaquam ambigendum est: sed et si hac quis exceptione uti velit, nihilo minus poterit: dolo enim facere eum, qui contra pactum petat, negari non potest.

(Ulpian in the seventy-sixth book on the Edict)

Regarding the first type of cases where this *exceptio* is relevant, the following matters can be discussed. If someone stipulated from another without grounds (*sine causa*) and then sued on this stipulation, the defense of deceit (*exceptio doli mali*) will generally bar him. For although he committed no *dolus malus* when the stipulation was made, still it must be ruled that at joinder of issue he acts with *dolus* by continuing to sue on this stipulation; and likewise, if he had just grounds (*causa*) when the stipulation was taken but appears to lack good grounds (*causa*) now. Further, if a person who was going to lend money took a stipulation and then did not lend it, and if there was a stated ground (*causa*) for stipulation which was either not pursued or not carried out, it will be ruled that the *exceptio* bars suit. (4) Likewise the question arises whether the *exceptio doli* bars suit if someone stipulated abstractly for a definite quantity because this was arranged, but after the stipulation was taken he agreed that the money not be sued for in the meantime until a fixed day. Indeed, there is no doubt that a defense concerning the agreement (*exceptio pacti*) can be raised. But if someone wishes to use this *exceptio* (the *exceptio doli*), he will nonetheless be able to; for it cannot be denied that a person who sues contrary to an agreement acts with *dolus*.

Discussion:

1. You stipulated that you would pay me 10,000 sesterces. There was no basis (*causa*) for this stipulation; for example, you may have made the stipulation because you thought you owed me 10,000 sesterces, when in fact you did

not. Why does the defense of deceit bar suit if I sue you for 10,000 sesterces?

2. You stipulated that you will pay me 10,000 sesterces. At the time of the stipulation, there was a basis for the stipulation, but that basis subsequently disappeared. Why does the defense of deceit bar suit if I sue you for 10,000 sesterces? How is this case different from the previous one? Can you give an example of how the basis for a stipulation might disappear? Suppose, for instance, that you promised to pay me 10,000 sesterces as a dowry for your daughter, but she then decided not to marry me. Why is it deceit for me now to claim the money from you?

3. As the previous question suggests, the *exceptio doli* was especially useful to defendants who had made an "abstract" stipulation that did not state the reasons for the stipulation. (For example: "Do you promise to pay me HS 10,000?" "I promise.") Such stipulations are troublesome because they seem to establish a debt, but state no reason for the debt. Through the defense, the defendant could introduce evidence concerning the circumstances in which the stipulation had been made; the defendant could also use the defense to point out other flaws in the plaintiff's conduct. What sorts of uses are described in this Case?

4. In the situation described in section (4), Ulpian holds that a defendant may choose to use either the defense of a pact or the defense of deceit. To what extent is the latter a generalized defense covering all wrongful use of legal procedure?

Part B: Duress (*Metus*)

Case 152: The Edict on Duress

D. 4.2.1, 3 pr. (Ulpianus, libro undecimo ad Edictum)

Ait Praetor: 'Quod metus causa gestum erit, ratum non habebo.' olim ita edicebatur 'quod vi metusve causa': vis enim fiebat mentio propter necessitatem impositam contrariam voluntati: metus instantis vel futuri periculi causa mentis trepidatio. sed postea detracta est vis mentio ideo, quia quodcumque vi atroci fit, id metu quoque fieri videtur. (3 pr.) Continet igitur haec clausula et vim et metum, et si quis vi compulsus aliquid fecit, per hoc edictum restituitur.

(Ulpian in the eleventh book on the Edict)

The Praetor says: "What is done because of duress (*metus*) I will not hold valid." Formerly the edict read: "What (is done) through force (*vis*) or because of duress"; force was mentioned on account of (a present) necessity imposed contrary to one's will, while duress was a mental disturbance because of an impending or future danger. But later the mention of force was removed, since anything done by serious violence is held to be done also by duress. (3 pr.) Therefore this clause covers both force and duress, and if anyone is forcibly compelled to do something, he is restored through this edict.

Discussion:

1. According to Ulpian, what was the original distinction between force (*vis*) and duress (*metus*), and how did the two concepts come to be merged? How plausible is his interpretation?

2. The remedy is described by Ulpian (D. 4.2.14.1):

    If someone does not restore, he (the Praetor) promises a trial for quadruple against him.... But after a year he promises an action for simple (damages); though not always, but only after investigating the circumstances.

    Why was the Praetor suspicious of suits brought after a year?

3. How is extortion through duress different from theft? Could the victim of extortion simply sue on theft or on robbery (Case 126)? But note that the action on theft lies only against the thief, who may be dead or insolvent.

Case 153: Objective Fear

D. 4.2.5 (Ulpianus, libro undecimo ad Edictum)

Metum accipiendum Labeo dicit non quemlibet timorem, sed maioris malitatis.

D. 4.2.6 (Gaius, libro quarto ad Edictum Provinciale)

Metum autem non vani hominis, sed qui merito et in homine constantissimo cadat, ad hoc edictum pertinere dicemus.

(Ulpian in the eleventh book on the Edict)

Labeo says that duress (*metus*) should be construed not as any fear, but (as fear) of a serious evil.

(Gaius in the fourth book on the Provincial Edict)

We will hold that the fear covered by this edict is not a weak man's fear, but that which a highly resolute man also justly shares.

Discussion:

1. Why do the jurists insist that only severe forms of duress are covered by the edict? Why do they use an objective rather than a subjective concept of fear, so that the exceptionally timorous are not completely protected?

2. Are only physical threats (e.g., death or bodily injury) covered by the edict? Paul (D. 4.2.4) also includes the fear of being made a slave; what sort of cases might he be thinking of? See Case 156.

3. I catch you in an act of theft or in adultery with my wife. In certain situations I am legally justified if I kill you (see Cases 69–70). Whether or not this is one of these situations, you give me a gift in order to escape my anger. Can you later successfully bring an action on duress against me? Pomponius (cited by Ulpian, D. 4.2.7.1) holds that you can. Why should this be so?

Case 154: Loss Due to Duress

D. 4.2.12.2 (Ulpianus, libro undecimo ad Edictum)

Iulianus ait eum, qui vim adhibuit debitori suo ut ei solveret, hoc edicto non teneri propter naturam metus causa actionis quae damnum exigit: quamvis negari non possit in Iuliam eum de vi incidisse et ius crediti amisisse.

(Ulpian in the eleventh book on the Edict)

Julian says that a person who used force (*vis*) to get his debtor to pay him is not liable under this edict because of the nature of the action on duress, which requires loss. But it cannot be denied that he (the creditor) has fallen under the Lex Julia on force (*de vi*) and has lost the right to what was lent.

The Hypothetical Problem:

Seius owes money to Titia. Titia tells Seius that unless he pays the money, Titia will have him beaten up. Seius pays the money to Titia. Can Seius use the action on duress?

Discussion:

1. Why did Julian hold that the creditor is not liable under the action on duress? Would the outcome be different if the debt was not yet due?

2. Ulpian states that the creditor falls under the Lex Julia *de vi* (a statute of Augustus that made it a crime to use force in order to obtain property), and that he also loses the right to claim the debt. If the creditor, through use of force, has lost the right to the debt and is in violation of criminal law, should he also be in violation of private law? Is Ulpian thus implicitly holding that Julian's view is wrong? As the following Case makes clear, Roman views on the use of force in collecting debts changed during the early Empire.

Case 155: Physical and Non-Physical Fear

D. 4.2.13 (Callistratus, libro quinto de Cognitionibus)

Exstat enim decretum divi Marci in haec verba: 'Optimum est, ut, si quas putas te habere petitiones, actionibus experiaris. cum Marcianus diceret: vim nullam feci, Caesar dixit: tu vim putas esse solum, si homines vulnerentur? vis est et tunc, quotiens quis id, quod deberi sibi putat, non per iudicem reposcit. quisquis igitur probatus mihi fuerit rem ullam debitoris vel pecuniam debitam non ab ipso sibi sponte datam sine ullo iudice temere possidere vel accepisse, isque sibi ius in eam rem dixisse: ius crediti non habebit.'

(Callistratus in the fifth book on *Judicial Examinations*)

For there exists a decree of the deified Marcus (Aurelius) in the following words: "It is best that, if you think you have some claims, you pursue them judicially. When Marcianus said: 'I used no force (*vis*),' Caesar replied: 'Do you think it is force only if men are wounded? It is also force whenever someone does not demand through a *iudex* what he thinks is owed to him. Therefore if anyone is proved to me to possess or to have taken, without intervention of a *iudex*, any of a debtor's property or money owed to him which the debtor did not give voluntarily, and to have declared his own law for this matter: he will have no right to the debt.'"

Discussion:

1. How does this decree of Marcus Aurelius modify Julian's ruling in Case 154?

2. Does it seem right that the creditor have no recourse at all against a debtor who is unwilling to pay, except to go to court? What is the Emperor presuming about the speed and effectiveness of the Roman judicial system?

3. If the debtor is forced to pay a debt, can he or she recover the payment? Does the Emperor allow the debtor to sue on the delict of duress if his or her property is seized by the creditor to satisfy the debt? What if the creditor does not use force, but only threatens the debtor?

Case 156: Fear of Non-Physical Injury

D. 4.2.8.1–2: (Paulus, libro undecimo ad Edictum)

Si is accipiat pecuniam, qui instrumenta status mei interversurus est nisi dem, non dubitatur quin maximo metu compellat, utique si iam in servitutem petor et illis instrumentis perditis liber pronuntiari non possum. (2) Quod si dederit ne stuprum patiatur vir seu mulier, hoc edictum locum habet, cum viris bonis iste metus maior quam mortis esse debet.

(Paul in the eleventh book on the Edict)

If a person will destroy documents proving my status unless I give (him) money, and he receives money, there is no doubt that he extorts through great duress (*metus*), at any rate if an action to have me declared a slave has already been brought and I cannot be adjudged free if these documents are lost. (2) But if a man or woman gives a gift to avoid being sexually assaulted, this edict is relevant, since for upright persons this fear ought to be greater than the fear of death.

Discussion:

1. You have documents that prove my free status, and threaten to destroy them unless I give you money; I do so. Why should it be relevant that a trial is underway concerning my status, or that I have no other means of proof? What concept of duress does Paul rely on?

2. You extort money from me by threatening rape. Is this threat similar to one of physical injury? What if I am not an "upright" person, but rather one of lax morals?

3. Note that money given for an immoral purpose (e.g., to avoid sexual assault, or to prevent destruction of documents) can in any case be recovered by a *condictio*. How is the plaintiff advantaged by having the action on *metus* as well?

Case 157: Inducing Duress

D. 4.2.21 pr. (Paulus, libro undecimo ad Edictum)

Si mulier contra patronum suum ingrata facta sciens se ingratam, cum de suo statu periclitabatur, aliquid patrono dederit vel promiserit, ne in servitutem redigatur: cessat edictum, quia hunc sibi metum ipsa infert.

(Paul in the eleventh book on the Edict)

If a (freed) woman showed ingratitude to her patron, and, knowing that she was ungrateful, she gave or promised something to her patron when her status was at risk, in order that she not be returned to servitude, the edict fails since she brought this duress on herself.

Discussion:

1. Under certain circumstances, a freedperson could lose his or her freedom by failing to exhibit sufficient gratitude to a former master. Reconstruct what happened in this hypothetical case.

2. Does Paul hold that the freedwoman's patron was justified in extorting payment from her? Can he recall her into slavery despite the payment?

Case 158: Third Parties

D. 4.2.14.5 (Ulpianus, libro undecimo ad Edictum)

Aliquando tamen et si metus adhibitus proponatur, arbitrium absolutionem adfert. quid enim si metum quidem Titius adhibuit me non conscio, res autem ad me pervenit, et haec in rebus humanis non est sine dolo malo meo: nonne iudicis officio absolvar? aut si servus in fuga est, aeque, si cavero iudicis officio me, si in meam potestatem pervenerit, restiturum, absolvi debebo. unde quidam putant bona fide emptorem ab eo qui vim intulit comparantem non teneri nec eum qui dono accepit vel cui res legata est. sed rectissime Viviano videtur etiam hos teneri, ne metus, quem passus sum, mihi captiosus sit. Pedius quoque libro octavo scribit arbitrium iudicis in restituenda re tale esse, ut eum quidem qui vim admisit iubeat restituere, etiamsi ad alium res pervenit, eum autem ad quem pervenit, etiamsi alius metum fecit: nam in alterius praemium verti alienum metum non oportet.

(Ulpian in the eleventh book on the Edict)

But sometimes, even if it is hypothesized that duress was used, the judgment brings absolution. For what if Titius used duress and I was unaware of this, but the object came to me, and this object ceases to exist without my *dolus malus*; should I not be absolved at the discretion of the *iudex*? Or likewise, when the (extorted) slave runs away, if at the discretion of the *iudex* I promise that I will re-store him should he come into my power, I should be absolved. Hence some think that a buyer in good faith, who purchases from a person who used force (to get the object), is not liable; nor is one who receives it as a gift or a legacy. But to Vivianus it quite correctly seemed that they too are liable, lest the duress I suffered be of loss to me. In his eighth book, Pedius also writes that the discretion of the *iudex* in restoration of property is so great that he may order a person who used force to restore the property even if someone else has it, but also (he may require restoration from) the person to whom it came, even though somebody else inflicted the duress. For it is not right that a third party benefit from duress inflicted by someone else.

The Hypothetical Problem:

You used force to extort a slave from Seius, and then sold the slave to me; I did not realize that the slave had been extorted. Under what circumstances should I be held liable to Seius for *metus*? Would I be liable if the slave had since died of natural causes, or run away?

Discussion:

1. If the slave is still alive, what arguments can be found in favor of and against allowing me to keep the slave? Which side seems to have the best argu-ments? How convincing do you find Ulpian's argument in favor of allowing

recovery by the person from whom the slave was extorted? Note that the seller of a slave would normally be liable to the buyer on the sale if the buyer lost the slave to a true owner.

2. What difference should it make whether you sold the slave to me, or rather gave the slave to me as a gift or left me the slave in your will?

3. The person who uses duress can be held liable even though he or she no longer has the extorted property. What are the practical consequences of this extended liability? Should the victim be required to proceed first against the perpetrator, and only then against a third party if satisfaction is not obtained from the perpetrator?

Case 159: The Defense of Duress

D. 44.4.4.33 (Ulpianus, libro septuagensimo sexto ad Edictum)

Metus causa exceptionem Cassius non proposuerat contentus doli exceptione, quae est generalis: sed utilius visum est etiam de metu opponere exceptionem. etenim distat aliquid doli exceptione, quod exceptio doli personam
complectitur eius, qui dolo fecit: enimvero metus causa exceptio in rem
scripta est 'si in ea re nihil metus causa factum est,' ut non inspiciamus, an is
qui agit metus causa fecit aliquid, sed an omnino metus causa factum est in hac
re a quocumque, non tantum ab eo qui agit. et quamvis de dolo auctoris exceptio non obiciatur, verumtamen hoc iure utimur, ut de metu non tantum ab auc-
tore, verum a quocumque adhibito exceptio obici possit.

(Ulpian in the seventy-sixth book on the Edict)

(In his Edict,) Cassius had omitted the defense of duress (*exceptio
metus*); he was content with the defense of deceit (*exceptio doli*),
which is general. But it has been held more useful to interpose the
defense of *metus* as well. For it differs a little from the defense of
deceit, in that the defense of deceit embraces (only) the person
who acted with *dolus*. By contrast, the defense of *metus* is directed
at the (entire) matter: "if nothing in this matter was done by
duress"; so that we do not examine whether the plaintiff did anything by *metus*, but rather whether duress was used in this matter
by anyone, not just by the plaintiff. And although the defense (of
dolus) may not be interposed for *dolus* by one's predecessor in title
(*auctor*), nonetheless our law is that this defense (of *metus*) can be
interposed with regard to *metus* used not just by a predecessor in
title but by anyone.

Discussion:

1. Give some examples of how the defense of duress could be used. How does
   it differ from the defense of deceit?

2. How convincing is Ulpian's argument against Cassius? This Cassius is the
   jurist Cassius Longinus, who was Urban Praetor probably in A.D. 27.

Part C: The Action on Corrupting a Slave

Case 160: The Edict on Corrupting a Slave

D. 11.3.1 pr. (Ulpianus, libro vicensimo tertio ad Edictum)

Ait Praetor: 'Qui servum servam alienum alienam recepisse persuasisseve quid ei dicetur dolo malo, quo eum eam deteriorem faceret, in eum quanti ea res erit in duplum iudicium dabo.'

(Ulpian in the twenty-third book on the Edict)
The Praetor says: "Against a person who is alleged to have acted with *dolus malus* by harboring another person's slave of either sex or by persuading something in order to worsen the slave thereby, I will give a trial for double the amount that the matter will be worth."

Discussion:

1. The edict applies to two actions: harboring another person's slave, and "worsening" the slave's value by urging some course of action. Why is the former not *furtum*? (See Case 111.) Why is the latter not wrongful damage to property?

2. Ulpian (D. 11.3.1.2) defines "harboring" as admitting the slave to one's property with the intent to conceal him or her. Why is this an offense against the slave's owner? Note that the slave must be harbored with *dolus malus*; Ulpian (D. 11.3.5 pr.) explicitly states that there is no liability if one harbors a slave for reasons of humanity or pity, or for some other accepted and just reason. Does this unduly restrict the action?

3. Note that the measure of damages under this edict (what "the matter will be worth") is the same as the measure under the Third Section of the Lex Aquilia. Does this mean that the plaintiff can claim not just the loss in value of the slave, but also the kinds of consequential damages that are available under the Lex Aquilia? Why does the Praetor allow recovery of twice the amount of losses?

4. Is it correct to regard the edict on corrupting a slave as basically a supplement to the Lex Aquilia, reaching cases of non-physical loss that the Lex Aquilia ignored?

Case 161: Defining Corruption

D. 11.3.1.4–5 (Ulpianus, libro vicensimo tertio ad Edictum)

Sed utrum ita demum tenetur, si bonae frugi servum perpulit ad delinquen-
dum, an vero et si malum hortatus est vel malo monstravit, quemadmodum faceret? et est verius etiam si malo monstravit, in quem modum delinqueret,
teneri eum. immo et si erat servus omnimodo fugiturus vel furtum facturus, hic
vero laudator huius propositi extitit, tenetur: non enim oportet laudando
augeri malitiam. sive ergo bonum servum fecerit malum sive malum fecerit deteriorem, corrupisse videbitur. (5) Is quoque deteriorem facit, qui servo persuadet, ut iniuriam faceret vel furtum vel fugeret vel alienum servum ut sollici-
taret vel ut peculium intricaret, aut amator existeret vel erro vel malis artibus
esset deditus vel in spectaculis nimius vel seditiosus: vel si actori suasit verbis
sive pretio, ut rationes dominicas intercideret adulteraret vel etiam ut rationem sibi commissam turbaret:

D. 11.3.2 (Paulus, libro nono decimo ad Edictum)

vel luxuriosum vel contumacem fecit: quive ut stuprum pateretur persuadet.

(Ulpian in the twenty-third book on the Edict)
But is a person liable only if he drove an honest slave to wrongdoing, or rather also if he encouraged a bad slave or showed a bad
slave how to act? The more correct view is that he is liable even if
he showed a bad slave how to act. Indeed, even if the slave would
run away or commit theft anyway, but he approves this project, he
is liable: for it is wrong to increase wickedness by praising it. So
whether he makes a good slave bad or makes a bad slave worse, he
is held to have corrupted. (5) He also makes (a slave) worse if he
persuades the slave to commit *iniuria* or theft, or to flee, or to incite
another's slave, or to entangle a *peculium*, or to become a lover or
a roamer, or to devote himself to evil arts or to spend too much time
at entertainments or to be seditious; or if, orally or by a bribe, he
persuades a slave-agent to tamper with or falsify the master's accounts, or also to confuse an account entrusted to him;

(Paul in the nineteenth book on the Edict)
or (if) he makes (the slave) extravagant or insolent, or persuades
him to submit to a sexual assault.

Discussion:

1. On the basis of this text, try to define concisely what the jurists mean by corrupting a slave. How do they conceive the offense? Is it interference with the
   owner's property rights?

2. How should the amount of loss to the owner be assessed? Should account
   be taken only of the decrease in the slave's value, or also of losses stemming

from the decline in the slave's value? Neratius (cited by Ulpian, D. 11.3.9.3) seems to take the former view. But Paul (D. 11.3.10) argues that, if the defendant persuades a slave to steal money, the defendant should be liable for the lost money even if he or she did not receive it; "for it is more just that the author of the delict be liable than that the recipient of the (stolen) property be sought for." Does this seem right?

3. I persuade a slave to falsify a document; I am liable for the loss the owner sustains thereby. But if the slave then becomes chronically untrustworthy, am I also liable for the owner's subsequent losses? See Ulpian, D. 11.3.11.1, who holds that I am not liable for the subsequent losses. Why?

4. Alfenus (D. 11.3.16) sets the following case: A master manumits his slave steward, and then discovers that the steward had falsified his account books in order to spend money on a disreputable woman. Can the owner sue the woman for corrupting the steward even though he is now free? Alfenus holds that the owner can sue; why and for what? Compare the logic in Case 36, on the Lex Aquilia; and see also Ulpian, D. 11.3.5.4.

5. What is it to "persuade" a slave? Ulpian (D. 11.3.1.3) appears to say that persuading means "compelling and forcing obedience"—considerably more, in other words, than just advising a course of action. Does this soften the impact of the edict? Compare Cases 110–111, on aiding and abetting theft.

6. Titius leads my slave into a lower-class tavern, or entices him to gamble. Under what circumstances will I have an action on outrage (*iniuria*), and when will the action on corrupting a slave be more appropriate? See Paul, D. 47.10.26, who gives the action on outrage if Titius intends to insult me, and the action on corrupting a slave if Titius is unaware of me; these actions are available even if the slave is a willing participant. Why?

Case 162: Intent to Corrupt

D. 11.3.3 (Ulpianus, libro vicensimo tertio ad Edictum)

Dolo malo adiecto calliditatem notat Praetor eius qui persuadet: ceterum si quis sine dolo deteriorem fecerit, non notatur, et si lusus gratia fecit, non tenetur. (1) Unde quaeritur, si quis servo alieno suaserit in tectum ascendere vel in puteum descendere et ille parens ascenderit vel descenderit et ceciderit crusque vel quid aliud fregerit vel perierit, an teneatur: et si quidem sine dolo malo fecerit, non tenetur, si dolo malo, tenebitur.

(Ulpian in the twenty-third book on the Edict)

By adding *dolus malus*, the Praetor censures the craftiness of the person who persuades. But if without *dolus* someone makes (a slave) worse, he is not censured, and if he did it for a joke, he is not liable. (1) So it is asked whether someone is liable if he urges another's slave to climb onto a roof or go down a well, and the slave obeys and climbs up or goes down, and falls and breaks a leg or something else, or dies. If he did this without *dolus malus*, he is not liable; if with *dolus malus*, he will be liable.

Discussion:

1. Why are you not liable if you jokingly suggest that someone's slave do something that is obviously dangerous? Is the slave also presumed to possess some common sense?

2. How easy would it be to tell, in a given case, whether the defendant had intended to corrupt a slave? What sorts of evidence might be used?

3. When someone persuades another's slave to climb a tree or go down a well, and the slave is in consequence injured, there is often Aquilian liability *in factum*; see Case 7. How does Aquilian liability differ from liability for corrupting a slave? If the person who persuaded had acted with *dolus*, would he or she be liable both under the Aquilian action and under the edict on corrupting a slave?

Chapter VII: Quasi-Delict

Quasi-delict is a murky category that was probably not accepted until the postclassical period, although the law teacher Gaius seems to know it already in mid-second century A.D. The category collects several types of liability, all established in classical law, that for one reason or another are not easily explained as delicts. In all of them, one person has suffered loss, and another person is held liable for that loss even if he or she did not directly inflict it; the defendant may not be at fault, but at least had the opportunity to prevent the loss from occurring. Since the defendant's fault is not necessarily involved, the liability is not delictual; rather, it is said to arise "as if from a delict" (*quasi ex delicto*).

The Praetor's Edict established that if something was poured or thrown from an upstairs dwelling onto a public way, and it caused damage to persons or property beneath, the principal occupant of the dwelling was liable even though he or she was not the culprit. In this sort of situation, a victim may find it difficult to establish the culprit's identity; but whether this is possible or not, the occupant is held liable, perhaps on the theory that he or she had failed to exercise sufficient oversight.

A similar theory may underlie the liability of ship-operators, innkeepers, and stable-keepers whose employees stole or did damage to the property of guests. In this instance a person is held liable for an act that he or she has demonstrably not committed; here too the issue seems to be one of inadequate oversight.

Perhaps the most difficult liability is that of a *iudex* who "makes the case his own." This expression appears to mean that the *iudex* makes himself liable in place of the defendant; but it is unclear when this would happen. The Praetor's edict was perhaps originally directed only at the failure of a *iudex* to hear a lawsuit and render judgment. But by the second century A.D., the *iudex* was also held liable for judgments that were objectively erroneous, even as a result (e.g.) of inexperience. This may have been regarded as a quasi-delict because the *iudex* was liable without regard to his own fault. Alternatively, it is possible that, since a misbehaving *iudex* vicariously assumed another's liability, his case was treated as broadly analogous to that of an occupant or a shipowner. In postclassical law, the *iudex* was made liable also for corrupt judgments.

Quasi-delict is mainly interesting for the ways in which it begins to go beyond the classical principles of delictual law, in order to establish liabilities based not on demonstrable fault (*dolus* or *culpa*), but on imputed failure of oversight — a form of strict liability that has become far more prominent in modern law.

Part A: Things Thrown or Poured Out of Buildings

Case 163: The Edict on Pouring or Dropping Objects

D. 9.3.1 pr.–1 (Ulpianus, libro vicensimo tertio ad Edictum)

Praetor ait de his, qui deiecerint vel effuderint: 'Unde in eum locum, quo volgo iter fiet vel in quo consistetur, deiectum vel effusum quid erit, quantum ex ea re damnum datum factumve erit, in eum, qui ibi habitaverit, in duplum iudicium dabo. si eo ictu homo liber perisse dicetur, quinquaginta aureorum iudicium dabo. si vivet nocitumque ei esse dicetur, quantum ob eam rem aequum iudici videbitur eum cum quo agetur condemnari, tanti iudicium dabo. si servus insciente domino fecisse dicetur, in iudicio adiciam: aut noxae dedere.' (1) Summa cum utilitate id Praetorem edixisse nemo est qui neget: publice enim utile est sine metu et periculo per itinera commeari.

(Ulpian in the twenty-third book on the Edict)
Concerning those who throw or pour out, the Praetor says: "Whence something is thrown or poured out onto a place where persons commonly go or stand, against the occupant I will give a trial for double the loss inflicted or done by this act. If a free man allegedly dies from this blow, I will give a trial for fifty gold coins; if he lives and is allegedly injured, I will give a trial for as much as it will seem just to the *iudex* that the defendant be condemned for this thing. If a slave allegedly acted without his master's knowledge, I will add in the trial: 'or make noxal surrender.'" (1) No one will deny the great usefulness of this edict of the Praetor; for it is publicly useful that people move through streets without fear and risk.

Discussion:

1. What is the apparent purpose of this edict? How do its provisions differ from Aquilian liability? Should the occupant be held liable for everything dropped or poured, no matter by whom?

2. The Praetor also gave an action against anyone who suspended objects where they could fall: Ulpian, D. 9.3.5.6. Although Gaius (D. 44.7.5.5) also describes this action as a quasi-delict, it apparently lies only against the wrongdoer; but it lies even if no loss results from suspending the object.

Case 164: Strict Liability

D. 9.3.1.4 (Ulpianus, libro vicensimo tertio ad Edictum)

Haec in factum actio in eum datur, qui inhabitat, cum quid deiceretur vel effunderetur, non in dominum aedium: culpa enim penes eum est. nec adicitur culpae mentio vel infitiationis, ut in duplum detur actio, quamvis damni iniuriae utrumque exiget.

(Ulpian in the twenty-third book on the Edict)

This action *in factum* is given against the occupant at the time something is thrown or poured out, not against the building's owner; for the *culpa* rests with the former. Nor (in the Edict) is mention made of *culpa*, or of (the defendant's) denial leading to action for double, although the action for wrongful loss requires both.

Discussion:

1. You lease an upstairs apartment to me; something falls from the window of my apartment and kills a slave. Why does Ulpian say that the *culpa* rests with me? Since *culpa* is not required for this action, is this just a fiction?

2. Ulpian (D. 9.3.1.9) defines an occupant as one who lives "either in his own dwelling or in a rented or gratuitously granted one." But he adds that a temporary guest is not liable "because he does not live there." How clear is this distinction? Only the principal occupant of the dwelling (the owner, or the tenant, or a long-term guest, as the case may be) is liable under this edict.

3. Who, other than the occupant, might actually be responsible for throwing an object from the window? Is the occupant liable if something is thrown down by a member of his household (whether slave or free), a guest or visitor, a craftsman who is in the dwelling temporarily, an employee, or even an uninvited intruder such as a burglar? Can the occupant realistically be expected to keep close watch on the acts of all these persons?

4. As this Case indicates, the action that results from the Praetor's edict on dropping or pouring is *in factum*. Like the Aquilian *in factum* actions, the action rests on the Praetor's power as a magistrate (*imperium*), not on the Roman legal system. How may this action be regarded as a praetorian reform of the Roman legal system?

Case 165: Multiple Occupants

D. 9.3.1.10 (Ulpianus, libro vicensimo tertio ad Edictum)

Si plures in eodem cenaculo habitent, unde deiectum est, in quemvis haec actio dabitur,

D. 9.3.2 (Gaius, libro sexto ad Edictum Provinciale)

cum sane impossibile est scire, quis deiecisset vel effudisset,

D. 9.3.3 (Ulpianus, libro vicensimo tertio ad Edictum)

et quidem in solidum: sed si cum uno fuerit actum, ceteri liberabuntur

D. 9.3.4 (Paulus, libro nono decimo ad Edictum)

perceptione, non litis contestatione, praestaturi partem damni societatis iudicio vel utili actione ei qui solvit.

D. 9.3.5 pr. (Ulpianus, libro vicensimo tertio ad Edictum)

Si vero plures diviso inter se cenaculo habitent, actio in eum solum datur, qui inhabitat eam partem, unde effusum est.

(Ulpian in the twenty-third book on the Edict)
If several persons live in the same apartment out of which something is thrown, this action will be given against any of them

(Gaius in the sixth book on the Provincial Edict)
when it is obviously impossible to know who threw or poured out,

(Ulpian in the twenty-third book on the Edict)
and indeed (the action lies) for the entire amount. But if an action is brought against one person, the rest are released

(Paul in the nineteenth book on the Edict)
by actual payment, not by joinder of issue (*litis contestatio*); (however,) through an action on partnership (*societas*) or an analogous action, they will owe a share of the loss to the person who paid.

(Ulpian in the twenty-third book on the Edict)
But if several persons live in an apartment divided among them, an action is given only against the one who lived in that part from which it was poured out.

Discussion:

1. This Case is a good example of a "chain" (*catena*); the compilers of the *Digest* have used a text of Ulpian as their base, and inserted snippets from Gaius

and Paul in order to make points that Ulpian omitted. What omissions did Ulpian make?

2. In this Case, several persons are jointly occupying an apartment; they are presumably co-tenants. Ulpian describes two situations. In the first, the co-tenants are sharing the entire space of the apartment from which the object fell. The victim can bring suit under the edict against any of them for the full amount. After this defendant pays the victim what is judged, he or she can seek contributions from the other occupants, normally through an action on the contract of partnership (*societas*). Why is this cumbersome procedure required? Why can't the plaintiff simply sue the co-occupants as a group? Note that the other co-occupants are not released from liability to the plaintiff merely because the plaintiff has successfully lodged an action against one of them (joinder of issue, *litis contestatio*, follows the Praetor's grant of the action in the first stage of a trial); the defendant must actually pay the plaintiff before this happens. Why?

3. In the second situation, the co-occupants have divided the apartment's space among them. The victim can sue the co-occupant whose area was involved. Is this a straightforward extension of the usual rule for occupants?

4. Gaius says that an action can be brought against any co-occupant "when it is obviously impossible to know who threw or poured out." But what if it is possible to know this? Can the plaintiff then bring an Aquilian action against the person who threw or poured out something? Must the plaintiff use the Aquilian action? See the following Case.

Case 166: Aquilian Liability of the Thrower

D. 9.3.5.4 (Ulpianus, libro vicensimo tertio ad Edictum)

Cum autem legis Aquiliae actione propter hoc quis tenetur, merito ei, qui ob hoc condemnatus est, quod hospes vel quis alius de cenaculo deiecit, in factum dandam esse Labeo dicit adversus deiectorem, quod verum est. plane si locaverat deiectori, etiam ex locato habebit actionem.

(Ulpian in the twenty-third book on the Edict)

Since a person is liable for this (kind of act) in an Aquilian action, Labeo says that if someone is condemned because his guest or somebody else threw an object from an apartment, he should be given an *in factum* (Aquilian) action against the thrower; this view is correct. Obviously if he had leased to the thrower, he will also have an action on the lease.

The Hypothetical Problem:

A vase is thrown from my apartment window; under the edict on throwing or pouring objects, I am condemned to pay the victim. Later I learn that you threw the vase. Are you liable to me under an Aquilian action?

Discussion:

1. Why does Ulpian hold that you are liable to me? What is the measure of my loss? Why is the action *in factum* rather than direct? What is the amount of the liability?

2. Could I have escaped liability to the victim in the first place by proving that you were the real culprit?

3. If your identity had been known, could the victim have sued you on an Aquilian action, instead of me on the action concerning things thrown? If he or she did, would the second action be excluded?

4. The *Digest* text of this Case is clearly corrupt; the Latin text cited above follows Mommsen's extensive emendation.

Part B: Liability for Theft: Ship-Operators and Innkeepers

Case 167: The Action Against Ship-Operators and Innkeepers

D. 47.5.1 pr.–2 (Ulpianus, libro trigensimo octavo ad Edictum)

In eos, qui naves cauponas stabula exercebunt, si quid a quoquo eorum quos ibi habebunt furtum factum esse dicetur, iudicium datur, sive furtum ope consilio exercitoris factum sit, sive eorum cuius, qui in ea navi navigandi causa esset. (1) Navigandi autem causa accipere debemus eos, qui adhibentur, ut navis naviget, hoc est nautas. (2) Et est in duplum actio.

(Ulpian in the thirty-eighth book on the Edict)
A trial is given against those who operate ships, inns, or stables if a theft was allegedly committed by one of the persons they had there, whether the theft was committed with the aid and advice of the ship's operator, or with that of a person who was on the ship for the purpose of sailing it. (1) "For the purpose of sailing it" we should apply to those persons who are brought on in order to sail the ship, i.e., the sailors. (2) The action is for double (the loss).

Discussion:

1. The first paragraph is a close paraphrase of the Praetor's edict with regard to ships. (The *Digest* compilers added the references to inns and stables, whose operators had a similar liability.) How does the liability established by this edict differ from the general liability for *furtum*? Can the victim elect to sue the actual thief instead?

2. The Praetor established a similar liability if the property of guests was damaged by the employees of ship-operators or innkeepers. Ulpian (D. 4.9.7 pr.) notes that this liability can be avoided by contract; is the same true of the liability for theft?

3. Why might the guests on ships or in inns have required special protection? Ulpian (D. 4.9.1.1) suggests, what literary sources also confirm, that ships and inns had a low reputation, and that problems with theft or vandalism were frequent. Could it also be that the employees were usually insolvent or nearly so?

Case 168: Extent of Liability

D. 47.5.1.5–6 (Ulpianus, libro trigensimo octavo ad Edictum)

Servi vero sui nomine exercitor noxae dedendo se liberat. cur ergo non exercitor condemnetur, qui servum tam malum in nave admisit? et cur liberi quidem hominis nomine tenetur in solidum, servi vero non tenetur? nisi forte idcirco, quod liberum quidem hominem adhibens statuere debuit de eo, qualis esset, in servo vero suo ignoscendum sit ei quasi in domestico malo, si noxae dedere paratus sit. si autem alienum adhibuit servum, quasi in libero tenebitur. (6) Caupo praestat factum eorum, qui in ea caupona eius cauponae exercendae causa ibi sunt, item eorum, qui habitandi causa ibi sunt: viatorum autem factum non praestat. namque viatorem sibi eligere caupo vel stabularius non videtur nec repellere potest iter agentes: inhabitatores vero perpetuos ipse quodammodo elegit, qui non reiecit, quorum factum oportet eum praestare. in navi quoque vectorum factum non praestatur.

(Ulpian in the thirty-eighth book on the Edict)

The operator of a ship who is sued in the name of his slave frees himself by making noxal surrender. Why, then, is the shipper not condemned for having so bad a slave on the ship? And why is he liable for the entirety in the case of a free man, but not in the case of a slave? Unless perhaps, in bringing on a free man, he ought to decide on his character; but in the case of his slave, if he is ready to make noxal surrender, he should be forgiven as for a household wrong. But if he brings on another person's slave, he will be liable as for a free man. (6) An innkeeper is liable for the conduct of persons in his inn for the purpose of running it, and also for persons who reside there, but is not liable for the conduct of travellers. For the innkeeper or stable-keeper is not held to choose a traveller nor can he turn away people making a trip; but in a sense he chooses long-term residents by not rejecting them, and he ought to be liable for their conduct. On a ship also he is not liable for the conduct of passengers.

Discussion:

1. How convincing do you find Ulpian's argument concerning the ship-operator's noxal liability for slaves? Can you think of a more convincing explanation for the distinction between slaves and free employees?

2. This Case makes it clear that the victim of the theft must be able to identify the thief, even though suit is brought against the ship-operator or innkeeper. How realistic is this requirement?

3. In what sense are the long-term residents of inns similar to employees? How convincing is Ulpian's argument that the innkeeper has chosen them by allowing them to remain?

4. What are the likely economic consequences of making ship-operators and innkeepers liable for theft by employees? Will the price of booking passage

or obtaining lodgings be higher? Is this economically desirable? Why or why not?

Case 169: Quasi-Delict

D. 44.7.5.5–6 (Gaius, libro tertio Aureorum)

Is quoque, ex cuius cenaculo (vel proprio ipsius vel conducto vel in quo gratis habitabat) deiectum effusumve aliquid est ita, ut alicui noceret, quasi ex maleficio teneri videtur: ideo autem non proprie ex maleficio obligatus intellegitur, quia plerumque ob alterius culpam tenetur aut servi aut liberi.... (6) Item exercitor navis aut cauponae aut stabuli de damno aut furto, quod in nave aut caupona aut stabulo factum sit, quasi ex maleficio teneri videtur, si modo ipsius nullum est maleficium, sed alicuius eorum, quorum opera navem aut cauponam aut stabulum exerceret: cum enim neque ex contractu sit adversus eum constituta haec actio et aliquatenus culpae reus est, quod opera malorum hominum uteretur, ideo quasi ex maleficio teneri videtur.

(Gaius in the third book of *Golden Words*)

Also a person from whose apartment — whether he owns it or leases it or lives there free — something is thrown or poured so as to harm another, is considered liable as if from a delict (*quasi ex maleficio*). But he is not properly regarded as obligated from a delict, since frequently he is liable for the *culpa* of another person, whether slave or free.... (6) Likewise the operator of a ship or inn or stable is considered liable as if from a delict (*quasi ex maleficio*) for loss or theft inflicted on the ship or in the inn or stable, provided he himself is not the wrongdoer, but a person through whose help he operates the ship or inn or stable. For since this action was not established against him from the contract, and he is to some extent guilty of *culpa* because he uses the help of bad men, so he is held liable as if from a delict (*quasi ex maleficio*).

Discussion:

1. In this passage (which may contain post-classical elements), Gaius tries to state the theory linking the two types of liability he describes. Is this theory convincing?

2. What legal differences are there between the liability for throwing or pouring things from windows, and the liability of ship-operators for thefts committed by employees?

Part C: Misconduct by a *Iudex*

Case 170: "Making the Suit One's Own"

D. 5.1.15.1 (Ulpianus, libro vicensimo primo ad Edictum)

Iudex tunc litem suam facere intellegitur, cum dolo malo in fraudem legis sententiam dixerit (dolo malo autem videtur hoc facere, si evidens arguatur eius vel gratia vel inimicitia vel etiam sordes), ut veram aestimationem litis praestare cogatur.

(Ulpian in the twenty-first book on the Edict)

A *iudex* is considered to make the suit his own when he deceitfully (*dolo malo*) gives a decision in breach of law — and he is held to act deceitfully if his partiality or enmity or also bribery is clearly proven —, so that he is forced to pay the true assessment of the suit.

Discussion:

1. The original nature of this liability is very obscure, and the few texts concerning it are believed to have been heavily altered by the *Digest*'s compilers. But it may be that the original liability was much more narrowly conceived: the *iudex* became liable to the plaintiff if he failed to hear the case at the appointed time, or if he failed to render judgment on the case, unless he had a valid excuse for not doing so. By the second century A.D., the *iudex* was liable also for judgments that did not correspond to the formula for the trial (Gaius, *Inst.* 4.52). As this Case shows, in the postclassical period the liability was expanded still further, to take account of judgments that resulted from improper influences such as bribery.

2. Scholars believe that the original Ulpianic text of this Case did not have the words "deceitfully (*dolo malo*)" and the entire clause within the dashes. How did these later additions change the meaning of the Case?

3. What is meant by "making the suit one's own"? When a *iudex* misbehaves, a litigant may lose legally guaranteed rights. Does it seem reasonable to you that the misbehaving *iudex* should be made liable to the litigant for the value of these lost rights? Should this be true under all circumstances, or just in some situations? Remember that in classical law the *iudex* was usually a layman with no special training in law, rather like a member of a modern jury.

Case 171: Quasi-Delict and Judges

D. 50.13.6 (Gaius, libro tertio Rerum Cottidianarum sive Aureorum)

Si iudex litem suam fecerit, non proprie ex maleficio obligatus videtur: sed quia neque ex contractu obligatus est et utique peccasse aliquid intellegitur, licet per inprudentiam, ideo videtur quasi ex maleficio teneri in factum actione, et in quantum de ea re aequum religioni iudicantis visum fuerit, poenam sustinebit.

(Gaius in the third book of *Common Matters or Golden Words*)

If a *iudex* makes a suit his own, he is not properly held to be obligated from a delict (*ex maleficio*). But because he is not obligated from a contract, but is considered to have done wrong somehow, although by lack of foresight, he is as a result held to be liable as if from a delict (*quasi ex maleficio*) in an action *in factum*, and he will suffer a penalty of as much as seems right in this matter to the conscience of the *iudex* (in the trial against him).

Discussion:

1. Why is it not possible to regard the *iudex* as having committed a delict? The answer may lie in the phrase "although by lack of foresight"; does this mean that the *iudex* may be liable even though he was not at fault? Note that Case 170 speaks of liability only if the *iudex* acts "deceitfully" (*dolo malo*). Does this Case support the view that Case 170 was altered by the compilers of the *Digest*?

2. What relation does this form of quasi-delict bear to those discussed in Case 169? This question is not easy to answer; but Gaius may be focussing on the possibility that the *iudex* can be liable without fault.

Appendix:
Biographies of the
Major Roman Jurists

(Jurists who are cited or referred to more than once in the Cases are marked by an asterisk.)

AFRICANUS. Sextus Caecilius Africanus was a student of Julian; in his nine books of *Questions* he generally seems to follow and comment on Julian's decisions. The *Digest* contains 130 fragments or citations of his writings.

*ALFENUS. Publius Alfenus Varus, Consul in 39 B.C. and a student of Servius, wrote 40 books of *Digests* that were excerpted and commented on by Paul in the late classical period. He is the only preclassical jurist whose writings are represented by numerous excerpts (81 fragments) in the *Digest*; they frequently report views of Servius.

BRUTUS. Marcus Junius Brutus, Praetor in 142 B.C., is counted among the three founders of Roman legal science.

*CASSIUS. Gaius Cassius Longinus, descended from an eminent Republican family, was Consul in A.D. 30, later Proconsul and Legate in Asia and Syria, but in 65 was banished to Sardinia by Nero (A.D. 54–68). A pupil of Sabinus, he helped found the school of jurists that is also called Cassian. His major work, a commentary on the *ius civile*, is known from excerpts reworked by Javolenus.

Cassius' tenure as Urban Praetor, probably in A.D. 27, is referred to in Case 159.

CALLISTRATUS is a late classical jurist whose writings are mainly concerned with extraordinary cognition and administrative law. The *Digest* contains 108 fragments of his writings.

*CELSUS. Publius Juventius Celsus (Praetor in A.D. 106, Consul for the second time in 128, Governor of Thrace and Asia, a member of Hadrian's Council) is one of the most prominent juristic personalities of the high classical period. His acuteness and originality were accompanied, at times, by aggressive polemics. Although along with Neratius he headed the Proculian school, Celsus appears to have contributed to overcoming traditional school controversies. Of special note are his abstract statements on the sources of law and the methods of legal interpretation.

Celsus' major work, the *Digests* in 39 books, follows the order of the Edict (books 1–27) and a standard list of statutes and decrees of the Senate (books 28–39). He is relatively well represented in the *Digest* (279 fragments).

FURIUS ANTHIANUS is an obscure jurist, possibly of late classical date, who wrote a commentary on the Edict.

*GAIUS (his family name and origin are unknown) was an outsider in classical jurisprudence; he was a teacher of law, probably without the *ius respondendi*. His writings (some twenty in number, dating from A.D. 150–180) were intended mainly to instruct (e.g., the material is carefully organized) and also show an interest in legal history (e.g., his commentary on the Twelve Tables); but they avoid casuistic discussion of legal problems. For this reason Gaius was not considered worthy of citation by his contemporaries, but he came to be recognized as a major jurist in the post-classical period and is frequently cited in the *Digest* (521 fragments). His main significance lies in the area of abstract doctrine and system-building.

Gaius' thirty books on the Provincial Edict are an extended commentary on the model Edict for the provinces; the Emperor Hadrian (A.D. 117–134) had ordered the Provincial Edict to be edited along with the Urban Praetor's Edict, and the two closely resembled each other. Governors were required to proclaim the Provincial Edict unchanged. Gaius' commentary was perhaps written as a basis for law courses in a provincial city.

Gaius' *Institutes*, a beginner's text in four books, was used as the basis for Justinian's *Institutes*, which have profoundly influenced Continental legal education and codification down to modern times. Gaius' *Institutes* is the only work of classical jurisprudence that survives to us in approximately its original form; the single manuscript (a palimpsest, in which the text of Gaius was overwritten with the letters of Saint Jerome) was rediscovered by the historian B.G. Niebuhr in Verona in 1816, and identified by the great legal historian Carl von Savigny soon thereafter.

Gaius also prepared an expanded seven-book edition of the *Institutes*, which he called the *Res Cottidianae* or *Aurea*. Scholars today believe that the preserved fragments from this work contain some postclassical additions.

GALLUS. Gaius Aquilius Gallus, a student of Q. Mucius Scaevola, was Praetor in 66 B.C. and one of the major jurists of his day; he apparently wrote nothing, and his opinions are mainly transmitted through Servius.

HERMOGENIANUS is an early post-classical jurist who wrote six books of *Legal Excerpts* under Diocletian (A.D. 284–305); he probably also compiled the Hermogenian Code, a collection of Diocletian's rescripts between 291 and 294.

*JAVOLENUS. Lucius Javolenus Priscus, head of the Sabinian school and Julian's teacher, wrote during the late first and early second centuries A.D.; he was Consul in A.D. 86, and later Governor in Upper Germany, Syria, and Africa, as well as a member of Trajan's Council (A.D. 98–117). The *Digest* contains 72 fragments from his most important work, the *Letters* (14 books), the longer fragments of which preserve the response format. He also prepared critical editions of the works of several earlier jurists (Labeo, Cassius, Plautius).

*JULIAN. Publius Salvius Julianus, a student of Javolenus, enjoyed a brilliant career under the Emperors Hadrian (A.D. 117–138), Antoninus Pius (A.D. 138–161), and Marcus Aurelius (A.D. 161–180), to whose Council he belonged. "Because of his extraordinary learning" (so an honorary inscription tells us) the young Julian's pay as Quaestor was doubled by Hadrian, who later entrusted to him the final edition of the Praetor's Edict. Julian reached the Consulate in 148 and served as Governor in Lower Germany, Nearer Spain, and Africa.

Besides his major juristic work, the *Digests* (90 books), he also wrote four books commenting on Urseius Ferox and six books of excerpts from Minicius (an otherwise unknown jurist of the late first century A.D.). Julian is praised especially for his clarity, elegance, and intuition, the concrete vividness and realistic persuasiveness of his decisions. He seldom makes citations, basing his decisions instead on virtuosic reasoning from case to case, and he does not hesitate to overstep doctrinal boundaries in order to achieve fair results. The late classical jurists, especially Ulpian, cite him as a towering authority; in the *Digest* the compilers include more than 900 direct excerpts or citations from Julian's work.

*LABEO. Marcus Antistius Labeo was a student of Trebatius; because of his creative originality, he is considered the preeminent figure in early classical jurisprudence. He allegedly declined the consulate because of his opposition to the Emperor Augustus (31 B.C. to A.D. 14). Labeo taught law extensively — the law school later called Proculian was traced back to him — and he also wrote at length. Labeo's voluminous works (over 400 books) are known to us only through two abbreviated versions: the jurist Javolenus epitomized and commented on Labeo's posthumous writings (in ten books), and Paul later did the same for the *Pithana* ("Arguments," in eight books).

*MARCELLUS. Ulpius Marcellus, a high classical jurist, belonged to the Councils of Antoninus Pius (A.D. 138–161) and Marcus Aurelius (A.D. 161–180). His major work is 31 books of *Digests*, a collection of problems influenced by Julian's *Digests*. Justinian's *Digest* contains 292 fragments of his writings.

*MELA. Fabius Mela is thought to have written during the reign of Augustus (31 B.C. to A.D. 14).

*Q. MUCIUS. Quintus Mucius Scaevola (the Pontifex), Consul in 95 B.C., is considered the most important preclassical jurist. He came from an aristocratic family that boasted many jurists, and his father P. Mucius Scaevola was one of the founders of Roman legal science. According to Pomponius, Q. Mucius was the first jurist to present the *ius civile* in systematic classifications. His 18 books on the *ius civile* were still commented on by Pomponius in the second century A.D.

OCTAVENUS appears to have written at the beginning of the second century A.D.; his work is cited fairly frequently by later authors.

NERATIUS. Lucius Neratius Priscus (Consul in A.D. 98, later Legate in Pannonia) headed the Proculian school after the elder Celsus; he belonged to the Imperial Council of Trajan (A.D. 98–117) and Hadrian (A.D. 117–138). His major works are collections of case law (*Responses, Letters, Rules of Law, Parchments*). He is well represented by 188 fragments or citations in the *Digest*.

NERVA. Marcus Cocceius Nerva (Consul in A.D. 21 or 22) was a close advisor of the Emperor Tiberius (A.D. 14–37). Along with Proculus, he led what was later called the Proculian school of jurists. Although later jurists often cite him, the titles of his writings are unknown. His son was also a jurist, and his grandson was the Emperor Nerva (A.D. 96–98).

OFILIUS. Aulus Ofilius was a student of Servius and a friend of Julius Caesar; no excerpts from his work survive in the *Digest*, but he is cited by other jurists more than fifty times.

PAPINIAN. Aemilius Papinianus rose to the summit of the imperial bureaucracy. In A.D. 198 Papinian appears to have taken over the Office for Petitions (*a libellis*), which drafted rescripts for the Emperor Septimius Severus and his son and co-ruler Caracalla (A.D. 193–211); Ulpian, who served as Papinian's Clerk (*Adsessor*), often refers to Severus' rescripts in his writings. From 203–211 Papinian served as Praetorian Prefect, with Paul and Ulpian probably acting as his Clerks (*Adsessores*) during part of this period. Papinian was executed in 211 or 212, allegedly because he objected to Caracalla's murder of his brother and co-ruler Geta.

Papinian's works (especially his 37 books of *Questions* and 19 books of *Responses*) preserve casuistry in its highest form. Despite their difficult style and their frequent extreme brevity of expression, Papinian is fascinating because of the richness of his thought and the sureness of his handling. The compilers of the *Digest* regarded him highly and made numerous excerpts from his writings (only Ulpian and Paul are used more frequently); and still today he is rightly regarded as one of the greatest Roman jurists.

*PAUL. The late classical jurist Julius Paulus was a student of Cervidius Scaevola; like Ulpian, he began his bureaucratic career as an Clerk (*Adsessor*) to the Praetorian Prefect Papinian. Along with Ulpian he then served on the Council of Septimius Severus (A.D. 193–211); under Alexander Severus (A.D. 222–235) he may have become Praetorian Prefect, the highest imperial office. Paul is considered more original than his slightly younger contemporary Ulpian, who seems to have inclined more strongly toward consolidating legal conceptions through dogma, thereby obscuring their original elasticity.

Despite his undoubtedly difficult and time-consuming official duties, Paul was astonishingly productive (notes on Neratius, Julian, Marcellus, and Scaevola; 16 books on Sabinus; 26 books of *Questions*; 23 books of *Responses*; dozens of monographs on specialized topics). Paul's commentary on the Praetor's Edict is a monumental work in 80 books, in which classical case law is critically assembled, examined, and presented from a relatively systematic viewpoint. The compilers of the *Digest* made numerous excerpts from his writings, amounting to about one-sixth of the entire *Digest*; but in the process they usually struck out Paul's extensive citations of earlier jurists and his reports of controversies.

The *Sentences*, attributed to Paul, are a collection of excerpts from the writings of Paul and (perhaps) other jurists; the collection was assembled in the late third century A.D. Until fairly recently the *Sentences* were considered a genuine and important work of Paul; as such, they had major influence on postclassical and medieval law. Today the *Sentences* are valued mainly because they preserve many texts of Paul in a pre-Justinianic form.

*SEX. PEDIUS. Sextus Pedius is known only through citations by Paul and Ulpian. He wrote a wide-ranging commentary on the Praetor's Edict and was probably a contemporary of Julian.

*PEGASUS, who succeeded Proculus as head of the Proculian school, served as Prefect of the City under Vespasian (A.D. 69–79) and under Domitian (A.D. 81–96), and also became Consul. His great reputation for learning led contemporaries to describe him as "a book, not a man"; but he is rarely cited by later jurists.

*PLAUTIUS, an adherent of the Proculian school, wrote during the Flavian period (A.D. 69–96). The writings of Plautius were regarded as highly as Sabinus' *Civil Law*; they were annotated by Neratius and Javolenus, and Pomponius (7 books) and especially Paul (18 books) wrote commentaries on his work.

*POMPONIUS. Sextus Pomponius, a contemporary of Gaius, like him represents an academic tendency in Roman jurisprudence. Nonetheless, he had great influence as the author of wide-ranging commentaries (39 books on Q. Mucius; an exhaustive commentary on Sabinus in 35 books; his commentary on the Praetor's Edict may have reached the impressive length of 150 books). Pomponius is frequently cited, especially by Ulpian, and there are numerous excerpts from him in the *Digest* (861 fragments or citations).

Case 21 is a good illustration of the organization of Pomponius' commentary; Q. Mucius is quoted directly, and then Pomponius adds supplementary remarks.

*PROCULUS. The early classical jurist Proculus wrote in the first half of the first century A.D. Probably in A.D. 33 he took over direction of the school that was later named for him. The *Digest* contains 33 fragments from his main work, the *Letters*. This work discusses legal problems in the question-and-answer format of responses; but the actual case is less prominent than its theoretical extensions. Proculus' numerous distinctions give his work a didactic schematism.

*SABINUS. Massurius Sabinus was an early classical jurist to whom the Emperor Tiberius (A.D. 14–37) gave the *ius respondendi*; Sabinus was the first member of the equestrian order to have the right. The Sabinian law school was founded by him. His most significant work, three books on the *ius civile*, was widely used throughout the classical period; Pomponius, Paul, and Ulpian wrote enormous commentaries on it.

SCAEVOLA. Quintus Cervidius Scaevola was Paul's teacher and an advisor of Marcus Aurelius (A.D. 161–180). His casuistic writings (six books of *Responses*, 20 of *Questions*, 40 of *Digests*) contain brief, precise decisions of cases, often without justifications. His writings are well represented by 344 excerpts or citations in the *Digest*.

*SERVIUS. Servius Sulpicius Rufus, Consul in 51 B.C., was one of the most prominent and versatile jurists of the later Republic. He taught a large number of students; Cicero also praised his eloquence as an advocate. Servius wrote, among other things, the first commentary on the Praetor's Edict. After his death a comprehensive collection of his responses was published by his students Aufidius and Alfenus.

TREBATIUS. Gaius Trebatius Testa, a friend and protégé of Cicero, also served as a legal advisor to Julius Caesar and Augustus. His opinions are known mainly through his student Labeo.

*ULPIAN. The late classical jurist Domitius Ulpianus was a student of Papinian; like Paul, Ulpian served as Clerk (*Adsessor*) when Papinian was Praetorian Prefect. Ulpian later became a member of the Imperial Council; under Alexander Severus (A.D. 222–235) he finally reached the office of Praetorian Prefect. In 223 he was murdered during a riot of the Praetorian Guard.

Ulpian's 83-book commentary on the Praetor's Edict had virtually the same breadth as Paul's; it contained extensive discussion of the views of earlier jurists. Ulpian's commentary on the *ius civile* (51 books on Sabinus) breaks off at the discussion of vindication; we do not know whether it was left incomplete at his death or a part has been lost. He also wrote numerous monographs and collections of legal opinions.

The compilers of the *Digest* drew more extensively on Ulpian's writings than on any other classical jurist; more than forty percent of the *Digest* comes from his work. Although Ulpian is often considered less brilliant than his slightly older contemporary Paul, the compilers were evidently attracted by the comprehensive character of Ulpian's writing, as well as by his openminded willingness to entertain divergent views of earlier jurists.

URSEIUS FEROX apparently wrote in the second half of the first century A.D.; Julian commented on his writings.

VENULEIUS. Venuleius Saturninus wrote extensive monographs on private and public law during the reigns of Antoninus Pius (A.D. 138–161) and Marcus Aurelius (161–180).

*VIVIANUS seems to have written a commentary on the Edict during the first century A.D.; later jurists cite him occasionally.

Glossary of
Technical Terms

References are to Cases or sections of the casebook. Definitions for Roman law terms rely heavily on A. Berger, *Encyclopedic Dictionary of Roman Law* (1953).

action (*actio*): a "lawsuit," or the claim upon which it is based. A "cause of action" is a legal basis upon which a lawsuit can be brought. In Roman law, the Praetor's Edict listed the available forms of action; see "Edict" and "formula." A "statutory action" (*actio ex lege*) is one based upon a statute such as the Lex Aquilia. An *actio utilis* ("analogous action") is one introduced by the Praetor by modifying an existing formula to cover situations for which the original formula did not provide; an *in factum* action ("action on the facts") is a form of action in which the defendant's liability results not from pre-existing law, but from a "fact" that the Praetor recognizes as a basis of liability. For the formulas that the Praetor grants on the model of the Lex Aquilia, the jurists use the phrases *actio utilis* and *in factum* action interchangeably (I. B). "Concurrence of actions" is the legal problem that results when a single event gives rise to more than one cause of action (III. C).

Aedile: an annually elected Roman magistrate, ranking below the Praetor and charged mainly with the keeping of order in public places in Rome. The Curule Aediles had jurisdiction over some minor criminal offenses (Case 40).

asportation: the removal of property from one place to another; a requirement for larceny in Anglo-American criminal law.

assumption of risk: voluntary acceptance of the possibility that another person may do one harm (Cases 58–59).

casuistry: the discovery and application of legal rules through discussion of particular cases.

cautio: a "formal undertaking"; see "stipulation. " The *cautio damni infecti* is an "undertaking against threatened damage" which the owner or occupant of land can demand from a neighbor when the rundown conditions of the neighbor's building may do damage to the adjoining property; the neighbor promises to pay for future damage resulting from this cause.

condictio: a form of action in which the plaintiff claims that the defendant has an obligation to give or to do something, without specifying the reason for the claim. The *condictio* on theft (*condictio furtiva*) is a claim for the recovery of stolen property, together with proceeds from that property.

contrectatio: the "handling" of another's property with a view to taking or appropriating it. *Contrectatio* is a requirement for theft (V. A. 1).

culpa: the "fault" of an individual, for which he or she may be held legally responsible. In Aquilian liability, *culpa* includes careless failure to foresee what a careful person would have foreseen (II. A–B). Depending on the context, *cul-*

pa means either unintentional fault (excluding *dolus*) or fault in general (including *dolus*).

custodia: the "safekeeping" of property belonging to another; a standard of care by which the holder is liable for all damage to the property except that occurring through "irresistible force" (*vis maior*).

damnum iniuria datum: "loss wrongfully inflicted," which gives rise to Aquilian liability (I–III). The concept of "loss" (*damnum*) is discussed in II. C.

delict (*delictum, maleficium*): a "misdeed" that is prosecuted through a private lawsuit brought by the offended individual and is punished by a money penalty that the defendant pays to the plaintiff.

dolus or *dolus malus*: the "intent" to inflict loss or hurt on another person. *Dolus* also means "deceit" in the delict established by the Praetor (VI. A).

Edict (*Edictum*): the proclamation of the Urban Praetor at the beginning of his year in office, in which he specified the forms of action he accepted. The Praetor's Edict contained numerous special edicts on particular causes of action. During the early Empire, the contents of the Praetor's Edict gradually became fixed, and a final "permanent" version (the *Edictum Perpetuum*) was issued under the Emperor Hadrian (A.D. 117–138). The "Provincial Edict" was issued by Governors in Roman provinces.

exceptio: a "defense" interposed by the defendant in order to render the plaintiff's claim ineffective; the *exceptio* was inserted into the formula for the action. The "defense of deceit" (*exceptio doli*) alleges that the plaintiff has acted or is acting deceitfully (Cases 150–151); the "defense of duress" (*exceptio metus*) alleges that the plaintiff's claim is nullified by prior use of duress (Case 159).

extra ordinem: judicial procedure "outside the regular order" of formulary procedure, and through judges appointed through the Emperor. "Extraordinary cognition" (*cognitio extraordinaria*) is the procedural system associated with these judges; in the post-classical period it replaces formulary procedure.

formula: a written document in which the Praetor appoints a *iudex* and orders him either to condemn the defendant if certain factual or legal circumstances are proved, or to absolve the defendant if they are not proved. "Formulary procedure" was the normal method of bringing private lawsuits during the classical period of Roman law.

freedperson (*libertus*): an ex-slave, who has been manumitted by his or her former master. The master becomes the freedperson's patron and is owed duties of respect and service.

furtum: "theft" (V. A). "Theft of use" (*furtum usus*) is the unauthorized use of property that the owner has entrusted to one (V. A. 3).

guardian (*tutor, curator*): a person legally appointed to supervise the affairs of a ward, who lacks full capacity because of age or mental condition.

in factum: see "action."

iniuria: "unrightfulness" and later "wrongfulness"; a requirement for Aquilian liability (II A–B, E). *Iniuria* also means "outrage" to another's dignity (V. B).

interdict (*interdictum*): an order issued by the Praetor upon the request of a claimant, directing another person to do something or abstain from some act. If the affected person does not comply or denies the applicability of the interdict, a trial on the merits of the claim results. The interdict *quod vi aut clam* alleges that the defendant used "force or stealth" to interfere with the plaintiff's property rights, and demands that the defendant restore the plaintiff to his or her former state by paying damages.

interest (*id quod interest*): a measure of the loss suffered by a plaintiff, based on what the plaintiff's material situation would have been had the defendant's act not occurred.

iudex: a "judge" in a private trial, appointed by the Praetor to listen to the parties to a lawsuit and decide the case on the basis of the formula.

ius civile: "civil law"; the private law peculiar to the Roman people, especially those portions of the law that are not of praetorian origin.

ius respondendi: a right granted by the Emperor to certain jurists, who are allowed to give legal responses that have quasi-official force. Most important early imperial jurists had this right.

jurist (*iurisconsultus*): an expert in private law.

legacy (*legatum*): a "bequest" that a deceased person leaves to someone other than the heir; the heir must pay legacies out of the inheritance.

lex: a "statute" passed by an assembly of the Roman people. For example, the Lex Aquilia is the statute making wrongful damage to property an actionable delict (I–III). The Lex Cornelia *de inuriis* is a statute of 81 B.C. punishing three types of "outrage" commmitted by violence (Case 128).

liability: legal responsibility for an obligation which courts recognize and enforce as between two parties. On "noxal liability," see "noxal surrender." See also "strict liability." "Aquilian liability" is liability either under the Lex Aquilia itself or under an *in factum* action modelled on the Aquilian action.

locatio conductio: "lease/hire"; a type of contract in which one person "leases out" his property, a job, or his labor to another.

manumission (*manumissio*): the release of a slave from the power of his or her master, by an act of the master. The ex-slave becomes a freedperson.

metus: "duress," the use of force or fear to compel another to act or refrain from acting (VI. B).

negligence: failure to conform to a standard of care that is legally required for another's or one's own protection from a specific kind of harm. In Anglo-American law, negligence is the basis of liability in the tort of negligence. "Contributory negligence" is a negligent act or omission by the plaintiff that "contributed" by helping to cause the loss on which the plaintiff is suing (Cases 60–61).

noxal surrender (*noxae datio*): an option given to the master of a slave who has committed a delict, whereby the master can transfer ownership of the slave to the plaintiff rather than accept liability for the delict. Noxal surrender is also used for children in the power of a *paterfamilias*, who can transfer them into the debt-bondage (*mancipium*) of the plaintiff.

ownership (*dominium*): legal title to property; the right to make use of it and dispose of it freely.

paterfamilias: the "head of a household," a Roman citizen who is not under the paternal power of another. The *paterfamilias* has sole ownership and possession of the property belonging to the family, as well as wide-ranging authority over all descendants in his power.

patria potestas: the "paternal power" of a *paterfamilias* over his natural and adoptive descendants, as well as over his wife in *manus*, the archaic form of Roman marriage. This legal power is very broadly conceived; the *paterfamilias* can treat those in his power more or less as he wishes, with few exceptions.

pauperies: "impoverishment"; loss caused to others by animals (IV).

peculium: property granted by a *paterfamilias* to his son or slave, for that person's free use and disposal.

pledge (*pignus*): property voluntarily given by a debtor to a creditor in order to secure payment of a debt; the creditor holds possession of the pledge and can sell it if the debt is not paid.

possession (*possessio*): the physical control of property, together with the intention to hold it, usually as the owner. Although possession is, in the first instance, a matter of fact, the right to possession is protected by Roman law, especially through the interdicts. "Good faith possession" is the control of property by a non-owner who incorrectly believes that he or she is the owner of it.

postliminium: the law governing questions that arise when Roman citizens are captured by enemies of Rome and later released.

power (*potestas*): see "*patria potestas.*"

Praetor: an annually elected Roman magistrate, ranking below the Consul. The Urban Praetor presided at the first stage of private lawsuits between Roman citizens. His Edict listed the causes of action that he accepted; the Praetor used the Edict to enforce existing law and create new causes of action.

private law (*ius privatum*): the law governing relations between individuals, on the basis of which lawsuits between them are judged.

Proculians: a "school" of jurists at Rome in the first and second centuries A.D., named for their first leader, the jurist Proculus. On numerous legal questions the Proculians adopt different positions from the Sabinians, a rival "school" named after the jurist Sabinus.

response (*responsum*): a jurist's answer to a question of law. In its normal literary form, a *responsum* consists of three parts: a statement of hypothetical facts, a question, and the jurist's answer.

Sabinians: see "Proculians."

servitude (*servitus*): a property right attaching to one piece of land over a neighboring one; the servitude gives the owner of the land the right to do or prevent specified things on the neighboring land. Examples are a right of way or a right to convey water. In Common Law, servitudes are called easements.

sesterce (*sestertius*): a Roman coin and a general accounting unit. Although it is hard to give a sense of its value, an unskilled workman at Rome could earn between three and four sesterces per day; while, at the other end of the social scale, Senators were required to have an estate of one million sesterces in order to remain in the Roman Senate.

standing: the legal requirements for being a plaintiff or a defendant in a lawsuit.

statute: see "*lex.*"

stipulation (*stipulatio*): a formal oral contract, concluded through the exchange of a question by the promisee (e. g. , "Do you promise to pay me 10,000 sesterces?") and a corresponding answer by the promisor ("I promise. "). The content of the promise becomes legally enforceable when the question-and-answer form has been properly observed. A *cautio* is a particular form of stipulation.

strict liability: liability without regard to the defendant's fault.

Trespass: a form of action in Common Law, whereby the plaintiff claims damages for an unlawful injury accomplished by the defendant's immediate force and violence against the plaintiff's person, property, or rights. Trespass on the Case is similar, except that the defendant's act is not accompanied by direct or immediate force, or the injury is only a secondary consequence of the defendant's act.

Twelve Tables: an early collection of fundamental rules of Roman law, written by a Commission of Ten Men (the *Decemviri*) in 451–450 B.C. and promulgated as a statute in 449.

usucapion (*usucapio*): acquisition of ownership of property that belongs to someone else, through continuous possession of it for a period fixed by law (two years for land; one year for movables). The right to usucapt is, however, narrowly restricted by legal rules.

usufruct (*usus fructus*): the right to use and exploit property belonging to another, without impairing its substance. A usufruct is usually created through a legacy.

vindication (*vindicatio*): a legal claim that property held by the defendant belongs in fact to the plaintiff and should be returned.

vis maior: an "irresistible force," such as an act of God or an enemy incursion, the consequences of which cannot be averted by foresight and planning.

Suggested Further Reading
for Students

The most important primary source for Roman law is Justinian's *Digest*, which has recently been translated into English: *The Digest of Justinian* (4 vols., ed. A. Watson, 1985). Besides the *Digest*, Gaius' *Institutes*, available in several English translations, is also essential. F. de Zulueta, *The Institutes of Gaius* (2 vols., 1946), has a fine commentary and is preferable on that basis to W.M. Gordon and O.F. Robinson, *The Institutes of Gaius* (1988). As for Justinian's *Institutes*, J.A.C. Thomas' *The Institutes of Justinian* (1975) is the best English version, but several others are available; Justinian's *Institutes* present Roman law in a somewhat "modernized" Byzantine version. Most other primary sources on classical Roman law have not received good English translations.

On Aquilian liability, F.H. Lawson, *Negligence in the Civil Law* (1950), provides full sources and discussion of not only Roman law but also its influence on later European Civil Law. Much of Lawson's book was reworked in F.H. Lawson and B.S. Markesinis, *Tortious Liability for Unintentional Harm in the Common and the Civil Law* (2 vols., 1982), which has up-dated references but is somewhat more focussed on modern law than the original. Unfortunately, for the other Roman delicts there is no book in English that is up to the Lawson standard; but H.F. Jolowicz, *Digest XLVII.2: De Furtis* (1940), can still be recommended on theft. The basic *Digest* titles on delict are translated by C.F. Kolbert in *Justinian, The Digest of Roman Law: Theft, Rapine, Damage and Insult* (1979), which however is rather difficult to use.

For a short general summary of Roman private law, B. Nicholas, *An Introduction to Roman Law* (1962), is hard to beat for brevity and clearness; Nicholas is particularly good at expounding Roman law for readers in the Common Law tradition. Among other available introductions, probably the fullest is M. Kaser, *Roman Private Law* (4th ed. transl. R. Dannenbring, 1984); Kaser looks at Roman law from a distinctively European perspective, and he is not always easy to read. W.W. Buckland's *A Text-Book of Roman Law* (3d ed. P. Stein, 1963) is intended, despite its name, mainly for advanced readers.

On the historical background of Roman law, W. Kunkel, *An Introduction to Roman Legal and Constitutional History* (2d ed. transl. J.M. Kelly, 1973), is brief and well organized. H.F. Jolowicz and B. Nicholas, *Historical Introduction to the Study of Roman Law* (3d ed. 1972), is fuller but may be hard to follow. A.A. Schiller, *Roman Law: Mechanisms of Development* (1978), offers a more institutional approach; the book also has an excellent bibliography.

J.A. Crook, *Law and Life of Rome* (1967), looks at Roman law from the standpoint of Roman social history; Crook discusses numerous surviving private documents that reflect Roman law in practice. Among the many other books discussing particular aspects of Roman law from a social perspective, readers may enjoy B.W. Frier, *Landlords and Tenants in Imperial Rome* (1980); J.F. Gardner, *Women in Roman Law and Society* (1986): and A. Watson, *Roman Slave Law* (1987). B.W. Frier, *The Rise of the Roman Jurists* (1985), recounts the emergence of the legal profession in the later Roman Republic and the effect of "legal science" on Roman society.

For a lively account of the main social values expressed in Roman private law, F. Schulz, *Principles of Roman Law* (transl. M. Wolff, 1936), can be recommended.

On the historical influence of Roman law, O.F. Robinson, T.D. Fergus, and W.M. Gordon, *An Introduction to European Legal History* (1985), present a good overview. W.W. Buckland and A. McNair, *Roman Law and Common Law* (2d ed. F.H. Lawson, 1952), survey the basic differences between the two systems. J.H. Merryman, *The Civil Law Tradition* (2d ed. 1985), is a good summary of the basic characteristics of modern Civil Law.

Bibliography on
Roman Delicts

The bibliography is intended to provide a selection of books and articles that represent modern scholarly approaches to the Roman law of delict. Some especially interesting works are marked with an asterisk. Abbreviation of periodical names mainly follows the standard usage in Max Kaser's *Das Römische Privatrecht*.

I. General Themes in Delict

* Albanese, B., "Cenni sullo Svolgimento Storico dell' Illecito Privato in Roma," in *Synt. Arangio-Ruiz* vol. I (1964) 104–122.
* Benöhr, H.-P., "Zur Haftung für Sklavendelikte," *SZ* 97 (1980) 273–287.
  Brasiello, U., *Atto Illecito Pena e Risarcimento del Danno* (1957).
  Daube, D., "'Nocere' and 'Noxa'," *Cambridge L.J.* 7 (1939) 23–55.
* De Visscher, F., *Le Régime Romain de la Noxalité* (1947).
  ———. "Il Sistema Romano della Nossalità," *Iura* 11 (1960) 1–68.
  Kaser, M., "Typisierter 'Dolus' im Altrömischen Recht," *BIDR* 65 (1962) 79–104.
* ———. "'Divisio Obligationum'," in *Römische Rechtsquellen und Angewandte Juristenmethode* (Forsch. z. Röm. Recht 36, 1986) 155–172.
  Longo, G., *'Delictum' e 'Crimen'* (Quad. di St. Senesi 37, 1976).
  ———. *Diritto Romano: Diritto delle Obbligazioni* (2 vols. 1954).
  ———. "La Complicità nel Diritto Penale Romano," *BIDR* 61 (1958) 102–207.
  MacCormack, G., "Fault and Causation in Early Roman Law: An Anthropological Perspective," *RIDA* 28 (1981) 97–126.
  Mayer-Maly, T., "'Divisio Obligationum'," *Irish Jur.* 2 (1967) 375–385.
  Sargenti, M., "Contributi allo Studio della Responsabilità Nossale in Diritto Romano," *Pubbl. Univ. Pavia, St. Sci. Giur. Soc.* 104 (1949) 59–135.
  ———. *Limiti, Fondamento e Natura della Responsabilità Nossale in Diritto Romano* (Pubbl. Univ. Pavia, St. Sci. Giur. Soc. 109, 1950).
  Serrao, F., "Responsabilità per Fatto Altrui e Nossalità," *BIDR* 73 (1970) 125–196.
  Stein, P., "School Attitudes in the Law of Delicts," in *St. Biscardi* vol. II (1982) 281–293.
  Vacca, L., *Delitti Privati e Azioni Penali nel Principato* (St. Econom. Giurid. Cagliari 49.1, 1978/1979).
  Watson, A., *The Law of Obligations in the Later Roman Republic* (1965).

II. Aquilian Liability and the *Actio de Pauperie* (Chapters I–IV)

Albanese, B., "Studi sulla Legge Aquilia," *Ann. Palermo* 21 (1950) 1–343.
———. "Note Aquiliane," *Ann. Palermo* 23 (1953) 253–257.

————. "Sulla Responsabilità del 'Dominus Sciens' per i Delitti del Servo," *BIDR* 70 (1967) 119–186.

Anderson, I., "'Volenti Iniuria Non Fit' and the Lex Aquilia in Roman Law," *Responsa Meridiana* 2 (1971) 103–118.

Andrews, N.H., "'Occidere' and the Lex Aquilia," *Cambridge L.J.* 46 (1987) 315–329.

* Ankum, H., "Das Problem der 'Überholenden Kausalität' bei der Anwendung der Lex Aquilia im Klassischen Römischen Recht," in *Fg. von Lübtow* (1980) 325–358.

————. "L' 'Actio de Pauperie' et l' 'Actio Legis Aquiliae' dans le Droit Romain Classique," in *St. Sanfilippo* vol. II (1982) 13–59.

————. "Actions by Which We Claim a Thing ('Res') and a Penalty ('Poena') in Classical Roman Law," *BIDR* 24 (1982) 15–39.

————. "'Quanti Ea Res Erit in Diebus XXX Proximis' dans le Troisième Chapitre de la Lex Aquilia: Un Fantasme Florentin," in *Mélanges à J. Ellul* (1983) 171–184.

Barton, J.L., "The Lex Aquilia and Decretal Actions," in *Daube Noster* (1974) 15–25.

Beinart, B., "'Culpa in Omittendo'," *THRHR* 11 (1949) 141–168.

————. "The Relationship of 'Iniuria' and 'Culpa' in the Lex Aquilia," in *St. Arangio-Ruiz* vol. I (1953) 279–303.

————. "Once More on the Origin of the Lex Aquilia," *S. Afr. L.R.* (1956) 70–80.

* Below, K.-H., *Die Haftung fur 'Lucrum Cessans' im Römischen Recht* (Münch. Beitr. z. Pap. u. Ant. Rechtsg. 46, 1964).

Bernard, A., "A Propos d'un Article Récent sur le Chapitre 3 de la Loi Aquilie. Contenu. Nature de la Réparation," *RH* 16 (1937) 450–460.

Birks, P., "Other Men's Meat: Aquilian Liability for Proper User," *Irish Jur.* 46 (1981) 141–185.

Biscardi, A., "Sulla Data della 'Lex Aquilia'," in *St. Giuffrè* vol. I (1967) 75–88.

* Cannata, C.A., *Per lo Studio della Responsabilità per Colpa nel Diritto Romano Classico* (1969).

Cardascia, G., "La Portée Primitive de la Loi Aquilia," in *Daube Noster* (1974) 53–75.

Cohen, B., "The Principle of Causation in the Jewish and the Roman Law of Damages," in *St. de Francisci* vol. I (1956) 305–336.

* Crook, J.A., "Lex Aquilia," *Athenaeum* 62 (1984) 67–77.

Dalla, D., "Giuliano e il 'Longum Intervallum' in Tema di Applicazione dell' Aquilia," *AG* 187 (1974) 145–176.

* Daube, D., "On the Third Chapter of the Lex Aquilia," *LQR* 52 (1936) 253–268.

————. "On the Use of the Term 'Damnum'," in *St. Solazzi* (1948) 93–156.

Del Portillo, L.E., "El Farol del Posadero," *Labeo* 29 (1983) 157–164.

Dias, R.W.M., "Obscurities in the Development of 'Damnum'," *AJur* (1958) 203–220.

Feenstra, R., "The Historical Development of Delictual Liability for Killing and for the Infliction of Bodily Harm," *AJur* (1972) 227–236.

Frier, B.W., "Bees and Lawyers," *Class. J.* 78 (1982) 105–114.

Giomaro, A.M., "Deperibilità dei Mezzi di Prova e Diritto Condizionato," *St. Urbinati* 45 (1976/1977) 3–52.

Gordon, W.M., "Dating the 'Lex Aquilia'," *AJur* (1976) 315–321.

Hausmaninger, H., "Zur Gesetzesinterpretation des Celsus," in *St. Grosso* vol. V (1972) 243–277.

* ———. *Das Schadenersatzrecht der Lex Aquilia* (2nd ed. 1980).

Honoré, A.M., "Linguistic and Social Context of the Lex Aquilia," *Irish Jur.* 7 (1972) 138–156.

Iliffe, J.A., "Thirty Days Hath Lex Aquilia," *RIDA* 5 (1958) 493–506.

———. "The Usufructuary as Plaintiff under the Lex Aquilia According to the Classical Jurists," *RIDA* 12 (1965) 325–346.

Jackson, B.S., "Liability for Animals in Roman Law: An Historical Sketch," *Cambridge L. J.* 37 (1978) 122–143.

Kelly, J.M., "The Meaning of the Lex Aquilia," *LQR* 80 (1964) 73–83.

———. "Further Reflections on the Lex Aquilia," in *St. Volterra* vol. I (1971) 235–241.

Knütel, R., "Die Haftung für Hilfspersonen im Römischen Recht," *SZ* 100 (1983) 340–443.

* Lawson, F.H., *Negligence in the Civil Law* (1950).

* ———. and B.S. Markesinis, *Tortious Liability for Unintentional Harm in the Common and the Civil Law* (2 vols., 1982).

Liebs, D., "'Damnum', 'Damnare' und 'Damnas'," *SZ* 85 (1968) 196–252.

Longo, G., "Appunti Esegetici e Note Critiche in Tema di Lex Aquilia," in *Ricerche Romanistiche* (1966) 713–732.

———. "Sulla Legittima Difesa e sullo Stato di Necessità in Diritto Romano," in *Fg. von Lübtow* (1970) 321–338.

* Lübtow, U. von, *Untersuchungen zur Lex Aquilia 'de Damno Iniuria Dato'* (Berliner Jur. Abh. 23, 1971).

———. "Die Aktionen im Umkreis der Lex Aquilia: Abwehr gegen Georg Thielmann," *Labeo* 30 (1984) 317–328.

MacCormack, G., "On the Third Chapter of the Lex Aquilia," *Irish Jur.* 5 (1970) 164–178.

———. "'Celsus Quaerit': D. 9.2.27.14," *RIDA* 20 (1973) 341–348.

* ———. "Aquilian 'Culpa'," in *Daube Noster* (1974) 201–224.

———. "Aquilian Studies," *SDHI* 41 (1975) 1–78.

———. "Juristic Interpretation of the Lex Aquilia," in *St. Sanfilippo* vol. I (1982) 255–283.

Macqueron, J., "Le Role de la Jurisprudence dans la Création des Actions en Extension de la Loi Aquilia," *Ann. Fac. Droit Aix-en-Provence* 43 (1950) 192–212.

———. "Les Dommages Causés par des Chiens dans la Jurisprudence Romaine," in *Flores Legum Scheltema* (1971) 133–153.

* Mayer-Maly, T., "'De Se Queri Debere', 'Officia erga Se' und Verschulden gegen Sich Selbst," in *Fs. Kaser* (1976) 229–264.

* ———. "Die Unzutreffende 'Confessio in Iure'," in *St. Biscardi* vol. III (1982) 303–314.

Nicholas, B., "Liability for Animals in Roman Law," *AJur* (1958) 185–190.

* Nörr, D., *'Causa Mortis'* (Münch. Beitr. z. Pap. u. Ant. Rechtsg. 80, 1986).

Pauw, P., "Once Again on the Origin of the Lex Aquilia," *S. Afr. L.J.* 95 (1978) 186–192.

————. "'Actio in Factum' and the Lex Aquilia," *S. Afr. L.J.* 97 (1980) 285–295.

Paoli, J., *'Lis Infitiando Crescit in Duplum'* (1933).

* Pernice, A., *Zur Lehre von den Sachbeschädigungen nach Römischem Rechte* (1867).

————. *Labeo* vol. II.1 (2nd ed. 1895).

Perrin, B., "La Caractère Subjectif de l' 'Iniuria' Aquilienne à l'Époque Classique," in *St. de Francisci* vol. IV (1956) 265–284.

Powell, R., "'Novus Actus Interveniens' in Roman Law," *Current Legal Problems* (1951) 197–226.

Pringsheim, F., "The Origin of the Lex Aquilia," in *Ges. Abh.* vol. II (1961) 411–420.

Pugsley, D., "'Damni Iniuria'," *TR* 36 (1968) 371–386.

————. "'Si Quis Alteri Damnum Faxit'," *AJur* (1977) 295–308.

————. "The Origins of the Lex Aquilia," *LQR* 85 (1969) 50–73.

————. "Causation and Confessions in the Lex Aquilia," *TR* 38 (1978) 163–174.

————. "On the Lex Aquilia and 'Culpa'," *TR* 50 (1982) 1–17.

Rodger, A., "Labeo, Proculus and the Ones that Got Away," *LQR* 88 (1972) 402–413.

————. "Damages for the Loss of an Inheritance," in *Daube Noster* (1974) 289–299.

Röhle, R., "Zur Frage der Sogennanten Verdrängunden Verursachung im Römischen Recht," *SDHI* 31 (1965) 305–311.

Rotondi, G., "Teorie Postclassiche sull' 'Actio Legis Aquiliae'," in *Scritti Giuridici* vol. II (1922) 411–464.

Sanfilippo, C., "Il Risarcimento del Danno per l'Uccisione di un Uomo Libero nel Diritto Romano," *Ann. Sem. Giurid. Catania* 5 (1951) 118–131.

* Schindler, K.-H., "Ein Streit zwischen Julian und Celsus," *SZ* 74 (1957) 201–233.

* Schipani, S., *Responsabilità 'ex Lege Aquilia': Criteri di Imputazione e Problema della 'Culpa'* (Mem. Ist. Giurid. Torino, ser. 2, Mem. 131, 1968).

Schubert, M., "Der Schlag des Schusters," *SZ* 92 (1975) 267–269.

Selb, W., "Kausalität in der Dogmengeschichtlichen Betrachtung," in *Fg. Herdlitczka* (1972) 215–222.

————. "Formulare Analogien in 'Actiones Utiles' und 'Actiones in Factum' am Beispiel Julians," in *St. Biscardi* 3 (1982) 315–350.

Sotty, R., *Recherche sur les 'Utiles Actiones'* (1977).

————. "Les Actions Qualifiées d' 'Utiles' en Droit Classique," *Labeo* 25 (1979) 139–162.

Thielmann, G., "'Actio Utilis' und 'Actio in Factum': Zu den Klagen im Umfeld der Lex Aquilia," in *St. Biscardi* vol. II (1982) 295–318.

* Thomas, J.A.C., "The Case of the Apprentice's Eye," *RIDA* 8 (1961) 337–372.

————. "An Aquilian Couplet," in *St. Biondi* vol. II (1965) 169–191.

————. "'Actiones ex Locato Conducto' and Aquilian Liability," *AJur* (1978) 127–134.

Thomas, J.M., "Who Could Sue on the Lex Aquilia?," *LQR* 91 (1975) 207–217.

Tilli, G., "'Dominus Sciens' e 'Servus Agens'," *Labeo* 23 (1977) 16–41.

Tomulescu, C.S., "Les Trois Chapitres de la Lex Aquilia," *Iura* 21 (1970) 191–196.

Valiño, E., *Acciones Pretorias Complementarias de la Acción Civil de la Ley Aquilia* (1973).

Velasco, M.A., "Viviano y la 'Castratio Puerorum' (A Proposito de D. 9.2.27.28)," *AHDE* 52 (1982) 733–749.

Visky, K., "Die Frage der Kausalität aufgrund des D. 9.2 ('ad Legem Aquiliam')," *RIDA* 26 (1979) 475–504.

Völkl, A., "'Quanti Ea Res Erit in Diebus Triginta Proximis': Zum Dritten Kapitel der Lex Aquilia," *RIDA* 24 (1977) 461–486.

Wacke, A., "Unfälle bei Sport und Spiel nach Römischem und Geltendem Recht," *Stadion* 3 (1977) 4–43.

Warmelo, P. van, "À Propos de la Loi Aquilia," *RIDA* 27 (1980) 333–348.

————. "Les Actions autour de la Loi Aquilie," in *St. Biscardi* vol. III (1982) 351–361.

Watson, A., "Narrow, Rigid and Literal Interpretation in the Later Roman Republic," *TR* 37 (1969) 353–368.

* Wesener, G., "Offensive Selbsthilfe im Klass. Röm. Recht," in *Fs. Steinwenter* (1958) 100–120.

* Wittmann, R., *Die Körperverletzung an Freien im Klassischen Röm. Recht* (Münch. Beitr. z. Pap. u. Ant. Rechtsg. 63, 1972).

Wolf, J.M., "D. 20.1.27 Marc. 5 Dig.: Zur Aktivlegitimation des Pfandgläubigers für die 'Actio Legis Aquiliae'," *SZ* 76 (1959) 520–534.

Wollschläger, C., "Eigenes Verschulden des Verletzten," *SZ* 93 (1976) 115–137.

III. Theft (Chapter V, Part A)

* Albanese, B., "La Nozione del 'Furtum' Fino a Nerazio," *APal* 23 (1953) 1–120.

* ————. "La Nozione del 'Furtum' da Nerazio a Marciano," *APal* 25 (1957).

————. "La Nozione del 'Furtum' nell' Elaborazione dei Giuristi Romani," *Jus* 9 (1958) 315–326.

Ankum, H., "'Furtum Pignoris' und 'Furtum Fiduciae' im Klassischen Römischen Recht," *RIDA* 26 (1979) 127–161, 27 (1980) 95–143.

Archi, G.G., "Asini e Cavalle in un Passo di Ulpiano," *Labeo* 19 (1973) 135–155.

Astolfi, R., "Sabino e il 'Furtum Fundi'," *SDHI* 51 (1985) 402–406.

Balzarini, M., *Ricerche in Tema di Danno Violento e Rapina nel Diritto*

Romano (Pubbl. Fac. Giurid. Padova 54, 1969).

Birks, P., "A Note on the Development of 'Furtum'," *Irish Jur.* 8 (1973) 349–355.

Bohacek, M., "'Si Se Telo Defendit'," in *St. Arangio-Ruiz* vol. I (1953) 147–172.

Burillo, J., "La Desprivatización del 'Furtum' en el Derecho Postclásico," *Rev. Estudios Hist.-Jur.* 7 (1982) 13–20.

De Robertis, F.M., "La Legittimazione Attiva nell' 'Actio Furti'," *Ann. Fac. Giurid. Bari* 10 (1949) 55–136.

Duff, P.W., "'Furtum' and Larceny," *Cambridge L.J.* (1954) 86–98.

García Garrido, M., "El 'Furtum Usus' del Depositario y del Commodatario," in *Accad. Rom. Costantiniana, Atti del IV Convegno Internaz.* (1981) 841–860.

Gaudemet, J., "À Propos du 'Furtum' à l'Époque Classique," *Labeo* 7 (1961) 7–19.

Haymann, F., "Grenzen zwischen Betrug und Diebstahl im Römischen Recht," *BIDR* 59/60 (1956) 1–45.

Hughes, D., "'Furtum Ferarum Bestiarum'," *Irish Jur.* 9 (1974) 184–190.

Huvelin, P., *Études sur le 'Furtum' dan le Très Ancien Droit Romain* vol. I (1915).

* Jolowicz, H.F., *Digest XLVII.2: 'De Furtis'* (1940).

Kaser, M., "'Actio Furti' des Verkäufers," *SZ* 96 (1979) 39–128.

———. "Grenzfragen der Aktivlegitimation zur 'Actio Furti'," in *Röm. Rechtsquellen und Angewandte Juristenmethode* (Forsch. z. Röm. Recht 36, 1986) 215–254.

———. "'Furtum Pignoris' und 'Furtum Fiduciae'," *SZ* 99 (1982) 249–277.

Klingenberg, G., "Das Beweisproblem beim Urkundendiebstahl: Die These der 'Quidam' und die Klassiker," *SZ* 96 (1979) 229–257.

Landsberg, E., *Das 'Furtum' des Bösgläubigen Besitzers* (1970).

Longo, G., "L'Elemento Soggetivo nel Delitto di Furto," in *Ricerche Romanistiche* (1966) 571–600.

MacCormack, G., "Definitions: 'Furtum' and 'Contrectatio'," *AJur* (1977) 129–147.

———. "'Ope Consilio Furtum Factum'," *TR* 51 (1983) 271–293.

Nicholas, B., "Theophilus and 'Contrectatio'," in *Studies J.A.C. Thomas* (1983) 118–124.

Olivecrona, K., "D. 47.2.21: Some Questions Concerning 'Furtum'," in *Three Essays in Roman Law* (1949) 43–51.

Pampaloni, M., *Studi sopra il Delitto di Furto* (1894–1900), repr. in *Scritti Giuridici* vol. I (1941).

Powell, R., "'Furtum' by a Finder," *Tulane L.R.* 33 (1959) 509–524.

Pringsheim, F., "'Servus Fugitivus Sui Furtum Facit'," in *Gesammelte Abhandlungen* vol. II ((1961) 152–170.

Pugsley, D., "The Plaintiff in the 'Actio Furti'," *AJur* (1971) 143–146.

———. "'Contrectatio'," *Irish Jur.* 15 (1980) 341–355.

———. "'Animus Furandi'," in *Sodalitas Guarino* vol. V (1984) 2419–2426.

Thomas, J.A.C., "'Contrectatio', Complicity and 'Furtum'," *Iura* 13 (1962) 70–88.

———. "D. 47.2.21," in *Synt. Arangio-Ruiz* vol. II (1964) 607–615.

———. "'Furtum' of Documents," *RIDA* 15 (1968) 429–444.

———. "'Infitiando Depositum Nemo Facit Furtum'," *St. Volterra* vol. II (1969) 759–768.

———. "'Furtum' of Documents II," *Iura* 20 (1969) 301–312.

———. "'Furtum Pignoris'," *TR* 38 (1970) 135–162.

———. "'Furtum Pignoris': A Commentary on the Commentaries," in *St. Sanfilippo* vol. I (1982) 587–600.

Vacca, L., *Ricerche in Tema di 'Actio Vi Bonorum Raptorum'* (Pubbl. Fac. Giurispr. Cagliari Ser. I.12, 1972).

Watson, A., "The Definition of 'Furtum' and the Trichotomy," *TR* 28 (1960) 197–210.

———. "'Contrectatio' as an Essential of 'Furtum'," *LQR* 77 (1961) 526–532.

———. "D. 47.2.52.20: The Jackass, the Mares, and 'Furtum'," in *St. Volterra* vol. II (1971) 445–449.

Wieacker, F., "'Furtum Tabularum'," in *Synt. Arangio-Ruiz* vol. II (1964) 562–576.

IV. Outrage (Chapter V, Part B)

Birks, P., "The Early History of 'Iniuria'," *TR* 37 (1969) 163–208.

———. "'Infamandi Causa Facta' in Disguise?," *AJur* (1976) 83–104.

Coolidge, F.L., "'Iniuria' in the Corpus Iuris Civilis," *Boston Univ. L.R.* 50 (1970) 271–284.

* Daube, D., "'Ne Quid Infamandi Causa Fiat': The Roman Law of Defamation," in *Atti Cong. Verona* vol. III (1953) 411–450.

Halpin, A.K.W., "The Usage of 'Iniuria' in the Twelve Tables," *Irish Jur.* 11 (1976) 344–354.

Kurylowicz, M., "Paul, D. 47.10.26 und die Tatbestände der Römischen 'Iniuria'," *Labeo* 33 (1987) 298–307.

Lavaggi, G., "'Iniuria' e 'Obligatio e Delicto'," *SDHI* 13/14 (1947/1948) 141–198.

Lübtow, U. von, "Zum Römischen Injurienrecht," *Labeo* 15 (1969) 131–167.

Manfredini, A.D., *Contributi allo Studio dell' 'Iniuria' in Età Repubblicana* (Pubbl. Fac. Giurid. Ferrara Ser. II.11, 1977).

———. *La Diffamazione Verbale nel Diritto Romano* vol. I (1979).

Marrone, M., "Considerazione in Tema di 'Iniuria'," *Synt. Arangio-Ruiz* vol. I (1964) 475–485.

Plescia, J., "The Development of 'Iniuria'," *Labeo* 23 (1977) 271–289.

Pólay, E., "Iniuriatatbestände im Archaischen Zeitalter der Antiken Rom," *SZ* 101 (1984) 142–189.

———. *'Iniuria' Types in Roman Law* (1986).

Pugliese, G., *Studi sull' 'Iniuria'* vol. I (1940).

* Raber, F., *Grundlagen Klassischer Iniurienanspruche* (Forsch. z. Röm.

Recht 28, 1969).

———. "Frauentracht und 'Iniuria' durch 'Appellare': D. 47.10.15.15," in *St. Volterra* vol. III (1971) 633–646.

Santa Cruz Teijeiro, J., and D'Ors, A., "A Proposito de los Edictos Especiales 'De Iniuriis'," *AHDE* 49 (1979) 653–659.

Santa Cruz Teijeiro, J., "La 'Iniuria' en Derecho Romano," in *St. Sanfilippo* vol. II (1982) 525–538.

Selb, W., "Formel der Injurienklage," *AJur* (1978) 29–38.

Simon, D.V., "Begriff und Tatbestand der 'Iniuria' im Altromischen Recht," *SZ* 82 (1965) 132–187.

* Völkl, A., *Die Verfolgung der Körperverletzung im Frühen Römischen Recht: Studien zum Verhältnis von Tötungsverbrechen und Iniuriendelikt* (1984).

Watson, A., "Personal Injuries in the XII Tables," *TR* 43 (1975) 213–222.

Wittmann, R., "Die Entwicklungslinien der Klassischen Injurienklage," *SZ* 91 (1974) 285–359.

V. Other Delicts; Quasi-Delicts (Chapters VI–VII)

Albanese, B., "'Actio Servi Corrupti'," *APal* 27 (1959) 5–152.

———. "La Sussidiarietà dell' 'Actio de Dolo'," *APal* 28 (1961) 173–319.

Birks, P., "The Problem of Quasi-Delict," *Current Legal Problems* 22 (1969) 164–180.

———. "A New Argument for a Narrow View of 'Litem Suam Facere," *TR* 52 (1984) 373–387.

Carcaterra, A., *'Dolus Bonus'/'Dolus Malus': Esegesi di D. 4.3.1.2-3* (1970).

Cremadez, I., and Paricio, J., "La Responsabilidad del Juez en el Derecho Romano Classico," *AHDE* 54 (1984) 179–208.

* D'Ors, A., "'Litem Suam Facere'," *SDHI* 48 (1982) 368–394.

Gallo, F., "Per la Ricostruzione e l'Utillizzazione della Dottrina di Gaio sulle 'Obligationes ex Variis Causarum Figuris'," *BIDR* 76 (1973) 171–224.

Gordon, W.M., "The Roman Class of Quasi-Delicts," *Temis* 21 (1967) 303–310.

———. "The 'Actio de Posito' Reconsidered," in *Studies J.A.C. Thomas* (1983) 45–55.

Hochstein, R., *'Obligationes Quasi ex Delicto'* (1971).

Hübner, H., "Zur Haftung des 'Iudex, Qui Litem Suam Fecit'," *Iura* 5 (1954) 200–208.

Longo, G., *Contributi alla Dottrina del Dolo* (1937).

———. "I 'Quasi Delicta.' 'Actio de Effusis et Deiectis.' 'Actio de Positis et Suspensis'," in *St. Sanfilippo* vol. IV (1983) 401–469.

Lübtow, U. von, *Der Ediktstitel 'Quod Metus Causa Gestum Erit'* (1932).

———. "Die bei Befreiung eines Gefesselten Sklaven Eingreifende 'Actio'," in *Mél. Meylan* vol. I (1963) 211–223.

MacCormack, G., "The Liability of the Judge in the Republic and Principate," *ANRW* vol. II.14 (1982) 3–28.

MacCormick, D.N., "'Iudex Qui Litem Suam Fecit'," *AJur* (1977) 149–165.

Maier, G.H., *Prätor. Bereicherungsklagen* (1932).

Palumbo, F., *L'Azione di Dolo* (1935).

Pugsley, D.F., "'Litem Suam Facere'," *Irish Jur.* 4 (1969) 351–355.

Rodriguez-Ennes, L., "Notas sobre el Elemento Subjetivo del 'Edictum de Effusis vel Deiectis'," *Iura* 35 (1984) 91–98.

Sciascia, G., "'De Servo Corrupto'," *Investigaçoes* 5 (1953) 48–54.

Stein, P., "The Nature of Quasi-Delictual Obligations in Roman Law," *RIDA* 5(1958) 563–570.

Stojcevic, D., "Sur le Caractère des Quasi Délits en Droit Romain," *Iura* 8 (1957) 57–74.

Wacke, A., "Zum 'Dolus'-Begriff der 'Actio de Dolo'," *RIDA* 27 (1980) 349–386.

Watson, A., "'Actio de Dolo' and 'Actiones in Factum'," *SZ* 78 (1961) 392–402.

———. "Liability in the 'Actio de Positis ac Suspensis'," in *Mél. Meylan* vol. I (1963) 379–382.

Wolodkiewicz, W., "'Obligationes ex Variis Causarum Figuris': Ricerche sulla Classificazione delle Fonti delle Obbligazioni nel Diritto Romano Classico," *RISG* 14 (1970) 77–227.

———. "Sulla Cosidetta Responsibilità dei 'Quasi Delitti' nel Diritto Romano e il Suo Influsso sulla Responsibilità Civile Moderna," in *La Formazione Storica del Diritto Moderno in Europa* vol. III (1977) 1277–1293.

Index of Sources

The following list includes all ancient sources cited in this casebook. Reference is to Cases. References in bold are to the Cases themselves; other references are to the Discussions.

I. Pre-Justinianic Sources

Collatio Legum Mosaicarum et Romanarum

2.3.1	84
2.4.1	38
7.3.2–3	**69**; 25, 34, 62, 63, 153
7.4.1	116
12.7.1–5	**50**; 10, 28, 42
12.7.7	24, 89
12.7.8	**42**; 10
12.7.9	91
12.7.10	**72**; 103

Aulus Gellius, *Noctes Atticae*

7.15.1	121
11.18.13	**118**
11.18.20–21	105

Gaius, *Institutiones*

2.50	114
2.51	118
3.183–194	Intro. to V.A
3.195–197	**105**; 116, 121
3.199	**119**
3.200	**117**; 123
3.202	**110**; 11, 22, 161
3.203–204	**123**; 117
3.205–207	**124**; 122
3.209	**126**; 152
3.211	**26**; 27, 58
3.214	36
3.217	**8**
3.219	**7**; 10, 20, 21, 56, 162, 164
3.220	**127**
3.221	**142**; 138
3.222	**133**; 92

3.224–225	**136**
4.6, 9	**15**; 4, Intro. to II.B and V
4.37	**75**
4.41, 43, 49	150
4.52	170
4.76	1
4.119	**150**; 52, 148
4.174–179	149

Paulus, *Sententiae*

1.15.1a	98
2.31.12	105
5.4.6–8	**128**

II. Justinianic and Byzantine Sources

Codex Justinianus

3.35.6	21

Digesta Justiniani

4.2.1, 3 pr.	**152**
4.2.4	153
4.2.5–6	**153**
4.2.7.1	153
4.2.8.1–2	**156**; 153
4.2.12.2	**154**; 155
4.2.13	**155**; 154
4.2.14.1	152
4.2.14.5	**158**
4.2.21 pr.	**157**
4.3.1 pr.–1	**144**
4.3.1.2	**146**; 145
4.3.7.3	**145**
4.3.7.6	97
4.3.7.7	11, 111

Scholiast on the *Basilika*

Printed in the United States
133524LV00001BA/171/A